PERRY ELLIS

PERRY ELLIS

Jonathan
Moor

ST. MARTIN'S PRESS   New York

A 2M Communications Ltd. Production

LIBRARY OF CONGRESS
Library of Congress Cataloging-in-Publication Data.
Moor, Jonathan.
   Perry Ellis : a biography / by Jonathan Moor.
      p.   cm.
   "A Thomas Dunne book."
   ISBN 0-312-01489-9 : $16.95
   1. Ellis, Perry, d. 1986.   2. Costume designers—United States—Biography.   I. Title.
TT505.E55M66 1988
746.9'2'0924—dc19
[B]   87-27345
                                                   CIP

TT
505
E55
M66
1988

First Edition   3 3001 00712 0297

10 9 8 7 6 5 4 3 2 1

This book is, dedicated to the memory of a kind, talented, and gentle man, Perry Ellis.
And to my mother and father, who taught me the meaning of our family motto: "Truth, Justice and Honour."

Acknowledgments

First of all I would like to thank my agent, Madeleine Morel, whose advice, support, and friendship did so much to keep me going throughout the long and sometimes painful process of writing this book, as well as my editor and publisher, Tom Dunne, who had faith in my untried ability to write Perry's tragic story and turned my verbose prose into modern English. I would also like to thank Laurie Holmes, my researcher, who helped so much in the six sometimes frustrating months of gathering and organizing the hundreds of files of information I needed to complete the work, David Harvey for his research in Europe, and Amanda Rubin for her research on the photographs.

There are many people I have to thank for their contributions, but especially my old boss at Fairchild Publications, Steve Stoneburn, whose help was invaluable. I also cannot forget the wonderful work done by the "girls" in Fairchild's reference library, especially Tish, Gloria, and Grace, who gave me so much of their time, as well as Anita in the syndication department and Mary Palmer, my old assistant, who also contributed to the research.

The book could not have been written without the hours and effort so generously given to me by Pamela Altman, Judy Beste, Erwin Isman, Ed Jones, and James Terrell. Without their professional knowledge of, and personal friendship with, Perry, much of his character and way of working would have remained hidden.

The insight I gained into Perry's early years is greatly due to the time that Troy Swindell and Jerry Yospin spent with me. I would also like to thank Catherine Bell, Michael Black, George Bryson, Kathy Gempp, Gloria Halbertstein, Gordon Mallonee, Carlos Mills, Barbara Oliver, Nina O'Connell, Sarah

Price, Avis Schumacher, Ed Steinberg, and Suzanne Tyler for their recollections of Perry as a young man.

There are many people who contributed to the book with their reminiscences of Perry during his New York years: for the six years Perry spent with John Meyer of Norwich my thanks go to Arlene Meyer Cohen. Among the many others are Marjorie Ambrogio, Bob Andrialis, Joe Armstrong, Eve Arnold, Richard Banks, Wilkes Bashford, Bill Blass, David Bottoms, Jr., Jean-Charles Brosseau, Richard Caples, Ron Cheng, Larry Crysler, Bruce Dunham, Linda Dyett, Ruth Finlay, Karen Fortier, Norman Fryman, Tom Gurtner, Carolyn Gottfried, Dr. Willam Graves, Bob Haas, Nigel Holmes, Barry Kieselstein-Cord, Ralph Lauren, Bob Lenzner, Stanley Lesser, Rea Lubar, Patricia Morrisroe, Keith Munroe, Pieter O'Brien, Robert Raymond, Frank Rizzo, Bill Robinson, Frank Rockman, Jean Rosenberg, David Rosensweig, Abbijane Schifrin, Matt Shaw, Alan Stenberg, Jim Thayer, Marvin Traub, Barbara Turk, and John Weitz.

Many of my fellow editors and writers were tremendously helpful in their appraisal of Perry's talent and work as a fashion designer, as well as with their insights into his character: I would like to thank Bob Beauchamp, Vincent Boucher, Melissa Drier, John Duka, Annie Flanders, Jean Guilder, Clara Hancox, Sandra Horvitz, Mary Lou Luther, Julie Moline, Nonnie Moore, Bernadine Morris, Patricia O'Brien, Art Seidenbaum, David Shaw, Audrey Smaltz, Diane Sustendal, Viviane Turbiana, and Judy Woolrich.

I would especially like to thank Cammy Sessa for the vital contribution she made to the book.

I am very grateful to Dr. Mathilde Krim for her advice on the medical aspects of the book, as well as to the other physicians who spoke to me. Larry Kramer and Roger McFarland were also very helpful in this area.

Several experts helped me with the introductory chapter and I would like to especially thank the Reverend Michael Donahue, S.J., Professor Alison Jolly, and Don Melnick.

There were times when the computer felt it was overworked and got sick. I thank Terry Greenan of Greenan Business Machines for his continued service of what became the most temperamental element in the writing of the book.

There were also many, many other people who allowed me to interview them for the book but wish to remain anonymous due to outside pressures. They know who they are and I thank them for talking to me, especially one very brave, courageous lady to whom I am extremely grateful.

Last but not least, I would like to thank Michael Childers, Harry Coulianos, Yvon Dihe, Michelle Hillman, Michael Hall, Margaret Muldoon, Tom Murray, Mike Nicklaus, Patricia Vigors, and my oldest brother, Anthony; all friends who gave me the support and encouragement I needed during the nine months it took to try to piece together all the brushstrokes of information that became this portrait of Perry Ellis.

Thank you.

PROLOGUE

*Yes, when this flesh and heart shall fail
and mortal life shall cease,
Amazing grace shall then prevail
in heaven's joy and peace.*

—John Newton
"Amazing Grace"

June 12, 1986, was a cold, dismal, rainy day in New York City, and, ironically, the backdrop to what would be the year's most important fashion show. It was not the typical eager crowd of retail and editorial personages that comprised the usual circus of the fashion scene—that group of self-important, self-appointed arbiters of taste who have the power to make or break a designer—that descended on the Society for Ethical Culture on that day, however. No. This was a collection of everyone of importance—and even people who weren't—in the American fashion industry, from heads of multimillion-dollar corporations to lowly editorial assistants. They had all congregated on Manhattan's Upper West Side simply to say farewell to one of the most beloved and adored figures in the industry, the designer Perry Ellis.

Fashion, style, and taste notwithstanding, Perry Ellis's memorial service that morning was an object lesson in lack of sensitivity, a star-studded ritual devoid of real feeling, even though most of the people present felt they had suffered a tremendous personal loss with Perry's passing. At times almost an exercise in bad taste, the morning had all the trappings of a Hollywood extravaganza, as other stellar designers, celebrities, limousines, and paparazzi crowded the street in front of the neo-classical building. It was a fashion presentation, but this time the crowd wasn't there to ogle, praise, or damn the latest creations of one of America's great designers; they were there to mourn him. Perhaps it was this that was wrong, along with the dark cloud that Perry's illness and premature death had cast over the whole industry. For Perry Ellis had been the most celebrated person in a very self-conscious industry to die at such an early age in circumstances most people in the industry wanted to deny.

The intention of the service at the Society for Ethical Culture was beautiful; its execution, however, was almost painful in its lack of emotion and the absence of a sense of genuine loss. One of Ellis's employees was running around greeting everyone in sight with a kiss, as though it was just another party. A fellow designer and his entourage were fashionably ten minutes late, even though most of the guests, including people equally as celebrated, had had the courtesy to arrive on time for once. It wasn't a good start. The music was provided by the Meliora Quartet, which played works by Beethoven, Mozart, and Benjamin Britten. Ten of Perry's friends, co-workers, and industry figures eulogized him, sometimes movingly, with their reminiscences and praise. But it was all so dry and austere.

The only time one got a hint of the real Perry was when Jed Krascella, one of his designers, stood up to speak and got everyone to laugh. "If Perry was here today he would say, 'Go up there and give them performance, darling! That's what they're here for!'" The remark evoked the sharp sense of humor that people remembered Ellis for, and which had helped make his clothes so witty and irreverent. It was pure Perry. The other side of Ellis, his sensitivity, was remembered when soprano Mavis Martin stood up and sang Perry's favorite hymn, "Amazing Grace." There were few dry eyes in the house after that.

Outside after the service the photographers snapped away in the rain, having a field day with industry royalty the likes of Bill Blass, Calvin Klein, Ralph Lauren, and Donna Karan. Perhaps Perry would have liked it all—he would certainly have made a wry comment about it—but it didn't accurately represent the Perry that his friends and colleagues had come to know and love.

Perry Ellis was a phenomenon. One of the most influential designers of the late seventies and eighties, he was a major creator of style and fashion in a period when fashion design in

America was at its most influential. His name, thanks to the most careful and calculated exposure by the country's media, had become legend. A personal appearance by Ellis, just as with Calvin Klein, Ralph Lauren, or Bill Blass, was a local media event. The country's preoccupation with style and fashion—image—was perhaps nowhere more evident than in Washington, D.C., where Nancy Reagan seemed determined to be First Lady with a vengeance; it was almost as though Jackie Kennedy's Camelot years had to be emulated and then surpassed. Seventh Avenue reaped the harvest of this obsession and its top designers became almost as well known as movie stars.

So who was Perry Ellis, and why did he deserve such attention? How could a man with no formal training as a fashion designer, someone who couldn't even sketch, much less draw a technical design—details that were left to his design team—achieve the summit of one of the most powerful industries in America, creating a fashion empire with retail sales of nearly three-quarters of a billion dollars a year worldwide in just ten short years?

To answer these questions, one must first understand the magnitude of the fashion industry in the United States. In 1985, for example, Americans spent a staggering $132,650,000,000 on clothes alone—more than the GNP of many smaller countries—a fact that gives tremendous financial power to the people who run the industry, as well as providing work for hundreds of thousands of people. It's the fourth-largest expenditure in American families' household budgets, after housing, food and beverages, and transportation,* and it also shapes the public's perception of style and beauty—something very dear to America's heart. For these reasons alone a designer as influential as Perry Ellis has an effect on the lives of millions of people—not because they buy his clothes; most

---

*Department of Labor statistics, 1982–1984.

people can't afford them—but because the trends he unveils one year will be reflected in popularly priced clothing the next.

To fully appreciate the extent to which the designers fashion taste, one must examine the socio-political and economic background of the industry today. Fashion is an incredibly complex subject. More than just an artisan craft manipulated by clever advertisers to make us spend tens of billions of dollars a year, it's endemic to our psychological makeup. It has been said that we only need three things for our existence—food in our stomachs, a roof over our heads, and clothes on our backs. Like all truisms, this one is only half correct: religious leaders would say we need the existence of a Supreme Being; nihilists might propose we need nothing more than our intelligence; romantics might argue we need only love; and humanists that we need an outlet for our creative impulses. Still, to many, it comes down to just three essentials: food, shelter, and clothing.

Even clothing is suspect in this group, however. After all, every species on earth manages to survive without garments except for Homo sapiens (though a few remaining primitive peoples manage to exist quite nicely without clothes). Maybe, despite Darwin, there is more to the myth of the fall in the Garden of Eden than we suppose; maybe it was knowledge that gave us our false modesty. (And given new research into our DNA, current theory holds that we are all descended from *one* single woman, in studies of our mitochondrial DNA, suggesting there was an Eve!)

The current theory is borne out by how little distinguishes Homo sapiens from our ancestors, the higher primates. Admittedly apes have longer arms and shorter legs, whereas we have proportionately larger craniums and genitalia, but we are formed in a very similar fashion (we even have the same number of hair follicles). It also now appears that apes are capable of conceptual thought—signing chimpanzees are quite capable of putting rudimentary thoughts together and asking related questions. As a result, the older definitions of the differences between man and ape have had to be revised.

Still, man is the only species that feels a basic need for adornment. Some species will cover themselves for the purposes of camouflage and protection, but even our nearest relatives, the higher primates, though they have the dexterity as well as a certain "artistic" sensibility, don't cover themselves. (Dr. Alison Jolly, professor of primate behavior at Rockefeller University in New York, does claim that some species of primates will put leaves on their heads as a sort of hat, but no more than that.)

Man, on the other hand, began to wear furs as soon as he discovered how to use clubs to kill other animals. Although such pelts were worn primarily as protection against the elements, primitive man soon began to string saber-tooth tiger teeth together to wear as necklaces, as well as daubing himself with berry juice. This primitive wish for adornment can still be seen in the few remaining Stone Age tribes residing in the jungles of the Amazon basin and Borneo. Such tribes do adorn themselves and it isn't always in the form of a loincloth. In many cases they are drawn more to rudimentary jewelry displayed on the head, around the neck, or on the arms and legs, as well as painting their faces and bodies.

The second factor in the evolution of fashion developed soon after in mankind's history, when he started to conceive of a structured society and the rules by which to govern such an arrangement. Over long, unremarked milleniums a class system deriving from authority was developed. Initially, authority was established and executed by brute strength, but that came to be considered "uncivilized," and dress ultimately became the symbol of authority and power.

Finally, there is a third factor which helps to explain the evolution of fashion—our unique sexuality. Homo sapiens, unlike any other species, utilizes clothing to attract mates of the opposite sex. Taken together with our use of clothing as adornment and as a symbol of status, one begins to get a sense of how powerful a force fashion is in our lives.

We also differ from other species in that normally it is the male of the species who is the "peacock." Among humans, on the contrary, it is the female who dresses up for sexual attention, though this is a relatively late development in Western culture. As recently as the seventeenth century men played the greater part in following fashion, bejeweling and parading themselves in their military costumes and clothes far more than women.

Up to that point all fashion was a manifestation of political power, a tool to be utilized by the aristocracy, to the point where one couldn't wear what one wanted to. The material or fabric, as well as its color, one could wear was often designated by codes called sumptuary laws in many European countries. For example, Edward III of England's 1363 sumptuary legislation on furs stated that only royalty and the higher echelons of the nobility could wear ermine, marten, and vair. The people on the next rung of the social ladder were permitted to use otter, and, in descending order, fox, beaver, lamb, goat, and finally, for the peasants, wolf. The same law proscribed anyone lower than the rank of baronet from wearing crimson, gold, or velvet. Such laws even prohibited the style of clothes one was allowed to wear and determined the length of jackets and cloaks. As a result, a person's rank was instantly manifest by the clothes he wore. Even in Renaissance Florence under the enlightened rule of Lorenzo di Medici, guild members could only wear certain cloths in certain colors, thereby identifying them by their trade. By the seventeenth century, however, most sumptuary laws concerning clothes and fashion had been repealed. (Though they have been revived from time to time, even in the United States as late as the 1940s, when the style of women's clothes was prescribed by law. However, these "M-" and "L- Orders" were wartime emergency measures.)

The sixteenth and seventeenth centuries saw two dramatic changes in fashion. First, women emerged as powerful entities in their own right, with the rise of Elizabeth I of England and, later, Catherine the Great of Russia, as well as Jeanne Antoinette Poisson, the mistress of Louis XV, who, elevated as Madame de Pompadour, became the power behind the French throne. All three ladies utilized feminine wiles—and fashion— to achieve their political goals. And second, in the first recorded historical reference to a "fashion designer," Michelangelo Bounarroti was commissioned by Pope Alexander IV to design the outfits for the Vatican's Swiss Guard, which they still wear today. (Furthermore, there must have been some Roman seamstress who decided that Julius Caesar would look more chic with a purple border round his regulation toga—or was it just a case of his tailor having an excess of Phoenician dye on hand that week? We will never know.)

However, it wasn't until the next century that an individual's name relating to matters of fashion came to real prominence. Mademoiselle Bertin, seamstress to Marie Antoinette from 1775 to 1786, was indicted for high treason. For better or worse, fashion had made its somewhat dubious entrance into the political arena, a situation that lasts to this day, if one considers the debates about the clothes of H.R.H. Diana, The Princess of Wales, and Nancy Reagan, not to mention the political effect of Imelda Marcos's opulently extravagant wardrobe. (It is interesting to note that in the twentieth century, the golden age of fashion, the woman to most successfully exploit fashion in the political arena—and meaning no disrespect to the late Indira Ghandi and Eleanor Roosevelt, as well as the Right Honourable Margaret Thatcher, M.P. P.M., remarkable and formidable ladies in their own right—was a hooker. The young Eva Duarte Peron instinctively knew more about how to use clothes, style, and image as a political force than anyone in recent years.)

The reason for this anonymity in fashion design up to the eighteenth and nineteenth centuries is simply that the ruling classes, who were the only people who could afford (or were allowed) to indulge themselves in fashion, used personal seam-

stresses and tailors. Fashion was very much an individual statement, even to the point of Frederick the Great of Prussia
designing the uniforms of his armies. (He was enamored of
gold braid and very much impressed by glitz.)

It wasn't until the middle of the nineteenth century that
fashion really became the creative province of every individual,
thanks in large part to an Englishman by the name of Charles
Frederick Worth and the prestige of his Paris salon. Immediately women who could afford it were wearing his creations,
and following his design dictates. His sartorial influence was
profound, reaching every country in the world, and his
emergence came just in time to save women from being further repressed by their outwardly virtuous and puritanical hus-
bands and fathers during the Victorian era. The stage was
finally set for the most varied and creative period in the history
of fashion, the twentieth century.

It was at the beginning of our century that Paul Poiret
took women out of the bondage of corsets, invented the bras-
siere, and set the stage for modern fashion. However, perhaps
just as important were the revolutionary changes that occurred
during the turbulent years of the First World War, which re-
duced class distinctions, gave women the vote, and put fashion
within the reach of everyone.

In the halcyon years after the Great War, there sprang up,
in Paris especially, more creative fashion designers than at any
previous period of history. The sheer variety of their work was
astounding and suddenly women's fashions were changing season by season in drastic ways. Hemlines, for example, would
suddenly rise above the knee, something that hadn't happened
since Greek times, then drop again; breasts and hips would be
given prominence, especially with the bias-cut dresses of
Madeleine Vionnet, then, as if in anticipation of the militarism
of the approaching Second World War, severely tailored suits
came into style. It was an extraordinary period, but the one
person who stood out above all others was an illegitimate or-

phan from central France, a girl with no training at all. Her name was Gabrielle "Coco" Chanel.

From the unconstructed day suit, to pants, to cardigans, even to the use of jersey, which she discovered how to cut on the bias, Chanel reinvented the way women dressed and freed them forever from rigid fashion constraints. She was and still is the single most important fashion figure of the century, and her influence will be with us well into the next. It's impossible to know where her vision came from; it was totally original, the mark of genius, but every designer since owes something to her, including Perry Ellis.

Ironically, Chanel got much of her inspiration from the sporting clothes of one of her boyfriends, the Duke of Westminster, who favored the relaxed, casual, hunting, shooting, and fishing clothes English gentlemen have worn at home on their country estates since the end of the nineteenth century. Men's attire had long since lost the splendor personified by Sir Walter Raleigh. (Even Beau Brummel, in the brief renaissance of male splendor at the beginning of the eighteenth century, only had to appear at a court ball in black frock coat and white tie—which set the trend for evening wear to our own day—to make the best-dressed list.)

It is only in the last two decades that men have begun to rediscover the true freedom of individual dressing. This male emancipation in matters of fashion started in the heyday of Carnaby Street and Haight-Ashbury in the sixties, but even today men are still somewhat regimented as to what is considered suitable attire (though now the rules are becoming relaxed enough so that a dark suit isn't considered "de rigueur" in the office and men are beginning to sport earrings again, a social taboo for men, apart from sailors and pirates, since the days of the Renaissance). Men's attire before then had been dominated by the influence of military uniforms—even the business suit is descended from a military jacket. Now, however, it is sportswear that's becoming the dominant force—

clothes directly descended from work clothes and from what
gentlemen wore for athletic activities—various layers of their
undergarments.

It is, of course, America that has given the world fashion
leadership in sportswear, after the initial thrust and inspiration
provided by Chanel and a French tennis shirt designed in
1927 by René Lacoste. Almost an amendent to the Constitu-
tion, the American love of freedom has found its fashion expression in easy, comfortable sports clothes that dispense with
the old rules of dressing (except for business and social functions, where America still is more strict than most other Western countries).

Perry Ellis's consummate achievement, the one for which
he will probably always be credited, was in breaking down the
barriers between sportswear and "couture." As heir to the
fashion legacy established by American sportswear designers
like Claire McCardell, John Weitz, Anne Klein, and Rudy
Gernreich in the fifties, Ellis brought together their impet-
uosity and freedom with the more established, tailored, "couture" tradition, a tradition started when American designers in
the late forties and fifties attended the shows of Parisian designers and were liberally "inspired" by their designs, finally
finding its home-grown expression in the fashions of such designers as Norman Norell, Pauline Trigere, Bill Blass, and
Geoffrey Beene.

It wasn't until the seventies, however, that the two tradi-
tions—sportswear and "couture"—were brought together in a
single fashion expression by designers both here and in Europe. Finally the "look" of an outfit was deemed more important than the time of day it was "meant" to be worn. It was the
ultimate freedom from the constraints of social convention and
destroyed class assumptions of what fashion should be forever.

Three American names became synonymous with this
movement—Calvin Klein, Ralph Lauren, and, especially,
Perry Ellis. Not surprisingly, their influence has not only per-
vaded the American fashion scene, but affected Europe as well.

(Italian designers such as Giorgio Armani and Gianni Versace have, for many seasons, looked to American sportswear for inspiration.)

The individually free dress code of these last decades of the twentieth century is, in large part, due to this "radical" view of fashion, and while catering to the elite, the freedom of expression championed by today's leading designers will continue to have an immense effect well into the twenty-first century. Of this movement, Perry Ellis was one of the undoubted leaders.

i

Some are born great, some achieve greatness,
and some have greatness thrust upon them.

—William Shakespeare
Twelfth Night (Act II, Scene V)

Nineteen hundred and forty was one of the pivotal years in modern history. Europe had fallen and Great Britain was rapidly using up the wealth and resources of its vast empire in a desperate struggle for survival against Adolph Hitler's Nazi Germany. It was, however, the year that would see the tide begin to turn against the Third Reich and the Axis powers with the Allies' victory in the Battle of Britain.

Against this backdrop, in a maternity ward in Portsmouth, Virginia, Winifred Alene Roundtree Ellis gave birth to her first and only child on the evening of March 3. By all accounts it was an easy delivery, and mother and child were soon allowed to return home to the large family house where Winifred and her husband Edwin lived with his parents.

With Perry's subsequent celebrity, much was written about his childhood in the South. Many newspaper and magazine accounts give the impression that he was the scion of an aristocratic Virginia family that lived in a grand house that looked much like Monticello. These accounts go on to describe a lifestyle that's more akin to the novels of Judith Krantz than the reality of the Ellis's situation.

Actually, Perry's childhood was much more interesting than the myth—a myth that certain close friends suggest Perry did not go out of his way to discourage. In reality, his was the story of the only son of a well-to-do Portsmouth family who

1

spent much of his life working in middle management on the commercial side of the fashion industry, and then blossomed to become one of the world's foremost creative talents, if not a genius, in the last eight years of his short life.

Winifred and Edwin named their son Perry Edwin, after his father and his maternal grandmother's family, the Perrys, and he was baptized in the Methodist church to which his father belonged.

His parents had first met in high school, and married some six or seven years later in 1939. Edwin was an incredibly hard-working and ambitious man who not only worked for the government as a draftsman in the naval dockyards at Norfolk but found the time to start a fuel business (called Ellis & West, Inc.) with a partner.

Just about the time Perry was taking his first steps, America was thrust into the global conflict by the Japanese attack on Pearl Harbor on December 7, 1941. However, Edwin's government job was important enough that he wasn't drafted. The fuel business, in the meantime, expanded rapidly and during those years Winifred would go into the office in the evenings and on weekends to help with the growing backlog of orders.

The Ellises were native Virginians, though Edwin's mother's family, the Karrakases, had originally come from Greece. The Roundtrees and Perrys were both old North Carolina families, though Winifred's parents moved to Portsmouth before she was born. The Ellis family, which was large, was especially close and the whole family doted on young Perry. His mother has described these early years very simply but with great warmth as "just a good life."

The family home, a large old frame house in the oldest part of Portsmouth, was by all accounts beautifully appointed and contained some fine antiques. One can surmise that it was this childhood environment that instilled in the young Perry an appreciation of style and taste, which would play such a central role in his later career, as well as the love of fine objects that would so mark his own lifestyle.

Another character trait that was developed early on was his love of fine clothes. One of Winifred's greatest joys was buying her young son's clothes, and even though he would quickly grow out of them, she would always buy the best, taking Perry to the most expensive stores in town for his wardrobe or having his clothes expressly made. Unlike most children, Perry enjoyed these outings with his mother and soon began to be able to determine different styles. On occasion he was even known to point out, precociously, to his mother or one of his aunts, "That looks like so-and-so."

Much later he would remark in an interview with *Vogue:* "Among my most vivid memories [of childhood] was how absolutely wonderful it was being dressed in clean cotton and linen pants and shirts, how all of that felt in the summer. . . . It seems that fabric was an important part of my childhood, as was color—they weren't things I seemed to care about too much then. I only look back now and realize that I noticed them."

Unwittingly, Winifred was educating her son's eye and developing his visual awareness. Certainly, at an early age Perry began to appreciate pictures in magazines and books and would spend a lot of his free time drawing. His mother can't recall whether he had any real artistic ability, but she encouraged his interest in art and took pains to take him to local art galleries. That he was a quiet, solitary child who used to spend much of his time reading did not worry her. It was his favorite pastime, he would later tell one interviewer, "because you do it by yourself." Invariably, he would be found at night asleep in his room with the light still on and a book lying by his pillow.

He apparently suffered from asthma, and though not sickly, was neither athletic nor outgoing. "I was terribly shy and introverted," he recalled later. In school he was terrified of being singled out to answer a question and having to stand up in front of the class, and for most of his childhood he was more comfortable in the company of one of the family dogs than children of his own age.

Winifred and Edwin had been aware of their son's shyness from the start and decided that he should go to school as soon as was possible in order to learn how to interact with other children. He had already shown a marked intelligence in kindergarten, and Winifred decided he should attend a private primary school, so he was enrolled in a certain Miss Weekes's establishment when he was only five years old. He quickly showed his earlier promise and was advanced to the second grade by the time he was six. Throughout his school years he was to remain a year ahead of other kids his age, yet his parents never considered him an exceptional student.

It was around then that Perry's parents felt it was time they lived on their own, and though it was wrenching to have to leave the rest of the close-knit Ellis family behind, they soon moved out of the big house into a much smaller one in another part of town that was only temporary until the house they were having built was finished. The new house, built in the ranch style so popular with suburban developers during the fifties, was situated outside the city limits of Portsmouth, in an area west of the city called Churchland that has since been incorporated into the city but was then a rural area.

The young Perry adapted to his new environment remarkably well and proved himself quite endearing. With his chubby, round face, a small button nose, wide-set eyes, and a large, generous mouth, he was irresistibly cute and would grow up to markedly resemble his mother. He also had a cheerful disposition and a ready smile for everyone he met. One of the Ellis's neighbors, who was an old man even then and lived alone, told Winifred much later that Perry would always take the time and trouble to stop and talk to him on his way back from school, while most of the other neighborhood children would shun or make fun of him. Winifred also recalls her son's thoughtfulness and remembers, "When Perry was given money to go to the cinema he wouldn't spend it all on himself and always came back with a flower for me from the market." Although he adored his father, Perry had a special bond with his mother. To the end of his life Winifred would write him notes two or three times a week, and Perry would speak to her on the phone nearly every day.

However, despite his sensitive nature, one shouldn't get the impression that Perry was anything other than a normally boisterous, mischievous boy. Though he never really got into serious trouble, he was always playing pranks and his unique sense of humor was developed early on.

Although he had attended private primary schools, his parents decided to send him to public high school rather than an exclusive establishment like the Norfolk Academy, where many of the "best" local families sent their children. The fact that Woodrow Wilson High School was then one of the finest public schools in the state, with a very high level of academic excellence and a lengthy list of graduates who had earned national scholarships, probably had much to do with their decision.

Perry entered Woodrow Wilson in 1953, at the age of thirteen, a year earlier than was normal. In the fifties, Woodrow Wilson had two "tracks," a college preparatory program and a vocational program. As Perry had already been groomed for college, he was placed in the former and soon found himself embarked on a regimen of rigorous academic study, including four years of English, history, and upper-level math and science courses, including biology and chemistry. According to his transcript, Perry's strengths lay in English and history rather than the sciences, though he must have had an interest in biology, since he was a member of the Biology Club. Interestingly, he only took art for a year, his first at Woodrow Wilson, and he appears to have been much more interested in drama and music, which he kept up for all four years of high school. He never learned to play an instrument, but he did sing in the mixed vocal chorale. He also got good grades in physical education, which would suggest that his asthma had disappeared by that time. And though he was not naturally athletic, he did well in track and field.

Most of his teachers remember him as exceptionally polite and well mannered, and all, to this day, remember his positive attitude and ready smile. He also must have been a diligent student, as he was only tardy for class once in four years despite his living about five miles from school. Still, given his natural intelligence, it seems he did not apply himself to his studies as he might have, as his grades suggest that he was only an average student.

He must have learned how to overcome his shyness during these years, however, since he became extremely popular among his fellow students. His mother had always told him "never to take a back seat and always be up front"—advice he obviously took to heart. The thoughtful and considerate side of his nature is testified to by two of the clubs he belonged to—the Wilson Hi-Y, which devoted itself to community works, and the Pan-American League, which was involved in furthering relations between the two American continents. He also served as director of publicity for the Student Cooperation Society, a particular talent that he would eventually exploit brilliantly in his years as a designer, just as he would theatrical production and music.

Ms. Avis Schumaker, the teacher who worked with him on the Student Cooperation Society, recalls that he was a "bright, intelligent, personable student. He was very likeable and pleasant; always smiling and very easy to work with." She admits to being very fond of him and remembers that he was always well dressed. Barbara Oliver, who still teaches at Woodrow Wilson, also remembers him as a good student and, even after all these years, says, "He stuck out. He had an outstanding personality, but he was never a blazing maverick."

In his senior year Perry was voted Best Dressed, and his sartorial élan got him his first piece of publicity. Woodrow Wilson used to have a "Baby Day" once a year when all the students would come to class dressed up in baby clothes and suck on lollipops. That year Winifred made him a short red jumper suit that he wore with a white shirt, much like the outfits he had worn when he was two years old. He won the competition, and was later photographed for the local newspaper with a little girl sitting on his knee.

It was also while Perry was still in high school that his father introduced him to what was to become one of the great joys of his life. One summer, Edwin took him alone to Greece to give him a sense of that part of his heritage. This vacation and a subsequent skiing trip to Switzerland instilled in Perry a passion for travel.

Judging by the entry in his senior yearbook, Perry had come to enjoy his high school years very much. In those days it was a tradition at Woodrow Wilson that the senior class make a "bequest" to the junior class; Perry's went as follows: "I, Perry Ellis, the last of the Terrible Three, leave behind all the good memories I've had at Wilson and give to some lucky freshman my non ability to date the Wilson cheerleaders."

In the fall of 1957, Perry entered Old Dominion University in Norfolk, Virginia, as a seventeen-year-old freshman. Old Dominion was then an annex of the College of William and Mary in Williamsburg, and Perry used to commute to Norfolk from Portsmouth every day via the tunnel under the Elizabeth River, driving the 1953 Chevy his parents had given him for graduation. Although Perry was popular in high school, having his own transportation made him even more sought after in college, since few kids had their own cars then and he was always willing to give fellow students from Portsmouth a ride to and from campus.

Ironically, he met his best friend from those days because he was unfashionably dressed. "I noticed him in an economic history class because he was the only one wearing black-and-white saddle shoes," recalls Troy Swindell. "By the time I got to college all the kids in Norfolk were wearing loafers. I guess they were behind in Portsmouth. . . . And you know how important things like that are at that age."

As there were only four hundred freshmen at Old Dominion, everyone got to know everyone else fairly quickly and, for the most part, they all used to hang out at Bud's, a drugstore in the student union. Perry and Troy soon became fast buddies because they had so much in common: they had both run track in high school, enjoyed playing tennis, and earned the sobriquet "Best Dressed" during their senior year. Their common interests and the camaraderie it engendered were to take them through the service together, and their friendship lasted well past Perry's move to New York and change in situation and lifestyle.

Troy says of Perry at this time, "Though he was a year younger than everyone else . . . he soon fit into the stream of things and was liked tremendously for his smile and witty personality." Like many of their peers, they spent much of their time at Bud's learning how to play bridge. "In those days you went to college to learn how to drink Scotch and play bridge. . . . Perry never learned how to drink Scotch, though."

However, Perry's devious sense of humor was, during his college years, the bane of his friends' existence. "Perry was a son of a bitch!" says Troy emphatically. "He never got into any real trouble, but he was real mischievous.

"I remember one New Year's Eve when Perry got Willie Smith, one of his oldest friends, and me to drive up to Richmond for a party. Willie was then attending the University of Richmond, and he told me that Willie had these friends who were giving this big New Year's Eve party and we had to go to it. Separately, he had told Willie that I had these friends in Richmond who were giving a party. . . . Of course, there was no party: Perry just wanted to go to Richmond for the evening.

"We were halfway there, about an hour on the road, when I asked Willie who his friends were. In reply, Willie asked me who my friends were. All through the exchange there was Perry in the back of the car laughing his head off! I seem to remember we weren't that amused, and we spent the evening driving to Richmond, having dinner in a deli, and driving home again. It wasn't exactly my idea of a good New Year's Eve."

Perry's parents were, by this time, well off and owned quite a bit of property in the Norfolk/Richmond area, so Perry had more money than most of the other kids at college, which enabled him to spend his summer vacations, at least his first few, at the beach. Troy had also been given a car by his parents, and a crowd of friends would pile into their cars and spend the afternoons at the unpopular end of Virginia Beach near Norfolk. "Perry was lucky," remarks Troy somewhat enviously. "I would have to rush out with my lunch, since there weren't a lot of places to eat at that end of the beach, and then rush back, so that I could get to my job in the afternoons, while Perry could spend all his time there."

In January of 1959 Perry transferred from Old Dominion to the main William and Mary campus. Situated on a hill overlooking the exquisitely restored Colonial town of Williamsburg, it is one of the most beautiful in America. The second-oldest college in the country, founded some sixty years after Harvard in 1693, it has the unusual distinction of having its original buildings designed by one of the great architectural geniuses of history, Sir Christopher Wren, and has played a distinguished role in the making of America, numbering among its alumni three Presidents—Thomas Jefferson, James Monroe, and John Tyler.

In those days William and Mary was a small college, with about 2,000 students, divided equally between male and female (and, like all schools in Virginia at that time, segregated). As a result, Perry would go back to Portsmouth nearly every weekend because the social life was better. Troy, who had remained at Old Dominion, says, "Perry would come home because there was so much going on in Norfolk. It's a naval town and there were big dances every weekend. He found it much more interesting than fraternity life in Williamsburg that first year."

That summer, after Troy had saved up enough from his summer job, he and Perry decided to take a holiday. They had heard about the pleasures of Miami Beach, and soon they found themselves in Perry's Chevy driving down to Miami. "We spent all our money in a week," says Troy, "because we met these two girls from Chicago. One of them had won a beauty contest and her prize was a week in Miami with a friend, so she had brought her girlfriend. Part of the prize was a free convertible for the week, and we spent all our time riding around with the top down. We had a great time spending our days on the beach and going out every night. They were really nice girls."

The summer over, Perry returned to Williamsburg for the fall semester. He continued with his liberal arts studies and became a member of the Kappa Sigma fraternity. He was living in the Bryan dormitory, according to one of his fraternity friends, David Bottoms, Jr., who says it was the "country club" on campus. Perry didn't take part in varsity sports at college, though he did play quite a bit of intramural baseball and basketball. Says Suzanne Tyler, one of his girlfriends at college, "Perry was different than most of the other students. He was a good time and a lot of fun, but he didn't have that macho image. . . . It wasn't that he didn't have it, he just wasn't after it as much as so many of those fraternity boys." Bottoms agrees with this assessment: "He was much more refined, more gentile. He wasn't a back-slapper . . . one of those good old boys from the South."

Suzanne was an art history student at William and Mary, and the two became very close. "I think we were friends because we both loved Frank Sinatra, who wasn't terribly popular then. He had all of Sinatra's albums, and we used to play them over and over and dance. He loved to dance!" He must have been fairly accomplished on the dance floor, since a couple of other students who were at William and Mary with

Perry also remember this about him. Another of his girlfriends recalls that he had a very commanding manner on the dance floor. "When you danced with him he had a certain way of dancing and would make you follow his pattern precisely. There was something quietly masculine about him."

Certainly he was popular with the girls, and his friendship with Suzanne Tyler made her the object of envy of many others. "He always looked wonderful! All the girls thought he looked so good, he was so well groomed. We would compare him to the jocks who were trying to prove their masculinity, and Perry never had to. He was incredibly handsome, and even then very well mannered. We all liked him."

He was also popular with the guys. As Bottoms says, "You couldn't help but like him. Although he wasn't overly outgoing, he made his presence felt. He was a good-looking man and charming. He was also very witty."

Although Perry wasn't active in sports, it would be too much of a cliché to think of him as a sensitive young man during his college days, and Tyler says there was definitely nothing fay about him. Still, it is quite likely that Perry himself did feel he was different. A hint of this can be seen in a quote he later gave to the William and Mary *Alumni Gazette:* "I have always felt inwardly creative. I always cared about art. Fine art courses were sort of the magic at school. . . . [I]n the '50s there was so much of life I couldn't let out. Everything was set as to what a young man in Virginia had to be like."

It was obvious that Perry still felt shy, even though he was much better able to deal with people than he had been as a young child, and although he was a diligent student he showed little of the flair and promise that was to come. "The first time I read about him as a fashion designer in the newspaper I said, 'No, it couldn't be,'" remarks Tyler. "And then in one article I saw his picture and it was really him and I was *shocked*. It just couldn't be! I thought. I had always imagined people like that were really aggressive, and that just wasn't Perry at all."

These were carefree days, and, as Perry was to remark in the *Alumni Gazette* in 1978, "It was before the revolution of the '60s and all the social changes that came about. . . . I just had a very good time in college. . . ." This must have been due in part to the comfortable size of William and Mary in those days. It was small enough so that everyone walked to wherever they had to go (as David Bottoms puts it, "You could get up at five of eight and still be in time for an eight o'clock class") and everyone knew each other. It was the sort of situation that brought out the best in Perry, and in his senior year he ran for vice president of the Student Association on a ticket with Bottoms. They won with their campaign slogan of "Bottoms Up!" and one of their ideas (actually, it was Bottoms's) was to introduce "Dress Up" days on campus aimed at improving the way students dressed. (Their efforts, for the record, did not meet with success, and Bottoms was even hung in effigy on campus.)

William and Mary was basically a liberal arts school, and it wasn't until near the end of his three years there that Perry decided to concentrate on business as his major—not because he had decided what he wanted to do with his life, but more because he knew what he didn't want to do. "I knew everything I didn't want to be—lawyer, doctor, Indian chief. Business seemed to be a catchall," he later told Holly Brubach in an August 1980 interview in *Vogue*. The end result: he graduated in the summer of 1961 from William and Mary with a B.A. in business administration.

Since he still didn't know what he wanted to do, Perry spent the summer working for his father, probably to see if he wanted to go into the family fuel business. At the same time, there was a much more pressing question in his life that summer: the draft.

David Bottoms seems to recall that Perry was in the ROTC in college but had no wish to enlist in the service, and with some devious research he discovered a way to avoid military duty. Well, not avoid it exactly, but certainly a way to circumvent the rigors of active service.

"I'll never forget it, "says Troy. "Perry came round to the house very excited and said, 'We're going into the Coast Guard!'

"I didn't know what he was talking about for a moment, but then he explained that he'd researched the whole thing and if we enlisted in the Coast Guard reserve we would only be on active duty for six months, and then all we'd have to do is attend reserve weekends once a month after that for the next eight years.

"It seemed a much better deal than going into the Navy or the Air Force at the time, and we certainly couldn't have gone into the infantry. . . . After all we were from a naval port!

"So Perry and I joined the Coast Guard together. His service number was 2017970 and mine one before, 2017969."

Immediately after their induction in August they were ordered to report to boot camp at Cape May, on the southern tip of New Jersey. "We traveled all night on the train and the next thing I remember was someone shaving our heads," says Troy rather ruefully. "That was our rude introduction to thirteen weeks of boot camp." Perry must have been feeling homesick, since he picked up a lock of his hair from the floor and saved it to send home to his mother.

Coast Guard boot camp turned out not to be as arduous as Troy and Perry had initially feared. "It wasn't too dissimilar to gym in college," comments Troy. "All we had to do was climb ropes and learn how to march." Yet Perry's childhood asthma was soon acting up again, causing him distress. He wouldn't report to the infirmary, however, because it would have meant losing a week toward his six months, so he came up with a ruse instead that would get him and Troy relieved of their routine duties.

Unlike the other services, the Coast Guard's Presidential

Honor Guard component is selected from new recruits. Perry, with another piece of research, had found out that you only had to be a certain height and look presentable to get accepted, so after five weeks of basic training he and Troy applied and met the qualifications: Perry was five-eleven and Troy six-one and they could both "handle a piece."

Life in the Honor Guard turned out to be much easier. They drilled separately from the other recruits and would go to Washington every time there was a State occasion. Since it was the first year of a new administration and nearly every head of state in the world was anxious to meet the young new president, John Fitzgerald Kennedy, Troy and Perry saw a lot of duty at Andrews Air Force Base and spent much of their time being transported between Washington and Cape May. "It wasn't like it's made out in the press," comments Troy. "I mean to read the accounts now it sounds as though we were in the White House all the time and sleeping with Jackie and JFK in the Lincoln bedroom.

"As I said," he continues, "most of our duties consisted of being there when the president was receiving heads of state. I can remember when Nehru came in, and also the president of Finland, but that was probably only because we noticed Jackie was wearing the same brown outfit on both occasions. Perry and I were probably the only two people in Washington who realized she wore the same dress twice!"

Their most memorable moment in their months as members of the Honor Guard came when they were present at Arlington National Cemetery to honor veterans of the two world wars. "It was a very moving occasion," says Troy, "and then they gave us a weekend pass, which was unheard of when you were at boot camp. The pass was only for Washington, though, but the moment we were dismissed Perry said, 'We're going home!'

"I replied, 'We can't, if we get caught we'll be court-martialed.' I guess Perry was much more daring than I was. I'm too by-the-book and was afraid we were going to get caught."

Needless to say, they went into Washington and caught the train home. And though they had to remain in uniform because they were recruits, Perry's solution to their dilemma was to take off their gaiters, which made them look more like naval ratings. (Fortunately, they didn't get caught, even though anyone who had looked closely enough would've seen the crease in their pants where the gaiters had been.)

Perry's irreverent humor wasn't always appreciated by his fellow grunts, however. "You have to realize that we're not talking about the brightest balls in the chandelier here," comments Troy. "Those guys [in the camp] just didn't know what he was about. I remember one time they were showing some English film—I can't remember what it was, an Alec Guiness movie or something—and Perry wrote on the announcement board, 'American subtitles.' Well, most of those guys took it seriously!"

The Honor Guard was rotated continually, and soon it was time for Perry and Troy to leave for a stint at sea in the next phase of their active duty.

"We were ordered to report to our ship at the New London submarine base in Groton, Connecticut. Unfortunately, the ship we were posted to was in dry dock, so we spent the next few weeks in classes, and then they put us on the maintenance detail for the next six weeks," he continues. "You have to picture it. It was a joke. We were taken into this empty room the size of a huge barracks and told to clean it. The moment we were finished we were told to start over again.

"One time I was caught reading a book and was put on KP for a week. Naturally, Perry was more crafty: he was given the job of finishing some steps. It took him and this guy, Frank Percheck from Pittsburgh, who was six-three and weighed a hundred and twenty-eight pounds, three weeks to scrape these steps. I don't know how they drew it out that long."

They finally got a pass one weekend and decided to go

into New York to relieve the monotony of the maintenance detail. They hoped it would be a special weekend, because they had gotten tickets to see Bette Davis on Broadway in *The Night of the Iguana*. (Coincidentally, the film in camp the night before had been *A Pocket Full of Miracles*, starring Davis.)

They stayed at the Piccadilly Hotel, and after the performance went around to the stage door to try and get her autograph. Still a bit wet behind the ears, they spotted a black limousine and asked the chauffeur if he was Miss Davis's driver. He was, and told them to wait by the car till she came out. In the meantime they discovered that neither of them had anything to write with except a rather chewed-up pencil stub. Troy wanted to run across the street to the hotel to get a pen but was afraid he would miss the great actress. While they were debating what to do, La Davis herself came out of the theater and didn't seem to mind the pencil the two servicemen offered after asking for her autograph. Troy admits they were both wide-eyed, but Perry managed to stammer, "Miss Davis, the boys in camp saw *A Pocket Full of Miracles* last night and loved it."

With a dramatic flourish of her cigarette La Davis replied, "Well . . . *that* was one of the *fun* things that I did!"

Perry was avidly following film and theater by then, and Troy can remember the time they went to see *Breakfast at Tiffany's*. "Perry was mesmerized by Audrey Hepburn and wouldn't stop talking about her for days." (Coincidentally, it was another Hepburn—Katharine—who was to mesmerize Perry in the last year of his life.)

Although Perry could be naive when approaching someone like a movie star at that age, he was very sophisticated when it came to some of the finer things in life.

One of Troy's memories illustrates that Perry was more than capable of handling himself in public. "There was another time we got a weekend pass and went up to Boston. Perry decided that we were going to have dinner at no less than the Ritz Carlton. I was a little abashed, but Perry insisted and we walked in. Even though we were in dress uniform, they treated us like a couple of squids. I think they thought we were going to roll up our sleeves and have tattoos all over our arms." A waiter eventually came over to their table and was so condescending that Perry demanded to see the maître d'. When *he* came over he was equally supercilious. The young Coast Guard rating reacted angrily.

"Perry put him in his place in no uncertain terms," says Troy. "Although he was normally mild-mannered, if he got angry he really let it show. He was used to going to places like that with his parents and wasn't going to put up with any bullshit. Even then he knew how to get his way."

Perry and Troy finished their active Coast Guard duty at the end of February 1962 (ironically, without ever having seen service at sea), and again the question arose as to what he would do with his life. Obviously, his stint with his father's company the summer before had shown him that he didn't want to go into the family fuel business. "You can't see Perry driving a fuel truck or working on a furnace, can you?" asks Troy, laughing. And his parents, understanding as ever, put no pressure on him to get a job immediately.

It was a period of indecision in Perry's life, and he found the solution to his dilemma quite by chance. One early summer day, he and Troy went to visit the Old Dominion campus and while they were there Perry picked up a catalogue from New York University. After a few moments of flipping through it, he told Troy, "I'm going to go to graduate school." What had caught his eye was a six-month graduate course in retailing. He had always loved visiting stores with his mother, and the course description sparked his imagination. As he explained in a later interview with *Vogue:* "Somehow this seems so unimportant in the course of life, but I really liked stores. I was just fascinated by the way they smelled, by the cash registers, the bells ringing. . . . For a kid coming from a small town, it was some vicarious form of travel, wondering where all those things had come from."

That summer he and Troy didn't do much of anything, though Perry did take some easy work as a tennis coach for the city, and at one point they both worked for the city's traffic surveyor. "We would go out on assignment and count cars," recalls Troy. "It was a very boring job."

In the fall, Perry left Virginia for New York. It was the first time he had really left home, and he ended up taking a small studio apartment in Greenwich Village near where the old Women's Prison used to be, at the junction of Sixth Avenue and Christopher Street.

No one from NYU can recall anything much about Perry while he was there, probably because it was the first time he was completely on his own, away from home and friends, and most likely hid behind his shyness as if it were emotional armor. Those six months of his life are virtually undocumented, and it appears that he concentrated exclusively on his studies. Troy feels that although Perry was sophisticated in many ways, he must have felt uncomfortable and a bit intimidated by New York at that point because he was so young. Between October and the end of December, however, he did get his first taste of department store retailing, working at Stern's on Forty-second Street as part of his course requirements.

In March of 1963 he graduated from NYU with a Masters Degree in retailing and immediately returned to Virginia.

2

My salad days,
When I was green in judgement . . .

—William Shakespeare
Antony and Cleopatra (Act I, Scene V)

By 1963 Perry was ready to go out into the world as a man and start a career. What neither he, nor anyone else, could possibly imagine was that his life was already half over.

He decided to apply for a position at the venerable Virginia department store chain of Miller & Rhoads, even though he gave his family the impression he wasn't sure that's what he actually wanted to do.

There are only two department stores native to the Old Dominion state, Thalhimer's, founded in 1842, and Miller & Rhoads, in 1885. Their downtown-Richmond flagship stores, situated almost opposite each other on Broad and Sixth Streets in the center of the old Confederate capital, had been in direct competition for nearly three-quarters of a century. Thalhimer's, although the older of the two, was the more aggressive and fashion-oriented, and part of a major retail corporation. Miller & Rhoads, on the other hand, was *the* quintessential establishment store. Genteel and reserved, rather snobbish and conservative, it catered to the Virginia and North Carolina "carriage trade." It was probably this reputation that appealed to the socially less-than-top-drawer Perry Ellis.

Perry interviewed with Miller & Rhoads's training director, Katherine Bell, who can still recall the impression he made in that first interview: "The first thing that struck me was his

19

appearance. He had a sense of style and was clean-cut looking. Of course his credentials were right: William and Mary and then a graduate degree from New York University, but his intelligence was also very manifest. He had enthusiasm and a sense of purposefulness. He knew what he wanted and it was obvious he was willing to work hard to get it."

Ms. Bell accepted Perry for Miller & Rhoads immediately, and he joined the store's executive training program on July 1, 1963, at a salary of about $7,500. Katherine Bell paid special attention to the new trainee and took him under her wing. "We were about to open a new store in the Tidewater area [in Newport News] and I decided to take Perry down with me. He was the only one I chose from the training program, because he showed such promise." It was a big break for Perry, since the new store was being scrutinized by top management, and he acquitted himself well.

"He became known to top management then," says Bell, who adds, "He also had a knack of getting on with people: Perry had poise and he was never flustered by management."

Perry worked so well in the shakedown of the new store that the manager soon had asked Katherine Bell if he could stay for a while. She agreed, and instead of the initial three weeks he'd been scheduled to work there, Perry ended up staying six. For the last three, he fulfilled the duties of assistant manager, without the title. As Bell puts it, "By the time the store was open people [management] knew Perry."

The Miller & Rhoads training program was quite innovative for those days and exposed its young executives to all aspects of retailing. Perry was put through nearly every department in both operations and management, and it was while he was working in the toy department as assistant sales manager for the 1963 Christmas period that he met a beautiful young college intern named Sarah Price. Perry was obviously taken with her, and they soon started to date.

On a professional level, however, Sarah may not have been as enamored of Perry as she was on a more personal one.

She recalls that even then he had habit of delegating responsibility, which was not exactly the impression he conveyed to
his superiors. "Perry was great at delegating, and I did all the
work!" Though she found it annoying, Perry's considerable
charm always mollified her. "If you say 'please' and 'thank
you,' it goes a long way." She also stresses that Perry taught
her a lot in those early days of their respective careers. "It was
certain business principles that he taught me—to be sincere,
and when you're questioned, always to have an answer."

At the end of the executive training program trainees
were allowed to choose the area in which they wished to spe-
cialize, and since Perry was mainly interested in merchandising
he asked to be placed in the buying department. Accordingly,
his mentor, Katherine Bell, made him assistant to the chain's
finest buyer, Dorothy Sawyer, as buyer of budget dresses. "I
used to put all the most promising people under her," Bell
explains. "Not only was she a good buyer, but she could teach.
She wasn't insecure." (Coincidentally, Sarah Price was also
placed in the buying department, in lingerie and robes.)

Two years after joining Miller & Rhoads, in December
1965, Perry was promoted to junior sportswear buyer for their
stores, with a salary increase to $13,000. "He moved ahead
pretty quickly," says Gordon Mallonee, who was then vice
president and general merchandise manager of Miller &
Rhoads, and Perry's new boss. "Although he was a mild-mannered man, he was an aggressive kid and it was evident he
knew what he was doing."

Katherine Bell's original assessment of him as "one of the
most outstanding and brilliant young trainees I ever knew"
had been recognized by management, and it would soon be
borne out by his performance in the junior sportswear department, which he would take from a being relatively small con-
tributor to M & R's gross to the biggest money-maker in the
chain. He would later assume a self-laudatory tone when talking about his buying acumen in the interview with Holly Brubach for *Vogue:* "I was very clever about how to get the most

the fastest because I had training at a time when very few people in retailing had any college experience. I took a small department and made it the largest in the store, bigger than the furniture department." While the statement is basically true, it fails to take into account how naive he was and how much he still had to learn.

Certainly Perry had a talent for buying and merchandising, and as soon as he took over the women's junior sportswear department, he decided to change its image. The social climate was changing radically by the mid-sixties, and dress codes, even in conservative Virginia, were being relaxed. Perry sensed this and had definite ideas about what he wanted to do with his department, implementing them almost immediately. Unfortunately, one of his first decisions nearly cost him his job.

"I was working in the John Meyer showroom as a salesman for seventy-five dollars a week," recalls Jerry Yospin, who later became Perry's business partner, "and Perry was sent up to buy from the Villager and John Meyer lines, which shared a showroom in those days. It must have been about 1965. Anyway, Perry was given fifty thousand dollars to spend by the store, thirty-five thousand on the Villager line and fifteen thousand on our line. Perry liked our line a lot better and spent all but ten thousand on it. Norman Radd, the owner of Villager, was furious and tried to get Perry fired, but his bosses backed him up."

Gordon Mallonee says of the incident: "He was a very astute fashion merchandiser from the beginning. He had a nose for what young people wanted: he talked to people and kids in school. Both the Villager and John Meyer lines were very much in vogue then, cute little blouses and A-line skirts, but Perry realized that the Meyer line had a stronger youth appeal."

Mallonee views Perry's efforts with the Meyer line as first-class merchandising. "Perry pushed the hell out of the line. He worked well with Meyer as a resource and saw that we got good delivery. He also saw to it that it got exposed and good publicity. He developed John Meyer into the number-one biggest resource in the store."

With this retail success behind him, Perry quickly became one of John Meyer's largest customers, buying nearly a million dollars' worth of goods from them annually, which in those days was a considerable amount. (A John Meyer wool skirt wholesaled then for about $8.75. Its cost now is about $35, so Perry was buying the equivalent of between $3 and $4 million at today's prices from that company alone. At retail prices, which are generally calculated by the fashion industry as between two and two-and-a-half times the wholesale cost, that would now be the equivalent of about $10 million in sales.) That Perry was given this leverage to buy what he wanted from John Meyer, as well as any other company he chose to, is testimony to the tremendous business he was doing for Miller & Rhoads.

"He was brilliant, he really was," says Gordon Mallonee. "He had a fashion flair I haven't seen in anyone else. And he was daring and ambitious and had a look in his eyes like he was going to go where he wanted." Mallonee adds that Perry was very conscious of his budgets. "He was a good figure man. He stayed within plans pretty well and he didn't argue with management about budgets until he could prove he needed more."

Professionally, Yospin found that Perry was "an incredibly astute buyer. There was this buyer at Miller & Rhoads who taught Perry everything he knew. Her name was Frances Cleary and she was the sharpest, most animalistic buyer you could ever hope to meet. I was afraid of her. . . . Perry picked up a lot from her.

"I remember many times sitting in his office while he ranted and raved on the phone, cussing some poor manufacturer out, and I would look at him and smile and he would smile back! He was only acting out a role, but he certainly got everyone to do what he wanted."

Kathy Gempp, who became Perry's assistant in 1966, agrees. "He knew what he wanted and if the manufacturers didn't want to give it to him he would be on the phone cussing them out. I remember with John Meyer that he would always speak to one woman at the factory and yell and scream and holler at her and say, 'You're going to send me three hundred of these and four hundred of those.' And before she knew it she was finding them for him. He just had that way with him."

On the same Ellis ability, Sarah Price adds, "Perry wheeled and dealed. He'd get things off-price and bring them in and sell them at twice the markup."

Perry's work habits and attitude did not entirely endear him to everyone at the store. "I wouldn't say all the buyers were his buddies," says Price. "They didn't know how to take Perry." More often than not it was his animated nature that offended some of the staff of what was after all, a very staid establishment. "Perry wasn't mild-mannered in the office at all!" exclaims Kathy Gempp. "He would come into the office with a smile on his face and everyone knew he was there. He and Frances [Cleary] would shout across the hall at each other as if they were mad at each other and he was always doing outrageous things with Sarah Price."

On the other hand, he was always the perfect gentleman in public. "Our offices were not at the store, and Perry spent a lot of time on the floor with the saleswomen, who loved him," says Gempp. "A lot of them had been with the store for a long time, and because they liked him they helped make that department the success it was. They were absolutely dedicated to him."

A lot of the credit for the department's success was due to Perry's fashion flair, which was part and parcel of the same youthful exuberance that wasn't always appreciated in the office. "Perry was outrageous in the way he chose clothes," says Gempp. "For someone who was buying John Meyer for the conservative Richmond area, he put together outfits that were very similar to what he ended up designing in New York, with big, oversized coats and everything layered. He liked that oversized, layered look on women and was always trying things on Sarah, who was very small. His ideas were ahead of their time."

Michael Black, who was the coat and dress buyer for Miller & Rhoads at the time, doesn't quite give Perry the same credit for his fashion acumen back then as others do. His assessment of Perry's success at M & R is due more to what is called the "bottom line." "He was successful because he didn't give a damn about fashion. He didn't care what brand it was or what it looked like as long as it sold!"

Sarah Price agrees, but only because most of what was being sold in the department—blouses with Peter Pan collars and A-line skirts—was still the mainstay of his business. "He didn't care for most of what he was selling. But he knew what they wanted and catered to it in order to make the department look good." And even Gempp admits, "In a way the department almost ran itself; Perry just had to make sure what he bought, he bought enough of. . . . It sold out almost as fast as it came in."

Although he seemed to be more merchant than anything else at this stage of his career, Perry had to have had an instinctive sense of fashion to have bought and edited collections as well as he did. Not surprisingly, it was this side of the business that was beginning to interest him more and more.

Despite his aggressive professional attitude, he remained the polite and mild-mannered young man had always been. He was not very social and spent most of his time with Troy, Jerry Yospin, Sarah Price, and Michael and Joanna Black. Yet within this tight group he would relax, and his friends found him enormously funny. "He was always fun to be with," says Sarah Price. "We spent most of our time laughing together. Even when he would throw me on the couch and we'd start kissing, he would invariably break up laughing."

It was around this time that Perry stopped dating Sarah

and she and Jerry Yospin began to date. "We still remained friends, though, and were inseparable. . . . It was like the Three Musketeers."

There was also a more reflective side of Perry. Michael Black recalls, "Perry, Joanna, and I would go to Virginia Beach in the summer, and Perry would just go to the beach and sit on a stool, get out a book, and stay like that all day. He wasn't into meeting people or getting a tan to look good or anything like that, he just wanted to be quiet and read. I would tell him, 'Perry you're burnt on one side and white on the other,' and he'd reply, 'I don't care, I just like sitting by the sea.' He was real independent that way."

The same quirk was noticed by Sarah Price. "Perry would sit on the beach and never turn over. He would be black as the ace of spades in front and white as a sheet in back. I wouldn't walk down the beach with him unless he walked backward." Yet she has a different explanation for it. "I once asked Perry why he didn't bother to tan his back, and with that sharp wit of his he replied, 'They're only going to look at my face, dear. They only want to look at the front of me.'"

At first, these two unprompted recollections of the same story seem to contradict one another. Yet, in this case, based on the author's personal experience, the conclusions drawn are equally valid. Perry Ellis was, and continued to be to the end of his life, an introverted, solitary romantic. Yet he also had a puckish side to his character and was not above acting and playing to an audience, albeit only close friends and people he worked with saw this side of him. One can assume that as he became aware of his considerable talents, his ego and self-assurance grew to match his assessment of himself.

"He was very authoritative and did not hesitate to tell you what to do in no uncertain terms," says Kathy Gempp. "He made you work your butt off and the day went quickly even though he was always shouting orders, but he was very kind and would compliment you when you did something right."

Perry's ability to manipulate people with just the right

word at the right time was extraordinary. Jerry Yospin goes as far as to say, "To me it was Perry's gift of the gab that got him where he was. He pulled the wool over everyone's eyes. Perry could snow anyone—girls, guys, big shots, it didn't matter who. He was a cool guy."

Charming, witty, possessing business acumen and an instinctive fashion sense, Perry Ellis was not without his idiosyncrasies, among them a certain propensity to laziness. He was always the last one to arrive at the store in the morning, took long lunch hours, especially for business, and was one of the first to leave. And, as Sarah Price has noted, he was not above delegating his work.

In fact, in one area his laziness could have got him into serious trouble. During his years at Miller & Rhoads he was still a Coast Guard reserve and was supposed to report to Yorktown one weekend a month to fulfill his obligations. Failure to do so could have resulted in his being put on active service for two years. But the famous Ellis charm seems to have saved him from that fate. Troy Swindell, who was reporting in regularly, remembers, "Perry was hardly ever there. I don't know how he got away with it, but they kept accepting his excuses. He must have had more family deaths at that time than he had relatives."

If he wasn't above avoiding some of his responsibilities, he was very loyal to his friends and the people he worked with. Jerry Yospin, who had become a close friend through their work on the John Meyer account, states that it was Perry who was instrumental in getting him appointed to the lucrative Virginia territory for Meyer. "Perry was John's biggest account by then, and John was already listening to him, so I was given the Virginia sales territory, which was worth about two-and-a-half million a year."

Whenever Yospin was making his rounds in the Richmond area he would stay at Perry's apartment at 1005 Grove Avenue in the city's Fan district, which meant he lived there about eight months of the year. "It was a small one-bedroom

apartment in a building filled with old ladies who all loved
Perry, of course. There was a bedroom, the living room where
I slept on the couch, and a dining room like a closet. It was
nothing special . . . the rent was only about a hundred dollars
a month . . . but whatever Perry had in there was always the
best."

At the same time, Michael Black says, "We were the two
squarest-looking people you could hope to meet. . . . Perry
dressed in traditional Ivy League–style—natural-shoulder gray
suits, blue or white button-down shirts, and loafers. Jerry
Yospin remembers that Perry could be quite particular within
the dictates of this uniform. "In those days everyone wore Bass
Weegans, but Perry had to get his shoes from Brooks Brothers. You couldn't tell them apart, but the Brooks Brothers
shoes were twice as expensive and he would throw them out as
soon as he had worn out the soles. I remember asking him on
a number of occasions, 'You're not going to throw them out
are you?' He would always reply, 'They're worn out on the
bottom.' 'Mind if I take them?' I'd ask, and I would get a
nearly new pair of shoes from him."

Yospin also remembers that although Perry dressed conservatively, he had one fashion quirk: he would always wear
bright ties. "They were really ugly; either big Paisleys or loud
prints."

Perry was only earning $13,000 at Miller & Rhoads, but
he could afford to indulge in a number of personal extrava-
gances due to the generosity of his parents. In 1965, for example, they bought him a brand-new white Chevrolet. But Perry
hated to drive and would make Jerry drive it for him.

His generosity to his friends was also manifesting itself by
this time. Yospin recalls that on the occasion of the birth of his
first daughter, Perry bought her a solid-gold diaper pin. He
also remembers that Perry wouldn't allow him to share the
rent at Grove Avenue, so he used to take Perry out to dinner
instead, since Perry was a notoriously poor cook. "It would
only cost about five dollars for the two of us to eat back then.

But Perry always wanted to pay his share because we were friends, which was crazy, since he was also a legitimate business expense."

Dinners and quiet evenings with the group were about the extent of his socializing. "We were still very naive," muses Yospin, "and even then Perry didn't like to mix in big groups. Besides, Richmond was a very cliquish town and it was hard to break into, so we would just have dinner together or go out with friends like Sarah."

Michael Black also remembers Perry's aversion to crowds. "Every time I would ring him up when Joanna and I were having a party he'd try to beg off. Perry always had a small coterie of friends and was only really comfortable with them. Later on, in New York, you would only see him with Jim Terrell, or later, with Pat Ashley—he was always like that."

Yospin and Perry did try to help each other pick up girls, however. After all, it was Perry who had introduced Jerry to Sarah, but generally it was Jerry who would do the dirty work. On one occasion, their plotting backfired on Perry, but it did earn him Jerry's eternal gratitude: "In the summer of 1966, Troy, Perry, and I rented a house on Virginia Beach. I took the whole summer off, since it was the off-season for selling, and Perry used to come down from Richmond every weekend.

"One Sunday we were in a bar, and Troy and I were talking about something or other while Perry was chatting up the waitress. She was very pretty and he was obviously interested in her, but he had to leave for Richmond, so he asked me, 'How about getting me a date with her?'

"I went back to the bar the next day and arranged it, but for some reason or other she had to break the date, so she called me and said, 'How about the weekend after?'

"I said, 'Sure,' and told Perry that his date would have to be the next weekend. But then she called me up again the next week and broke that date with Perry.

"He never did get to date her, but since I was down there

all week I did. . . . And a year and a half later Bonnie and I got married."

By the end of 1966, Perry was beginning to feel dissatisfied with his job at Miller & Rhoads. He was the most successful buyer in the store, and would undoubtedly soon have been promoted to management level, but it wasn't enough. He had made his mark and was justifiably enamored of his accomplishments. Yet despite his self-effacing nature, he was extremely ambitious and a management position in the hierarchy of a Richmond department store, however prestigious, was not what he wanted from his future. He had become Miller & Rhoads's "golden boy," and the resulting hubris led him to overstep himself.

The first indication of his dissatisfaction was an approach Perry made to his dry cleaner, Ed Steinberg, with a proposition to open a fashion boutique in an empty eight-hundred-square-foot property that Steinberg had next to his cleaning establishment. "It was the building behind mine," says Steinberg. "It was rather like an art gallery, and we thought it would be a great place for a women's clothing store, since it's situated on the campus of VCU [Virginia Commonwealth University]. I didn't have the knowledge to open a fashion store, but Perry did as a buyer and he brought in Jerry Yospin as a third partner."

Perry was very involved with the store before it opened and even helped design it. "Perry knew what he wanted, he had definite ideas," says Steinberg. The best of these was to open up the front of the store and construct it out of glass. Since the building didn't have enough space for a display window, Perry's idea was to make the whole shop the display. The name of the store, A Sunny Day, was also Perry's idea. The three partners each put $9,000 into the store—$3,000 in capital and $6,000 in the form of a bank loan. Perry was given his $3,000 by his father.

Yet Perry's retail wizardry seemed to desert him at the beginning. "When we opened the store seventy-five percent of the merchandise was from John Meyer, and boy was that wrong!" recalls Yospin with a laugh. "It was in the Fan district and our customers were mostly students—the John Meyer stuff was far too conservative for them. Anyway, Perry got Marge [Anilowski, the plant manager] at the factory to take most of it back without making us pay for it. I don't know how he did it, because I sure didn't have the balls to do it!"

Once they got to know their customers, however, the store took off, and it's still there on North Harrison Street, where it opened in February 1967, though it has since been enlarged. Jerry and Ed were to remain partners in the business until after Perry's death some nineteen years later.

While Perry was involved in the planning stages of A Sunny Day, however, his extramural activities were brought to the attention of top management at Miller & Rhoads. Naturally, they were not pleased. "Perry and I got called out on the carpet," says Yospin. "They even brought John Meyer down from New York and bawled him out first because they found out we'd bought a lot of his merchandise, then they bawled us out."

"Yes, I didn't think he should go into competition with the people who were paying him, and I told him so in no uncertain terms," recalls Gordon Mallonee. "But he was a young kid and aggressive, and quite frankly we didn't think they would duplicate too much of what we were selling, so we didn't fire him for it. But I'm sure we scared the hell out of him!"

Whether this dressing down acted as a catalyst on his future is difficult to ascertain, but it was around this time that Perry started to make plans that were to have great consequences in his life, eventually taking him to New York. John Meyer had grown to admire and respect Perry for his buying acumen and fashion expertise and casually offered him a job. Perry took Meyer up on his offer, somewhat to Meyer's consternation according to Jerry Yospin. "John came to me and said, 'What do I do, Perry came to me for a job and that will take away my biggest account from me.' But John's business was slipping at the time, so he decided he could use Perry to merchandise his lines."

Perry left Miller & Rhoads on December 22, 1967, and, despite the uproar over A Sunny Day, their parting was amicable. "Perry had inclinations to get into the design end of the business and he left us to go with John Meyer, and there were no hard feelings about it at all," says Mallonee. "He talked with me about it, and I felt he had pretty much done his job and if he was going to get into the fashion business he should get up to New York."

His co-workers were surprised at his choice, however. "I couldn't believe it when he told me he was going to work for John Meyer, except for the fact he had such good rapport with them, because he really didn't fit, in my mind, the John Meyer image," says Kathy Gempp. "It was only when I heard he had gone to Vera that I got excited, because he used to bring in Vera scarves to the office—they were the big thing then—and ooh and aah over the colors and designs. I thought it funny he bought such conservative things for our department, because what he really liked were outlandish colors and design that was unusual."

They all agreed, though, that Perry was moving his career in the right direction. "Perry needed to be in New York," says Gempp. "We all thought he needed to be in New York."

3

The mid-sixties in America were a time of change. It was an era of civil rights protests and political assassinations, of Woodstock and a growing conflict in Vietnam, of *Hair* and Rowan and Martin's "Laugh-In," of Leonard Bernstein and Black Panthers, of radical chic and rebellion. It was the half-decade during which the country lost its innocence; people protested in the streets or "turned the other cheek" and went to live in communes in Haight-Ashbury. The very fabric of American society had been ripped apart by a bullet on the streets of Dallas, and the wholesomeness of Mom and apple pie had been replaced by miniskirts and marijuana. The buzz-words and catch phrases of a society in turmoil filled the air: Berkeley; Hanoi; the draft; running the Canadian border; the Tet Offensive; Mayor Daley; Martin Luther King, Jr.; segregation; escalation; free love; bussing; the Second Vatican Council; Chairman Mao; Ho Chi Minh; Flower Power; LBJ; Che Guevara. . . . American culture was in a state of shock, and out of these profound changes a new more permissive "counterculture" emerged full-blown: liberation was suddenly the new gospel.

Ever a barometer of social change, fashion was rapidly

radicalized. Even in the heartland of the country, the old styles emulating the grace and glamor of Jackie Kennedy with her Chanel suits and Halston pillbox hats succumbed to the onslaught of bell-bottom pants and peasant shirts, except among the most reactionary and matronly.

Needless to say, the East Coast establishment clung to its safe, familiar sweater sets, jackets, sensible shoes, and demure skirts—a sporty, quintessentially American look that had been advocated by designers such as Claire McCardell and John Weitz in the fifties. Two of the most successful companies in the country to sell this look for young women of breeding were Villager and John Meyer of Norwich. John Meyer, as has been seen, was integral to the rise of the young Perry Ellis, who was buying junior sportswear for a conservative establishment store in Virginia, but Meyer's sales were beginning to slip by the middle of the decade. Youth was in the final throes of its rebellion against parental authority, a generational movement that had started in the late fifties with Elvis Presley and *Rebel Without a Cause.* Even housewives were ready for the coming of Gloria Steinem, Helen Gurley Brown, and *Cosmopolitan.*

Meyer needed help, and despite his original reluctance to hire him, he instinctively felt that Perry Ellis was just the man to revitalize his company. Perry was in tune with what the younger generation was beginning to ask for and, as a result of his retail experience, could gauge just how far Meyer could go without losing his more traditional-minded clientele. As Arlene Cohen, John Meyer's widow, puts it, "Perry became very important to John as an editor of the line just by what he bought and what he was looking for in fashion."

A good buyer can become important to a fashion house by suggesting what will or will not sell, both in terms of color and style. Many companies use buyers from their top accounts as a sounding board, since it is the buyer who ultimately knows what *is* selling. It was in this capacity that Perry had been of inestimable value to John Meyer. In fact, Arlene Cohen, whose admiration for Perry's contribution to the success of the company has not lessened over the years, goes as far as to say, "The middle sixties was a time when the John Meyer label was so sought after that girls were cutting the label out of our clothes and putting it into their own. And it was Perry that made this happen."

"I am sure that we weren't the only company Perry was dealing with at that time," continues Cohen. "He already had an innate sense of style and was directing us as to whether women really wanted their skirts as short as everybody was saying they did. He kept us pretty much on the ball. He could have gone anywhere, but he and John respected each other so much that he decided to come to New York and join the company."

It was a big step for Perry, perhaps the most significant of his career. In his new position he would be working continually with Meyer's designers, choosing fabrics and going on buying trips to Europe. In effect, he would control the look of the whole John Meyer operation. And though it had only been five years since he first studied retailing at NYU, he had by then grown in confidence enough to enjoy the challenge of the new job as well as what Manhattan had to offer. The stimulus of New York and the sudden freedom from the constraints of Virginia society were to profoundly change him, both professionally and personally.

Yet, though he was obviously talented, there was very little about Perry Ellis at this time that suggested his tremendous potential, which would only be unleashed when he finally made his own statement as a designer. Indeed, one of his oldest friends describes him as "quite ordinary" at this stage of his career.

Arlene Cohen basically concurs with this assessment. "I don't think he thought about fashion intellectually at that time . . . that came later. Of course he always dressed very well and he was into that, but people don't work in fashion unless they *are* interested in clothes.

"You have to remember that Perry was a preppie and

dressed conservatively; he wore suits, shirts, and ties, and he had the genteel manner of someone brought up in the South. Still, there was something different. . . . It was the way he wore things. I can remember the way he used to swing his necktie over his shoulder when he was working. There was a style in the way he did it, a style that was unaffected and natural, but slightly different."

The move to John Meyer was the beginning of the final stage in Perry's thirteen-year apprenticeship in fashion before becoming a designer. He had by then acquired comprehensive knowledge of the retail side of fashion—a knowledge he would use to great advantage in later years—and at John Meyer he would learn whatever he didn't already know about the production and manufacture of clothes, as well as fashion styling and the publicity side of the business. It was while he was there that he learned, among other things, how to deal with the press and became convinced of the importance of image and advertising. These are the building blocks of the fashion industry, and Perry was to become expert in them all.

By all accounts John Meyer was an exceptional man. Sophisticated, widely traveled, and cultured, he was a far cry from the usual Seventh Avenue garment manufacturer and despised many aspects of the industry. His ethics were exemplary, causing him once to be described as "one of the few honorable people in a dishonorable industry." He was also outgoing and demonstrative, yet he would take the time to listen and was respected as a good teacher. That many of the same things would later be said about Perry suggests just how great an influence Meyer had on his career. It is certain that, at least in his respect for John Meyer, Perry looked upon him as a father figure.

Although Arlene Cohen says, "When Perry came to us he was a full-blown merchandiser," he still had a great deal to learn about the business. John Meyer was a textile engineer, and from him Perry acquired first-hand experience working with fabrics. It was from Meyer that he learned how to "build" a plaid, as well as the different techniques utilized in printing fabric. They visited mills together, which taught Perry what could or could not actually be done with woven fabrics, and Meyer shared his expertise in knitwear as well as the technology of dyeing (John Meyer had its own color laboratory) with his new employee. The impact of this knowledge would later be seen in Perry's own designs, where fabric and yarn would prove to be the starting point and inspiration for all his collections.

The other great contribution John Meyer made to Perry's development as a designer and individual was in exposing him to Europe. Twice a year John and Arlene would make buying trips to England, France, and Italy, and shortly after Perry joined the company they began to take him along. John and Arlene were used to the very best that Europe had to offer, always staying at first-class hotels and eating at the finest restaurants, and their style in these respects was one Perry would emulate for the rest of his life.

Although such trips always sound glamorous to people outside the industry, they are in fact tremendously hard work. Visiting fashion houses or mills, buying samples, and watching fashion shows may sound like heaven to any dedicated follower of fashion, but the strain and responsibility can be incredibly demanding; the perks of beautiful scenery, haute cuisine, and a generous expense account don't always make up for the hours of work one actually puts in. Yet, because of this same intensity, these trips very often create strong bonds of friendship and camaraderie. And, for some unexplained reason, they always seem to be filled with their share of humorous incidents. As Arlene Cohen recalls about one of Perry's first trips to London: "We were booked into Claridge's, where John always stayed, but we got in so late that they couldn't hold our reservations. However, Claridge's had booked us into the Mayfair, in the 'Maharajah's Suite,' and I remember our reaction on first seeing that vast suite decorated to look like an Indian palace yet all a little seedy. I think there were at least five bedrooms, and we spent the whole night laughing and trying out every single one of them!"

On another trip they went to Scotland to buy cashmeres from Ballantyne, and Perry went wild over the colors, with the result that when they landed at JFK in New York there were literally trunks full of sweaters, scarves, hats, and socks—so much, in fact, that when the customs officer opened their luggage he couldn't believe it. As Arlene puts it, "We had so many samples, it looked like we were going to set up shop in the airport!"

Most of their time on these trips would be spent checking stores and boutiques in every capital they visited. When asked what Perry would look for in those days, Arlene Cohen replies, "We weren't really a fashion house so much as a company that capitalized on style and taste. We weren't innovators. Perry understood that very well and what he would go for were the unusual details—a special shoulder, an exceptional collar, interesting fabrics . . . things like that." These very same details would eventually become the hallmarks that made his own designs so individual.

What had so impressed John Meyer from the beginning was Perry's understanding of the customer. Not surprisingly, he knew exactly what John Meyer of Norwich's customers wanted and who they were. He also knew how to keep those customers buying Meyer's clothes season after season by carefully updating the line. It was a talent that was also recognized very early on by Jean Guilder, who was then fashion editor of *Glamour* magazine. "The John Meyer customer in the early seventies was the same customer who read the magazine—upscale young women eighteen to thirty-five, and Perry knew what the customer wanted and understood exactly what the magazine was about as a result. In our trend seminars, which we gave for the industry twice a year, he would always be more interested in what our reader was about than a certain style or color trend. What mattered to him was the lifestyle of the consumer and what kind of clothes she wanted and what was important to her. He instinctively understood that the American girl wasn't the fashion-aware customer in New York but came from the rest of the country. In this he was different from every other designer, and it was one of his greatest strengths."

Perry also instinctively understood the importance of the fashion press and became close to many of its editors. As a result, John Meyer's clothes received prominent exposure in fashion magazines.

His friendships with certain of the more prominent editors were real, however. Perry was an intellectual snob and did not suffer fools gladly, and it was as true of his personal life as it was of his professional one. If he didn't admire an editor, however important he or she might be, he wouldn't bother to spend time or energy on them. Editors he liked, on the other hand, were cultivated very carefully. Jean Guilder, who became very close to him, recalls: "Perry would call me up about once a month for lunch. It would never be a simple business lunch, though—with Perry it was always something special. He introduced me to Trattoria Alfredo in the Village, for instance. He would bring a bottle of wine, and we would try all the different pastas. This was around the time SoHo was being developed, and we would go down to places like Harriet Love [a boutique that specializes in antique clothing] and spend hours browsing and checking out the Victorian clothes and artifacts and old scarves and things. It was some of the best fun I've ever had."

He was also careful to give previews of the John Meyer lines to his favorite editors—obtaining advance information this way can be a godsend to a fashion reporter trying to scoop the competition—and, as a result, they would return the favor with increased magazine exposure. It was skillful manipulation of key members of the fashion press, and remained his style even after he had a corps of publicity people working for him.

In previews he was also careful to edit the line down to a manageable size. This not only helped save time, a valuable commodity for high-level editor, but was also a great help to buyers from the stores. Perry would preselect looks that went well together and exhibit the line packaged in a way that could be easily ordered. The clothes would never be bunched up side by side on endless racks, but presented instead on wall fixtures to show complete outfits in silhouette and by color. (It was a method of presentation that was later used to great effect in James Terrell's brilliant designs for the Perry Ellis showroom, and was copied so widely by other houses that it is now virtually the standard in the industry for presenting a line.) His reason for developing this method was quite simple. The experience and knowledge of buyers from retail stores had begun to diminish, and in many cases buyers simply didn't know what they were looking at. (Of course, there are many brilliant buyers from stores all over the country, but there are also vast numbers of them who have to be shown what to buy.) It was, in any case, an important contribution to John Meyer's flagging sales.

The difficulty the company had keeping up with the fast-changing times was considerable. Fashion had swung from careful to "kookie," and much of Meyer's merchandise simply wasn't in touch. "John, Perry, none of them really knew what to do and they kept looking for new avenues," says Jerry Yospin. It could partly have been that Perry was trying to bring the company along too quickly. Yospin recalls that when shorter skirts were becoming popular Perry insisted they show a line of the new minis. "They bombed," he says now. The difficulties at John Meyer might have been just in Yospin's conservative Virginia territory, but he insists it was common to all the Meyer sales areas and he cites the fact that his annual sales figures slid from $2.8 million when he took over Virginia to around $600,000 by the time he left the company in 1974.

Despite these setbacks, Meyer himself had complete confidence in Perry's merchandising skills, and Perry, for his part, began to get more involved with the styling of the lines, although he didn't actually design; that was the province of a talented young lady named Pat Ashley, who eventually became one of Perry's closest friends. One area in which Perry did meet with success, however, was in galvanizing the support of the sales reps and generating enthusiasm for the new collections. This is vital to the success of a large company like John Meyer, which relies on its regional salespeople to sell the line to the smaller stores across the country who can't afford to come into New York to buy the collection, as well as to service the large retail stores throughout the season with re-orders. Perry would give the reps a fashion show at each season's sales conference. Yospin recalls that one fall season Perry sent the models out without bras and in wet T-shirts (remember this was in 1969 or 1970) and even now remembers that, "We were so excited that we didn't even look at the clothes and none of us realized it was really the same shitty stuff!"

Another area in which Perry became proficient during his "apprenticeship" at John Meyer was advertising. Arlene Cohen was spending less time at the office while she brought up her children and soon had handed over responsibility for the company's advertising to Perry figuring it would flow naturally from his merchandising skills. (It was a selling tool whose power he recognized instinctively, and from then on he would control the advertising for all of his fashion companies and licensees through Perry Ellis International.)

The move to New York had a profound effect on Perry's personal life as well as his career. Almost immediately his metabolism seemed to change. According to Sarah Price, he lost a lot of weight. "When Perry first came to New York I would come to visit him and we'd go out to lunch and he'd order two big bologna sandwiches. They'd each have about three inches of bologna on them. . . . I've never seen anyone eat sandwiches like Perry did.

"And then in the evening we would go out to dinner and we'd both order steaks and then have seconds sharing another one. In Richmond he couldn't eat like that because he'd gain weight." Losing the weight he carried as a youth made Perry's looks striking.

It was at this point in his life that Perry began to express his homosexual tendencies, and though he would remain bisexual for the rest of his life, his coming to New York seems to have acted as a sort of catalyst on the former. Whether he knew of these feelings before is open to speculation. Prior to moving north, even his closest male friends have said that there was never any hint of an attraction to other men, and if he was aware of this side of his nature it is almost certain that he kept it totally repressed until then.

His first apartment in New York was at 57 West Sixty-ninth Street, where he rented a one-bedroom apartment on the parlor floor, but since he spent much of the week in Connecticut at the John Meyer factory, he also lived with a friend, Robert Barth, in New Haven. In contrast to Perry's paneled Upper West Side apartment, Barth lived in the already famous apartment architect Paul Rudolph had designed for himself while he was dean of the department of architecture at Yale University. (It has since become a design classic and its clean, uncluttered spaces set the tone for the whole Minimalist movement in interior design.) The apartment at 31 High Street soon became the site of a chance encounter that would result in one of Perry's closest friendships and most important professional relationships.

"I was studying architecture at Yale and I lived across the street in a high rise," recalls James Terrell. "I had always wanted to see the Rudolph apartment, which was very famous and had been publicized many times, so finally I got up the nerve and knocked on the door, and there was Perry standing there. He'd been playing cards or solitaire or something, and he asked me in to tea and that's how I met him."

Although he kept up with his friends from Virginia, Perry was beginning to surround himself with new ones in the city. He was obviously attracted to intelligent, handsome, WASPy, Ivy-League types, and one of these was Robert McDonald, a very good-looking young man working in the film business. In time he became Perry's third lover, after a short affair Perry had with one of his neighbors, an interior decorator. (Perry and McDonald were to remain lovers for at least six years, and now he is one of his heirs, guardian of Perry's daughter Tyler, and head of Perry Ellis International.)

By this time, the early seventies, Perry was much more outgoing than he had ever been, leading a very social life and taking advantage of all the amusements the city had to offer, though there was a part of him that always needed to be alone and which he appeased with reading and music. And, unlike his Richmond days, he was also becoming domesticated. Michael and Joanna Black had moved to the city near Perry on the Upper West Side, and Joanna has some very amusing anecdotes about Perry's first attempts at cooking for himself. One time he called her up and said, "Don't ever go to that grocery store on Columbus Avenue again!"

"Why not?" Joanna asked.

"They don't carry clarified butter!" said Perry indignantly.

On another occasion he called her and told her that he had had two eggs on the stove for an hour and a half and they still weren't hard-boiled.

"Did you turn the stove on?" asked Joanna. Perry replied that he had, so Joanna asked him if he had put any water in the pot.

"Do you have to put water in?" asked Perry innocently.

It is apparent that Perry had everything going for him at this point in his life. He was in New York at an exciting period of its history, and he was young, handsome, and had a good job with a good salary. (Jerry Yospin recalls that Perry once told him he was earning $60,000 a year, but that seems high in light of the starting salary he would pull down at his next job.)

Whatever the exact figure, it is a fact that by 1974 Perry had enough money saved to start thinking about buying his own town house. He had been living on West Sixty-ninth Street for approximately four years and had finally persuaded the owner to sell. The negotiations dragged on and on, and the house when he finally got it was in terrible condition. As Jean Guilder recalls: "Perry took me over to show me the place, and in those days the Upper West Side wasn't as chic as it is now. There were rats in the basement and we practically had to wear hip boots to enter it." On closing the deal Perry immediately asked his friend Jim Terrell to draw up plans for renovating it.

The town house still had other tenants in it, and Perry only took over the raised basement below the parlor floor in which he was already living. Perry and Terrell decided from the start on two ground rules for the renovation: to keep the old intact and, wherever they did have to build, not to emulate the past. "There was a juxtaposition between the old and the new elements side by side and it worked," says Terrell. "It was a style I associate with Perry." The renovation turned out to be a huge success and was featured in several interior design magazines, as well as making the cover of the book *Living Well*.

Upstairs was the bay-windowed "piano room," complete with a baby grand piano. It was a long, airy, south-facing room overlooking the street, and situated behind it was a warm, paneled living room (originally Perry's bedroom). Downstairs, which was reached via a striking glass-roofed stairwell designed by Terrell, were the kitchen, dining room, bedroom, and bathroom. The lower half of the duplex was much more modern, with clean, uncluttered spaces filled with reproduction furniture by the Virginia cabinet maker Hugo Beyermann, who had been brought to Perry's attention by his old college friend, Troy Swindell. Beyermann's reproductions were so good that they added to the myth of Perry's aristocratic Southern background and were regularly referred to by the press as family heirlooms. Certain pieces in the apartment were in fact from his parents, among them a seventeenth-century French provincial writing table, a Biedermeier fire screen, and an eighteenth-century love seat. But for the most part the furniture was new—and expensive. (Even then Beyermann was charging upwards of $4,000 a piece.)

Perry found that he and Terrell worked well together on the renovation, which was the first substantial manifestation of what would later be called the "Perry Ellis style." But, in fact,

Perry's contribution to the interiors Terrell designed for him was not as great as has been suggested in many articles about his homes and, eventually, the showroom. Still, as in everything else, Perry knew what he wanted and his demands often proved quite frustrating for Terrell. Perry was a perfectionist, and on one occasion Terrell remembers him nearly going too far. "I designed this dining room table for the house. It's an enormous oval glass-topped table with an acrylic stripe running through it, and it rests on a cylindrical base. It's still quite avant-garde, and it took about a year to have made. The specifications required it to be ordered in pieces from several manufacturers, and we assembled it on site. Just as we were finished, Perry came in and said, 'Couldn't it just be about a quarter of an inch smaller all around?'

"Well, there were about twenty people standing around looking at this huge nine-foot glass table they'd moved into place and no one knew what to say!"

Terrell believes that Perry could have been joking, given his rather wicked sense of humor. Perry was such a perfectionist, however, that he probably half meant it.

One surprising aspect of the house was the comparative lack of art on the walls even after Perry could afford any painting he wanted. In the bedroom he did have a series of lithographs called "Stones," which is the result of a collaboration between Perry's favorite poet, Frank O'Hara, and O'Hara's lover, the painter Larry Rivers.

Despite these diverse elements, the 69th Street house was a warm, comfortable, unpretentious home that Perry would live in until the end of 1983 when the big town house on 70th Street was completed.

The Sixty-ninth Street town house quickly became a place of refuge for Perry, and although he enjoyed giving candlelit dinner parties for friends, it was a home he more often than not liked to enjoy with whomever he was living with or seeing at the time and one or more of his beloved Brittany spaniels.

While his domestic situation had become settled with the

completion of the renovation and he was still very much involved with McDonald, things were not proceeding as well at work. He still loved what he was doing, especially his involvement in choosing all the colors, fabrics, and prints for the John Meyer lines, but, at the same time, he wasn't feeling challenged anymore and a certain dissatisfaction with his employment situation was setting in. As he told journalist John Duka in an article in *The New York Times Magazine* in July 1978: "It was an interesting period for a company like John Meyer. They were trying to be relevant, but after six years, even the challenge of that didn't interest me. I had too much time on my hands."

The company was also facing a tragic development. John Meyer, Perry's mentor for so many years and a man who had become almost as close to him as his own father, was dying of cancer. In July of 1973, while the company was still grossing nearly $100 million a year, it was sold to W.R. Grace & Company, a giant conglomerate, and it could have been this that caused Perry to start thinking about a new job. (Sadly, Meyer died six months after Perry left the company, on July 19, 1974.) The fact was that, despite certain setbacks in John Meyer of Norwich's performance over the preceding few years, Perry's reputation in the industry was superb, and toward the end of 1973 he was approached by The Vera Companies.

The person who had decided to feel him out was Matt Shaw, president of Vera Sportswear. "In some ways this is a very small business and you quickly hear about people. I knew what Perry had done for John Meyer and felt he would be the right person to help us develop Vera's sportswear. We needed a merchandiser who would understand The Vera Companies' philosophy and could work with double-knit polyester, which is where we were at, at the time."

Perry obviously must have felt stymied by the situation at John Meyer to have left a company that was working in the natural fibers he loved in order to go with a company that only used man-made fibers, and he was to later tell John Duka that he "wasn't really interested until I met Vera herself. She was an earth mother, and I loved her immediately."

Vera was the legendary Vera Neumann. Already sixty-four years old in 1974, she had founded her company in 1946, screen-printing her floral and abstract paintings onto linen place mats. "That's all we had room for on our kitchen table," she once said to Sally Kirkland, the well-known *Life* magazine fashion editor. Utilizing the surplus of parachute silk available just after the war, she began to design scarves that were also stitched together into blouses. She soon had become so famous that by 1966 the *New York Herald Tribune* only had to give a simple clue—"designer of scarves and blouses"—to elicit the correct four-letter answer in its crossword puzzle. A long-time collector of art, she not only had the Bauhaus architect Marcel Breuer design her house overlooking the Hudson River but also her showroom at 1411 Broadway. Viewed in context Vera's showroom was incredible. Apart from a few of the top designers, the level of showroom design in the garment district makes a Holiday Inn look tasteful. Certainly Vera's talent, reputation, and artistic connections would have appealed to the thirty-four-year-old Perry Ellis, but the company he was joining was primarily a cheap fashion house selling Nyesta dresses for $15 wholesale.

Perry officially began his tenure at The Vera Companies as vice president and merchandise manager of their sportswear division on January 21, 1974. It was a step up from his title of merchandise director at John Meyer and, according to Matt Shaw, his salary was $30,000—not a tremendous amount in today's inflated dollars, but a good salary then. (It is difficult to believe that Perry, who had told Jerry Yospin he was earning $60,000 a year at John Meyer, would have gone to Vera for half that amount. It is more likely that Shaw's recollection is accurate and that Perry was simply boasting to Yospin.) By joining Vera Sportswear, Perry became an employee of Manhattan Industries—at the time, a second-grade but highly successful company that had acquired Vera. He was to remain in their employ until his death twelve years later.

4

High flying, adored;
Did you believe in your wildest moments,
All this would be yours. . . ?
High flying, adored;
What happens now, where do you go from here?
For someone on top of the world;
The view's not exactly clear. . . .

—Tim Rice,
"High Flying, Adored" from *Evita*

One lazy evening sometime during the summer of 1975, Perry Ellis got a laugh from his weekend guests on Fire Island when he recounted what the eminent psychic Frank Andrews had predicted for his future—"Within five years I'll be as famous a fashion designer as Halston!" In those days, with the preeminence of Halston, Klein, and Blass on the American fashion scene, it was an unbelievable prediction and put down by his friends as a merry, late-night boast.

The year before, at a dinner party for about eighteen that Jim Terrell had given, the subject of fortune tellers, astrologers, and psychics had come up. Perry was quite adamant in his rejection of anything having to do with a sixth sense and decried the whole subject. Eventually, however, he called up Andrews, who was very much in vogue then, and said, "I have a feeling I should see you." Andrews intuitively said, "Come right down."

Perry never revealed all that Andrews told him, but he did tell Terrell, among others, that he had been warned not to fly in a small plane for the next five years and that his name would in fact some day be as famous as Halston's. Despite his skepticism, Perry did cancel his seaplane flight to the island that weekend . . . and the flight he was booked on crashed, killing all its passengers.

Still, Perry's circle of acquaintances remained skeptical about Andrews's prediction for their friend's future. What they did not know is that Perry's thirteen years in the fashion industry were about to pay off and his talent about to be recognized.

He had been working at Vera for about a year when Frank Rockman, the new president of the sportswear division, gave him the chance to design. Up to that point he had been doing much the same sort of work as he had at John Meyer, choosing fabrics and colors and suggesting different styles that might appeal to prospective buyers. One fashion editor says, "You have to realize that Vera wasn't anything like John Meyer. The first few times Perry showed me the line he was quite embarrassed. We couldn't feature anything in the magazine."

Yet Perry had been allowed considerable creative rein in adapting Vera Neumann's paintings. "He would interpret them into fabrics," says Terrell. "Of course it was all polyester . . . it's hard to imagine Perry into polyester! . . . But what he would do with them was either shrink them down so they became the smallest possible design, or enlarge them so that you got only a corner of the original on the fabric." (It should be noted that Perry learned from his experience at Vera and utilized many of the same techniques in his own collections later on, especially when he was working with plaids.)

It's a safe bet to assume that Perry didn't much enjoy his work at Vera that first year. He was traveling a tremendous amount, both to Europe on business, as well as on as many personal vacations as he could get away with. Jim Terrell says of this period, "I was working for a firm and I don't know where I found the audacity, but I used to take off all the time. Perry and I would go to Florida every three weeks or so and stay at the Royal Biscayne Hotel. It looks like the Beverly Hills [Hotel] now, but then it was absolutely out of the fifties. We used to have so much fun. There were no pressures, and when something would come up we would just start laughing and rolling around on the floor with tears in our eyes."

It wasn't all a lark, however. Jean Guilder recalls one time in Paris during the Prêt à Porter (ready-to-wear) collections when she took Perry to a Kenzo showing. "You remember, it was the famous collection he showed at the Bourse [the old Paris stock exchange]," she says. "Perry's eyes were so round . . . he had never seen anything like it, either the clothes or hair or the whole atmosphere of the thing. Afterwards we went to dinner with Bernadine Morris [of *The New York Times*] and Julia Schoen [of *Glamour*]. Perry couldn't stop talking about it."

For anyone outside the fashion industry it is difficult to imagine the power and excitement of a Kenzo show in Paris in those days. One literally had to fight one's way in, even if you represented one of the most important fashion magazines in the world, and the crush was so severe that there were armed *flics* (policemen) at the door. At one such show, one of the most dignified fashion matrons in the world was dragged away screaming with her carefully coiffed hair and couture Chanel suit in total disarray. It was the best theater in town and the excitement of the shows themselves was magical.

Perry was undoubtedly influenced by the experience to the end of his days. His clothes, even after they became much more sophisticated, had a whimsy that bore marked reference to Kenzo's collections of the mid-seventies (he even copied the irreverent skipping of Kenzo's models down the runway . . . until *Women's Wear Daily* started to make ugly remarks about it), and he always publicly acknowledged his admiration of, and debt to, Kenzo in those years. (More privately, the only other two designers he would admit an admiration for were Karl Lagerfeld and Elsa Schiaperelli, both of whose clothes also exhibit a remarkable irreverence.)

All the different facets of Perry's career up to that time had given him such a insight into fashion that when Frank Rockman joined Vera Sportswear in June of 1974, he discovered that much of the input and many of the ideas used in the Vera Sportswear line were coming from Perry rather than from their soon-to-retire designer. "She was a lovely lady, but in watching her I could see that Perry was the one that had all the ideas," Rockman says. Consequently, some time around December of that year he called Perry into his office and asked if he'd like to design the line. Perry immediately replied in the negative.

"He said he didn't want to be a designer, and obviously he felt badly about the designer we already had and didn't want to usurp her authority. I told him that as far as the company was concerned, she was about to go," Rockman remembers.

Perry insisted that he didn't want to be a designer. Rockman responded, "I don't care what I call you, but with you designing the line and me merchandising it I think we can have a good time with it."

Perry remained unconvinced. Rockman asked him to think about it, and by the time Perry reached the door he said, "You know, I *would* like to do a collection."

"Perry came back from the door and sat down again," Rockman remembers, "and said, 'Maybe someday I would like to design different things.'

"I said, 'Like what, Perry?'

"'I would like to design a blue-and-white dish pattern for Tiffany's.'

"And that's exactly how the conversation went and how Perry started to design."

It is interesting to note that within those few moments Perry's mind had already soared beyond the opportunity Frank Rockman had offered him—the chance to be a fashion designer—and was already thinking beyond just clothes. It indicates that his creative impulses were never directed solely toward fashion, but rather that his mind was exploring many different avenues and outlets.

The result of the conversation with Frank Rockman was that Perry became the designer of the Vera Sportswear line (which at that point mainly comprised print blouses and double-knit polyester pull-on pants) from January 1975 to the appearance of the first of what would be called his Portfolio collections in the fall of 1976.

Given Perry's penchant for style and natural fibers, he soon began to implement changes in the sportswear line. "The pants and the print tops were Vera's forte at that time, but Perry began to do small groups that took our customer forward," admits Rockman.

It was one of these groups that first caught Jean Guilder's eye with regard to Perry's design talent. "I can remember it quite well," she says. "Perry showed it to us at the end of 1975 and it was a very small group of about fifteen pieces—skirts, jumpers, and shirts in denim and French toweling. They were very simple peasant-type looks and it was quite charming. We photographed it for the magazine."

The success of Perry's forays into a more contemporary look caused Frank Rockman to go to the top executives at The Vera Companies and their parent company, Manhattan Industries, and ask them to allow him to start a new contemporary fashion line. Tom Costello, president of The Vera Companies, agreed to Rockman's proposal, figuring that the cost of starting up a new collection wouldn't be that high with Perry designing both lines. The only major expense, apart from sampling, that Rockman needed would be for another assistant for Perry to help with the sportswear line. Rea Lubar, who handled the press for Vera and was one of the most influential fashion publicity people in New York, happened to be in Rockman's office when he asked Perry if he would like his own line. "This is exactly how it happened," she says. "Perry walked into Frank's office and with no preface Frank said, 'Perry, I think you ought to do your own collection.'

"'I don't know how,' Perry replied.

"And Frank said, 'Why don't you think about it overnight?'

"Twenty minutes later Perry walked back into the office and said, 'I'll do it!'

"And that's how Portfolio was born."

Perry was never a designer in the purest sense of the word, in that he could barely sketch and wasn't able to make a *toile* (the muslin shape constructed on a mannequin from which the pattern is actually made), but he did supply the creative ideas and was articulate enough to express them to his assistants, who were technically proficient in the areas Perry was not. The first of these was Patricia Pastor, a young graduate of the Parsons School of Design in New York, who joined Perry on the Vera line at the end of 1975. With the implementation of the new arrangement, Rockman hired Charlotte Neuville for Vera and Patricia was moved over to Portfolio. There was also a pattern maker, Claire Newman, who worked with Perry in translating his designs into cloth and proved to be very important to him in these early years.

Among the European fashion cognoscenti the question of what constitutes a designer in America remains a bone of contention. Europeans expect their designers to be able to follow through on the original inspiration, from the sketch, toile, and pattern on through the finished garment. This is, in the European mind, the art of couture. In America we expect less: most of our homegrown designers are incapable of carrying out this transmutation and rely instead on numerous assistants to bring to life their nebulous ideas.

Perry belonged to the latter school of design. Yet he was a master of proportion and could oversee fittings as well as any of the grand couturiers in Paris. Certainly he supplied the ideas. But it should also be noted that Patricia Pastor's contribution to Perry's success was incalculable, and after Perry's death she was chosen to design the Perry Ellis women's collection with Jed Krascella, who was hired as his second assistant on Portfolio in 1977 or '78.

Perry was given a considerable raise by Manhattan Industries as soon as his appointment as designer of the new collection was made official, as well as a bonus based on the profitability of both Vera Sportswear (for which he would continue to oversee the design) and Portfolio. (At first the collection was called Portfolio by Vera, which Perry hated, and soon the Vera tag was omitted.)

His ideas proved to be deceptively simple—loose, flowing, easy shapes in natural fibers, all shown in natural earth colors. Although it doesn't sound revolutionary now, in the mid-seventies it was a complete change from the fussy, tightly fitted sportswear most Americans were used to seeing. "At the time it was so refreshing and very, very easy," comments Carolyn Gottfried, then one of the editors at *Women's Wear Daily*. "It all looked so right. When you're in the fashion industry as long as we have been, you go along with your gut feeling. As you know, we do our job and go along and look at clothes and don't get very excited, but every now and then someone comes along . . . it's hard to put it into words. You just know it's right and it makes you realize again why you're in the fashion business.

"Perry was one of those people."

Gottfried was covering the sportswear area in the summer of 1976 when June Weir, who was then fashion editor of *WWD,* asked her to do a story on the new design talent in New York. As a result, Perry, along with China Machado, Tibout Bouet, Regine Sicart, and Charles Suppon, were photographed together for Page One of *Women's Wear Daily.* It was the first of what would prove to be many covers for Perry in *WWD* and came out on November 22, 1976, the day of his show unveiling his first spring collection.

The show was small, with an audience that consisted of a small coterie of some of the most influential fashion editors in New York, gathered together partly by Rea Lubar and partly by Perry's own press contacts. "You have to realize he wasn't the instant darling of the press that people say he was," says Lubar. "It was very difficult to get editors up to see him at that time. Edie Locke [Edith Locke, one of the most important fashion editors of the seventies, who now has her own successful television fashion show] still reminds me of the time I called her up and said, 'You have to see my Perrele [a Yiddish diminutive]!' She replied, '*Who* is that?'"

Despite the difficulty they had in attracting attention, Lubar and Perry, with the contacts he had forged while working for John Meyer, rounded up more than a respectable turnout for a first collection. June Weir and Carolyn Gottfried were there, as were Anne Marie Schiro and Bernadine Morris of *The New York Times,* Nonnie Moore and Sandy Horvitz of *Mademoiselle,* Jean Guilder of *Glamour,* a couple of editors from *Vogue,* and Bill Cunningham, one of the best fashion photo reportage editors in the world. Perry had asked Gottfried's advice on how to stage a show, and it must have worked, since one of the editors present has said, "It was like 'instant designer.' I'd seen the collection while he was still working on it and suddenly there it was perfectly accessorized, worn layer over layer, and presented on some of the most beautiful models in town. It was a perfect, professional show, and you knew that Perry had arrived."

Adds Guilder, who had been watching Perry's career as long as anyone, "He was like an IBM machine. Everything he had done in his career up to then—all that input—came together, and, of course, there were those special ingredients of his wit, talent, and knowledge of the consumer."

One of the first people to take notice of that initial *WWD* cover story was the astute retailer Kalman Ruttenstein, then president of Bonwit Teller, who quickly got in touch with Perry, went to see the collection, and placed an order. As a result, by early 1977 his spring collection was gracing Bonwit's Fifth Avenue windows and heralding Perry as *the* designer of the future.

In the meantime, *Women's Wear* continued to cover Perry extensively, and he soon had met the single most powerful person in fashion publishing, John Fairchild, chairman of Fairchild Publications, which publishes the industry journals *WWD* and *Daily New Record,* as well as *"W"* and *"M"* magazines. Says Carolyn Gottfried, who introduced them, "Mr. Fairchild was as smitten with him as we all were."

Two days before Perry's first fall show, which was scheduled for Wednesday, April 27, 1977, Fairchild gave Perry his second cover—a photograph of him and two of his models wearing what either Perry or *Women's Wear* (which loves to invent sharp, witty labels) dubbed the "Slouch" look. It was apparent that Perry had gained a very powerful ally, and one who was to be instrumental in promoting his career. Fairchild's power was such that Gottfried took Ellis aside and said, "Perry, do you have a good lawyer? . . . You're about to become famous."

The power of Fairchild's exposure can be seen in the way that, the second time around, Lubar had no difficulty getting the press and retailers to attend the show. In fact, the response to the invitations was so overwhelming that Perry called her to his office one day and asked her how they were going to fit everyone in. "How's about bleachers?" Lubar replied. They agreed it might be an idea. Cathy Williams, Lubar's vice president, got the Yellow Pages and found a supplier, and soon the three of them had jumped into Perry's car and were driving to Staten Island to look for bleachers. "We drove deep into the heart of Staten Island," recalls Lubar, "to this terrible neighborhood where a company run by Italians provided bleachers for sports events. I don't know what the bleachers we saw had been used for, but they were very rusty; so Perry quietly said, 'Can you paint them?'

"'Painta the bleach?' they asked. 'Yes,' said Perry in that quiet way of his, and they painted those bleachers orange to match the color scheme of One-four-one-one [the Ellis showroom on Broadway]!"

The "slouch" look was inspired by Perry's going to the door of his office one day to pick up a lunch delivery from Gristede's (one of the more fashionable food emporiums in Manhattan) and noticing the long, slouchy, green Gristede's jacket the delivery boy was wearing. Perry startled him, so the story goes, by saying, "I'll buy your jacket for five dollars." The boy acquiesced and his jacket became the basis for what is now a famous fashion silhouette. Supposedly the silhouette for the trousers came into being when Perry came into the office one morning with his trousers uncuffed and falling around his ankles. Pastor saw him looking in the mirror rather pensively, and then he asked her to start sketching.

The resulting collection consisted of long oversized jackets with wide roll-up sleeves, pants that bunched softly below the knee, baggy "hobo" pants, long mohair sweaters with drawstrings running around the hips, tunic dresses over flaired petticoats, and bibbed shirts. The various looks, reminiscent of many things that Kenzo had done, were to become signature Perry Ellis styles. Like his first collection, the palette was limited, based on deep earth tones and lichen greens. In addition, the almost ill-fitting clothes were shown ever-so-casually on the runway. It was an irreverent attitude that caused a sensation and captured the imagination of the editors and retailers packed into the showroom. One of the more special items in the show perfectly demonstrated Perry's flaunting of convention and his sly sense of humor: a stunning fox fur coat made for him by Alixandre, the company that does Yves Saint Laurent's furs. Worked vertically and dyed a soft shade of lichen green, with a khaki cotton lining and a drawstring at the hem, it was shown with a real run-of-the mill backpack at Perry's insistence.

The press raved, buyers placed orders, and Perry Ellis's reputation was made.

Every year, just after New York's fall shows, the most important fashion editors in the country, with the exception of Fairchild's women's editors, would get together for lunch at the Plaza Hotel and nominate the best designers of the year for Coty Awards (more properly called the American Critics Awards for Fashion). Although they have since been cancelled, in the mid- to late seventies they were the fashion equivalent of the Oscars. (John Fairchild didn't agree with the policies of the cosmetics company Coty, the sponsor of the ceremonies, and therefore boycotted the nominations and awards for his women's publications, *WWD* and *"W,"* but not for his men's publications, *Daily News Record* and *Menswear* magazine.) That year, the central committee, in an almost unprecedented move, nominated Perry solely on the strength of his first two seasons, along with Stephen Burrows, Donna Karan and Louis Dell'Olio (who were responsible for designing the Anne Klein collection), and another relative newcomer, Charles Suppon. Perry didn't win, but the fact he had been nominated for the highest accolade granted by the fashion industry in his very first year of designing immediately thrust him into the ranks of the country's top designers.

Still, he managed to cause quite a fuss by insisting on using his own models for the show. He had already set a precedent by using only the top photographic models in the shows for his first two collections, and he wasn't about to go back to the regular show models that Coty used for their awards ceremonies in front of such a select and critical audience. He had his models come on in dyed body suits and carrying a bundle of clothes; they then proceeded to put them on until they were fully clothed and Perry's new fashion statement was revealed. It was a novel way to present a collection in a five-minute show and was further indication that Perry was thinking hard about every aspect of his individual design statement. In essence, he had already become the designer the press was lauding him as.

However much Perry might have worried over the minutiae of his Coty presentation, his main concern that summer was his forthcoming 1978 spring/summer collection, to be shown in the fall.

It's a strange fact of life in the fashion business that spring/summer clothes are shown in the fall and fall/winter clothes in the spring. This allows time for orders to be taken by stores, for fabric to be ordered, for clothes to be manufactured according to size and style, and for delivery. It also means the designer is working on a collection a year before the clothes are seen and bought by the public, certainly a major reason why fashion design is such an ephemeral art. Quite simply, it means the designer has to anticipate what the public will want to wear a year ahead of time. Much of the greatness of a world-class designer lies in his or her ability to predict the mood of the public a year hence, which in turn can depend on many things, including political, economic, and sociological factors. There is more to designing clothes than shape or style: a designer almost needs to be a soothsayer as well.

For the new spring collection, unveiled on November 9, Perry did nothing new. Instead, he simply evolved the slouch shapes of the winter collection into easier, slimmer summer silhouettes. It was a masterful merchandising ploy. Perry obviously wanted to show retailers—who, though interested, had not bought Portfolio in great volume—that he was a "stable" designer and therefore "bankable." All the Ellis signature shapes and details were present, including his preference for no buttons at all, or, at most, hidden closures (another tip picked up from avant-garde designers like Kenzo in Paris), and his trademark layering. Executed in beautiful natural fibers like linen and cotton, as well as more textural hemp and hopsacking, the colors were still neutral, but this time there were some dark accents like burgundy included, and the palette had a much greater range than before. Cream, seagull, wild honey, blush, and olive gray, they suggested the softness of a beautiful spring day.

Of course, nothing Perry did was ever totally straightforward, and for this show he decided to resurrect an idea he had used at John Meyer: for the finale he planned to have the models come out soaking wet. "How are we going to get the models soaking wet?" Rea Lubar asked. Cathy Williams came up with the idea of buying a small inflatable toddler's pool. But then they hit a snag—Frank Rockman absolutely refused to let them put a pool in his office.

The morning of the show arrived, Rockman walked into his office, and there was the pool. "I told you you couldn't put a pool in here," he said angrily.

"Do you see a pool?" asked Lubar in her most beguiling manner.

Rockman gave in, the models jumped into the pool in their beautiful cotton outfits at the end of the show, and then walked out on stage with mesh bags over their shoulders filled with mussels and clams. To this day Lubar is still not sure how Cathy got the pool and the water out of the office with Rockman still walking around fuming.

Once again the press hailed the collection, but, more importantly, now the buyers were beginning to sound fanatical. "We love him," Barbara Honsberger, fashion director of Lord & Taylor, was quoted as saying in *WWD*. "What he has for me are all the great contemporary looks for which we go to Europe for three weeks to find," added Koko Hashim of Bloomingdale's.

The last was high praise indeed. In those days Europe was considered the only place to find evolutionary fashion: American designers, while very good, were not perceived to be in the vanguard of fashion. For a retailer as astute as Hashim to put Perry in the international league was quite remarkable.

Such reactions were positive enough and frequent enough to soon have Perry champing at the bit; he now felt he was ready to design under his own name with his own company. The next chapter in his career was about to unfold.

The breathtaking speed of Perry's rise was undoubtedly due in part to the fashion press, which was now pushing him to the full extent of its considerable power. Perry fully understood this power, and realized it was the quickest way for him to gain the recognition of the public. Praise from the press, though mostly inspired by his considerable talent and fresh, new, witty clothes, was in part the result of his cultivation of it. At the same time, Perry also recognized the power of the retailers and was careful to foster special friendships with key people in that community. But it was with the press that he would have a special relationship throughout his career. In fact, he would later admit to John Duka in *The New York Times* piece how beneficial it had been to him. "The press has been extraordinarily good to me. Without them, in the early years, the company would not be in existence today. The press can do for you overnight what it would take years to accomplish otherwise."

Of course, Perry understood instinctively that the fashion industry, like the film, music, and theater industries, has always been dependent on the print and videotronic media to get its message across to the masses. Something as ephemeral as style cannot be simply sold—it has to be perceived as desirable, or at least publicized as the latest fad. This, in turn, has led to the concentration of unprecedented power in the fashion press as to who the editors wish to promote or decry in any given season. Their influence not only affects the perceptions of the public directly through their articles, but also is instrumental in whom the stores decide to promote.

At the top of the fashion press hierarchy lies Fairchild Publications, which, with its trade papers, *Women's Wear Daily* and the *Daily News Record,* speaks directly to the retailers, advising them who is good or bad, "in" or "out" (a more subjective classification invented by Fairchild). As such, Fairchild comes as close to dictating fashion in America as is possible nowadays, and is also extremely influential worldwide.

Almost of equal importance in the fashion world are the consumer magazines such as *Vogue, Harper's Bazaar, Glamour, Mademoiselle, Elle, Gentlemen's Quarterly,* and *Esquire,* as well as the country's most influential newspapers like *The New York Times, The Washington Post,* and the *Los Angeles Times,* which, within their respective communities and with their extensive syndication networks, suggest to the rest of us what we should wear and what's "in" in fashion. However, these are more dependent on what is actually in the stores for their coverage, since they have to appeal directly to the consumer.

The industry itself, of course, is totally aware of this Damoclean sword hanging over its metaphorical head and plays to the press with sycophantic vigor. Just as the top New York critics can make or break a Broadway show, so the fashion press can make or break a designer, a judgment that can literally run into tens of millions of dollars. Not surprisingly, a venal element can enter into this relationship, and it's an open secret in the industry that fashion editors do not always obey the rules of journalistic ethics. While one hesitates to accuse anyone of bribery and corruption, it has to be admitted that the Fourth Estate is not always as principled as it should be.

Perry Ellis, more than any other designer, manipulated the press and would sometimes augment editors' notoriously low salaries with "perks." Outside of what goes on in Italy between the Roman and Milanese fashion houses and the Italian magazine editors (where gifts of expensive jewelry are almost expected), Ellis was one of the most considerate and generous designers in the world to the fashion press. To call this practice bribery may be putting too harsh a light on it. However, "goodwill" is a factor in the way that fashion style is presented to the consumer, and Perry was a master of the game.

In defense of the editors, the vast majority of whom are totally innocent of these charges, the magazines themselves have a subtle form of persuasion exercised over them. It is a publishing fact that no magazine or newspaper can survive on the money generated by its cover price and circulation alone. The hard economics of publishing are such that the advertisements pay for the majority of the print and pictures we buy publications for. This, in turn, gives major advertisers a subtle power over the editorial content of a publication. Very few publishers will go out on a limb and ignore this delicate situation for the sake of a story—John Fairchild is one of the few. Most publications, whatever their area of interest, have "must" lists of advertisers who they feel they should feature in their prime editorial pages if they want to maintain their revenue sources.

Ellis, because of the power the press helped him achieve so quickly, utilized this form of persuasion most effectively. Like very few designers—Yves Saint Laurent, Giorgio Armani, Calvin Klein, and Ralph Lauren among them—he was able to insist that his clothes only be photographed as ensembles, and generally in full-page spreads. If this "rule" was ignored, he either threatened to withhold advertising pages, or would fail to deliver clothes to the editors.

One can certainly argue that in this way a designer can keep his creations and statement of the moment "pure," which is an argument not lacking in merit, but the pressure it puts on an editor, who is generally merely trying to provide a public service for the consumer, is considerable.

Without being unkind, one of Perry Ellis's greatest talents lay in his ability to make most editors believe they were doing him a personal favor by adhering to his dictates. Where perhaps he overstepped the boundaries of good faith was in his overt generosity to certain key editors. I'm not talking about the odd jacket, skirt, or shirt that might be perceived as friendship, but in gifts of whole collections of clothes for a particular season, lavish foreign vacations, or even monetary "consulting" fees—*all* of which took place.

5

PUCK: *"What hempen homespuns have we swaggering here?"*

—William Shakespeare
A Midsummer Night's Dream
(Act III, Scene I)

To anyone who has never witnessed the reality of Seventh Avenue, the name sums up the ultimate in chic—the center of creation, as it were, of the style of the greatest consumer society the world has ever known. The truth of this is as much a fable as that which holds that the American network TV shows "Dallas," "Dynasty," "Miami Vice," and "Moonlighting" epitomize the dubious heights of American style.

The eight-block section of the Seventh Avenue canyon in Manhattan renamed "Fashion Avenue" in 1972 is almost as tawdry a locale as Times Square itself. Known by the somehow philosphical and definitely practical New York cabbies as an avenue to avoid, this stretch between Macy's and Times Square is filled with triple-parked delivery vans, racks of off-price garments being hurried to unknown retail outlets, and drug pushers. Giving added flavor to this screaming, shouting, environment is the all-pervasive aura of the Italian and Jewish "garmento" families who literally rule the neighborhood and an industry that accounts for the fourth-largest budgetary expenditure by American consumers.

In the middle of this morass stand "the designers." How they manage to create amidst this rough, turbulent background one can only guess, as it's the antithesis of the atmosphere one will find in the more traditional environments of London's Savile Row, Paris's Faubourg Saint Honore, or

Milan's Via Della Spiga. Simply put: Seventh Avenue, for all the reverence accorded it in the press, is conducive not to pure design but rather to big business.

With the obvious critical success and acclaim that Perry's Portfolio collections had received, including the Coty nomination, it was obvious to Laurence C. Leeds, Jr., chairman and president of Manhattan Industries, that he had a star in the making and a major money earner on his hands, and if he wanted to keep Perry, who was determined to get his own collection and company, he had better start negotiating.

Whether Perry looked to another company to back him before he began serious negotiations with Manhattan Industries is a matter of debate, but it's quite likely, given reports that Leeds's board of directors didn't want to sign Perry, not believing his track record was good enough for the investment they would have to make in launching a new division under the Perry Ellis name. To a certain extent their fears were justified: Portfolio hadn't reached the market levels expected of it, and its sales volume was less than $1 million a year, despite all the press exposure.

It costs a tremendous amount of money to launch a new fashion company—$2 million is now regarded as the very least it would cost to set up a company and keep it going for the first few seasons until profitability and sales reached stable levels. With the grandiose schemes Perry had in mind, it was going to require far more than that in his case. And, as it happened, Leeds would reportedly have to invest over three million dollars in him before the first Perry Ellis Sportswear collection was actually seen.

Unlike most designers when they are first discovered, Perry was not a callow youth. At thirty-seven he had far more experience than, say, the nineteen-year-old Yves Saint Laurent when he came to prominence as the new designer at the House of Dior. Perry knew what he wanted, and what he wanted was perfection. The showroom had to be right, the samples had to be right, the advertising had to be right, the shows themselves had to be right, even the most insignificant members of the staff had to be right: no detail was too small for Perry, the perfectionist, not to require that it be absolutely perfect. And, to Perry's way of thinking, "right" meant freedom of choice and the latitude to spend money as he saw fit.

Perry had taken Carolyn Gottfried's suggestion and found himself a good lawyer—one of the best. Stanley Lesser, of the firm of Traub and Lesser, had represented, and continues to represent, some of the top Seventh Avenue designers. The deal he worked out for Perry, while seemingly not extraordinary at first glance, proved to be brilliant and laid the cornerstone of what was to become one of the most financially sound fashion empires in the business.

The negotiations commenced sometime in 1977. It has been stated that they took eight months, though it could have been more, since the deal wasn't actually formalized until Thursday, August 17, 1978. However, the negotiations were far enough along for Larry Leeds to reveal Manhattan Industries's plans to establish a separate Perry Ellis division as early as April of that year, which he did at the fall Portfolio show on the twenty-fourth. Lesser had negotiated a contract in which Perry would have his own division of Manhattan Industries as president and designer of Perry Ellis Sportswear, Inc. As such, he would be a salaried employee of Manhattan Industries—at about $150,000 a year—with extensive benefits and a generous expense account, as well as a percentage of the profits of the new company, with a base guarantee in six figures.

The percentage-of-the-profits clause was obviously a negotiated compromise. Most designers, in a deal of this sort, get a percentage of the sales (generally about seven percent), not the profits, which are much less. The clause in Perry's contract was probably the compromise that enabled Larry Leeds to get the deal past his board, who were still unsure of Perry's value to the company and undoubtedly aware of his lack of concern about spending company money to achieve his design and publicity ends. In a statement made later to *The New York*

Times Magazine, Leeds revealed the argument he probably used in front of the board of Manhattan Industries. "The major incentive for Ellis would be in profit sharing. I would not permit a percentage of the sales to go to him. We're here to make money. With profit sharing, there's an incentive to keep costs in line. It would be unfair for a large business to be losing money on a designer while he got a percentage on volume. Perry understood that. He's a part of Manhattan Industries."

Perry may have understood it, but what Leeds possibly didn't realize was that he had a tiger by the tail. Events were to prove that Perry could not—or would not—curtail his spending or be controlled by management. And what Manhattan's board of directors could not have realized at the time was that, with Lesser's deal for Perry signed, sealed, and delivered, Perry wouldn't even need the backing of Manhattan Industries within three years.

The negotiations were not only long, but also tough. Leeds was quoted in the same *New York Times* article as saying, "There were times when we would leave the table and not know where it was going. But, underneath it all, Perry and I both knew it would happen, that we would work it out."

What they worked out, and the heart of Lesser's legal masterpiece, was that Perry would retain control over his own name and be free to license it to other companies outside the women's sportswear field as long as Manhattan Industries did not already produce apparel within the category proposed (in which case Perry would have to offer it to Manhattan first, but as a licensee). The deal left Perry with tremendous room to negotiate with Manhattan and gave him leverage that would, eventually, lead to great dissension between himself and his employers.

Manhattan, for their part, felt they would be earning money from Perry's endeavors on all sides, since they were being given a percentage of the money that Perry might earn from any licensee ventures, as well as receiving twenty-five percent of the net profit of Perry Ellis International, which would derive its income from Perry's percentage of the sales of his licensee lines. (This figure was approximated from the mean aggregate of a complex sliding scale dependent on sales and other factors, according to sources.)

At first glance it seemed to be a remarkably favorable deal for Manhattan, and, in fact, it was to serve them well, earning them millions of dollars a year (which compensated somewhat for the huge operating expenses and overall losses that the Perry Ellis Sportswear and Men's collections would incur), but in the larger scheme of things, Manhattan's deal would be nothing compared to the sums that would pour into Perry's personal coffers. The mechanism that accomplished this for him was the simultaneous formation of Perry Ellis International, Perry's wholly self-owned company, which was to play the most important role in his business affairs.

Perry was obviously thrilled by the deal, as well he should have been. In *WWD*'s announcement of the deal on August 18, 1978, he said, with characteristic understatement (at least for public consumption), that he was particularly excited by "the nice creative license" allowed by his status as both president and designer of the new company, and added a statement that should have made him blush. "The arrangement leaves me free to be involved with only my own clothes, which is what I most care about."

While these negotiations were in progress, Perry was still designing, with his team, the Vera Sportswear and Portfolio collections. The April fall show was an exceptional triumph, and in it Perry demonstrated both his showmanship and his rapidly burgeoning ego.

The Vera showroom was packed to the gills. *Women's Wear Daily* had just done another cover story on Ellis, this one one of their influential feature stories. Entitled "Ellis in Wonderland" (a play on Perry's nickname around the office, "Mary Alice"), the article went on to quote two of America's top designers. Said Oscar de la Renta, "His clothes are wonderfully American in their look, the essence of what sportswear should look like, young and fresh." Added Ralph Lauren, "I consider him one of the few upcoming designers who is trying to develop his own style instead of looking like other people. He's very, very good."

As a result, everyone in the fashion industry was there. At the end of the runway was a a screen with a large red P on a black background. The upbeat disco music began to pound from the speakers and out came the Princeton University cheerleaders dressed in white sweaters (with red applique P on them, naturally), pleated black miniskirts, and white bobby socks. They started to do their number, and of course the audience went wild. With the finish of their routine, the handsome captain of the Princeton football team crashed through the screen, ran down the runway in his Tiger jersey, and the show started.

Most fashion editors get worried about antics such as these: they generally denote a lack of content in the clothes themselves. In this case, however, no one in the audience had to worry. It was Perry's best collection to date.

It was also Perry's most extensive collection to date, lasting over thirty-five minutes and packed full of ideas, styles, and silhouettes. All the signature Ellis looks were present—the slouchy tops, the long anoraks, the big jackets and full petticoated skirts, but there was also much that was new. In the collection Perry played with proportion, fabric, and silhouette, often simultaneously. There was corduroy in jackets, long slim skirts, and miniskirts. There were long sweaters and *very* important new short skinny sweaters, worn both separately and as snug waist-length twin sets, and knitted in tweedy natural wool that looked homespun. There were skirts over trousers and leg warmers over trousers under skirts. There were big, oversized, down-filled cotton poplin jackets, as well as what was to become one of Perry's most identifiable signatures, the large rounded shoulder. There was also men's wear for the first time, a hint of things to come. . . .

Any way one looked at it, Perry had outdone himself. The

previous singularity of his palette had been dropped and there were now deep tones of rose quartz, olive, slate blue, and mustard, often mixed together. It was as though he had looked into a kaleidoscope and mixed and matched everything in the most unusual and irreverent way he could. To everyone who was there, Perry had proved himself the most creative new designer in America. It was the collection that made his reputation.

The finale of the show was as much of a circus as the opening. Out came the twelve cheerleaders, sporting sweaters with a **P, E, R, R**, then two blank sweaters, another **E**, then an **L, L, I, Y**, followed by a very late **S**. They were followed by the football player with his outfit torn and showing rather a lot of skin. Then the girls reappeared, this time properly spelling out **P-E-R-R-Y E-L-L-I-S**, followed by all the models and the new talent himself, skipping down the runway.

The show was a swaggering virtuoso performance. Not only was the fashion press ecstatic, the retailers themselves were head over heels with glee. Said Koko Hashim, who had by then moved to Neiman Marcus, to *WWD*, "Now he's there. He's on target. Each collection gets better and better. The wonderful thing about his clothes is the free spirit. They have no time, no rules." "His proportions are exceptional," said Bernie Ozer, vice president of AMC (the Associated Merchandising Corporation). And from Kal Ruttenstein, who had joined Bloomingdale's as vice president and fashion director, "For such a new trend, Ellis has developed a style all of his own—truly a style and a way of dressing. . . . These are truly inventive clothes." It was truly an auspicious moment for Leeds to announce the formation of Manhattan's Perry Ellis division.

It is to Larry Leeds's credit that he pushed through the formation of Perry Ellis Sportswear, Inc. Without his support, it is doubtful that Perry Ellis's name would have become as big as it did as quickly. Although they were to have their differences—and these became quite serious—the Perry Ellis story would not have been the same without Leeds's contribution to his career. In the *Times* story Leeds told Duka, "I was behind Perry because the women and retailers I knew told me his clothes were fabulous. My own opinion? I liked his clothes, but that was not nearly as significant. My wife, Dalia, however, always liked his clothes. She convinced me to go forward. I am personally gratified." This is an uncharacteristically self-effacing statement by Leeds, who, though he has made errors of judgment that have been detrimental to the company founded by his grandfather, is one of the more astute and creative businessmen on Seventh Avenue. Certainly, he has always possessed the courage of his convictions, and his instinctive belief in Perry Ellis and the lengths he went to in backing the designer cannot be understated.

And even though Perry Ellis women's wear (and later the men's wear) would never earn Manhattan Industries the profit it should have, it did become the biggest feather in Leeds's cap. Up until then, Manhattan Industries had been a second-class fashion company, with some good, profitable lines like John Henry and Vera, but no top-of-the-line designer names except the Halston VI license (which was a relatively cheap dress line capitalizing on the Halston name and owing very little to his designs). In fact, their Frost Bros. chain of retail stores in the Southwest was, in 1977, creating over a third of their annual revenue of $270 million (about $103 million, compared to $170 million in sales for the Manhattan apparel lines). Although the Perry Ellis lines would eventually achieve about $80 million in sales by 1985 (overall apparel manufacturing sales for Manhattan Industries were approximately $244 million that year), the Ellis collections were far more important to Manhattan—and Leeds personally—in terms of prestige than they ever were as a percentage of overall sales.

Although the deal would not be made official till the middle of August, Perry had already signed his first licensee, Alixandre, the fur company, through his new company Perry Ellis International. His first collection for them came out just a month after the triumphant "cheerleader" show; Perry told *WWD*, "I look at fur coats as overcoats," and the small fifteen-piece collection definitely had all the hallmarks of Ellis irreverence, including deep armholes and no lining (unless they were reversible).

As a result of his year's work, and especially the fall collection, Perry would be nominated for his second Coty in 1978. And again he would not win.

Perry had two more collections to design for Portfolio, a small "resort" collection of thirty-five pieces (the resort is a pre-spring collection made available to the stores for the holiday selling season. It's a peculiarly American phenomenon; European designers don't bother with it, due to their more defined seasons), and at the beginning of November his spring/summer 1979 collection. The latter was well received, but less of a blockbuster than his previous fall collection. More of an evolution of style, the silhouette was still wide over skinny and it was still layered. His palette continued to expand and deepen, though the colors remained soft, with rose, carob, taupe, and silver among the highlights. It was a much more sophisticated collection than Perry had shown before, though his wit and irreverence continued to shine through in some very, *very* short miniskirts, often shown over cutoff colored tights.

Meanwhile, plans were going ahead for the new Perry Ellis Sportswear company. Sometime at the end of August or the beginning of September, Erwin Isman, who was administrative vice president of the M.I. Group, Manhattan's ladies' wear division, was asked by Larry Leeds to head Perry Ellis Sportswear, Inc., for the corporation as executive vice president, an arrangement that was soon changed, with Perry being named chairman and Isman president. Isman met with Perry for an hour and, though he felt Perry wasn't too keen on him, was given the job. "We were completely different types," says Isman. "I was business and he was creative, but there was some spark there and we decided to give it a try.

"I don't think he knew what he needed at the time," adds Isman. "At that time the product was everything to him and it was only later that he realized how well we were working together."

Perry, with Isman, Pastor, and Krascella, moved into part of a loft that Manhattan had at 148 West Thirty-seventh Street until they could find a permanent space.

"When we first started we had no place of our own," recalls Isman. "Perry had left Vera and I had left the Manhattan group that I had been working for. So we went down to the loft and said, 'Can we use part of the loft and we'll share the rent?' It was sort of an internal negotiation.

"We had one big cutting table and Perry sat at one end with Jed and Patricia while I sat at the other with all the projections and who we were going to hire. . . . We even had one discussion about what our working hours were going to be. It was that new."

The new company quickly began to grow, however. Isman bought in Steve Braverman as comptroller and Judy Beste, and Perry hired another assistant. "We just sort of grew around this cutting table!" exclaims Isman.

"It was the most fun I've ever had," says Beste, who was hired as merchandise manager (Perry's old job at John Meyer and Vera) and continued as vice president of merchandise for Perry Ellis until the designer's death. "We were such a small group. There were no egos and everyone was excited. Everyone pitched in, and even Perry swept the floor. Though it may sound trite, we were almost like a family."

While they were working on the first collection they were also looking for a permanent home. They finally found it, an old banking hall that had belonged to Manufacturers Hanover Trust at 575 Seventh Avenue and 1441 Broadway (the building straddles the block at Forty-first Street.) "The building wasn't really prestigious at the time; it was, to the best of my recollection, only a third full," says Isman. "We walked into this space and it was filled with rubble. But there were beautiful high ceilings supported by marble columns, and deco sconces on the walls. The floor was a mess, piled up with plaster, and Perry fell in love with it."

They negotiated with the Minskoff organization (who owned the building at the time) and obtained what Isman calls "a very favorable lease. We committed to putting in a good deal of taste and we got a very good rental agreement, which I believe is still in effect, since it had two five-year renewal periods," he continues.

Perry again hired James Terrell, who was by then a partner of his own architectural firm, Hambrecht Terrell International, to do the extensive renovations he wanted. The result was one of the most beautiful designer showrooms in the world, one on a par with the architectural masterpieces the Italian designers lavish on themselves in their Milanese palazzos. (It would eventually be featured in major publications like *Architectural Digest,* newspapers as august as *The New York Times,* and win one of *Interiors* magazine's annual awards in 1981.) Terrell used a restrained color scheme in shades of beige, and accentuated the inherent architectural features with light English sycamore paneling, Ondagata marble columns, and a two-story-high mirrored wall to offset the windows of the banking hall. Although Terrell maintains that Perry "had no concept of what to do with an interior," he goes on to say, "We originated all of it. He would say I want the proportions to be vertical or the details to be a little bit narrower."

A primary concern was Perry's insistence that all his shows be presented in the new showroom (normally, fashion shows in New York are presented outside the showrooms due to the relatively small size of most designer's headquarters). To solve this problem, Terrell came up with a runway system and carpeted bleachers that could be easily erected and dismantled. This meant the space would be open most of the time, so Terrell designed curved six-foot-high rolling modules in sycamore that created private "stations" that could be used when selling. The stations also featured one of Perry's ideas—horizontal bars to show off the clothes in silhouette. In addition, over each selling space and in the middle of each vault of the hall's roof, Terrell hung Art Deco chandeliers. The end result was wonderfully restrained and tremendously luxurious.

Trouble, however, was already looming between Perry and Manhattan Industries because of his profligate spending, which not only included the showroom but also the expense of things such as sample fabrics. This, in turn, put Isman in a difficult position between Ellis and Manhattan in his efforts to keep costs down and still keep Perry happy (which, it should be noted, Manhattan wanted, but at reasonable levels). Perry would listen, and go merrily on his way. In the case of the showroom, Isman recalls, "When I complained to him about the amount of money we were spending on fixing up the place, Perry's response was to cut me out of the meetings and meet with the architect privately!"

That there were problems over the cost of the renovation at this stage, which added up to approximately $750,000 (or $1.5 million, depending on whom you talk to), did not augur well for the future (especially when one considers that the second stage, started in 1982, would eventually cost somewhere between four and a half and six million dollars).

It would prove to be the opening skirmish of a long struggle between Perry and Manhattan Industries.

6

PUCK: *"And those things do best please me
That do befall preposterously."*

—William Shakespeare,
A Midsummer Night's Dream
(Act III, Scene II)

Perry was already thirty-eight years old when the deal for-
malizing Perry Ellis Sportswear, Inc., was closed in August
1978, hardly the young new talent that *Women's Wear Daily*
had heralded him as just a couple of years before, but with his
youthful demeanor, sparkling eyes, and ready smile he still
seemed to fit the description. Already a mature man with tremendous experience in the fashion industry, his courtly manners and soft-spoken approach belied his purposeful nature.
Yet it was this same youthful manner and good looks that cat-
apulted him into the public eye.

Perry at this stage of his life was a totally different person
from the sophisticated, elegant, thirty-four-year-old who had
joined Vera. Outwardly, he had undergone a metamorphosis.
The short-haired well-groomed preppie of previous years had
matured, for lack of a better word, into a neo-hippy. His hair
was down to his shoulders and he had taken to wearing what
was to become his signature outfit—a light-blue, oxford-cloth
button-down shirt, chinos without a belt, and Topsiders, with
or without white athletic socks (admittedly Eastern establishment items in themselves, but not in the rather eccentric way
Perry wore them). He had broken out of his shell, and
whether it was a result of his growing consciousness of his
status as a top-flight fashion designer, or of changes in his

private life, is a matter of conjecture. More than likely it was a combination of both: certainly the way he was expressing himself in his clothes had gone far beyond the prim looks of the John Meyer lines or the simple sportswear of the early Vera days. Here was someone who was teaching America how to dress in a fresh, youthful style that was more akin to a European attitude than it was to anything in his own country, even though it had its basis in traditional American looks.

But his personal life had also changed considerably. As a result of his new status as *the* up-and-coming American designer, he was meeting new and influential people all the time and having to be more social. (Both Jim Terrell and Rea Lubar concede that Perry actively pursued famous and influential people after he himself gained the limelight.) Though he undoubtedly enjoyed it, he would continue to do it on his own terms.

He had also found a new lover. Since sometime around 1977 Perry had been seen constantly in the company of a young, part-time model named Robert Tropper, known generally as Beau. His relationship with Robert McDonald had undergone a change, though a number of Perry's oldest friends say that McDonald was never really out of the picture until Laughlin Barker came on the scene around 1980. Whatever the truth, Perry and McDonald remained close, even though Perry was spending most of his time with Beau.

(It should also be noted that Perry had at least one girlfriend during this period. He was never totally faithful to the person he was then currently seeing, and often indulged himself in small "affairs" on the side, though by the standards of the time and the milieu in which he worked, he was remarkably restrained.)

Beau Tropper was twenty-one or twenty-two when Perry first met him, a handsome young man with long tightly curled blond hair. Though his looks were unconventional, he was certainly arresting. Almost the complete antithesis of Perry's usual circle of sophisticated college graduates, Tropper was a hedonist and lamentably irresponsible. In a way it is puzzling what Perry saw in him, but he was certainly attracted enough to spend a considerable amount of time with him, both in California, where Beau was going to college in Santa Barbara, as well as taking him on some of his European trips.

The amount of time they spent together was surprising in light of the responsibilities and work load Perry had assumed. But then Perry had never been a person to keep normal office hours. On his visits to Santa Barbara, where Beau was also acting as caretaker on the estate of Michael Butler (the producer of the play *Hair*), Perry would spend days at the beach in the laid-back surfer environment Beau was most comfortable in, as well as attending some of his college classes with him. All things considered, it was odd behavior for the up-and-coming superstar of American fashion.

Tropper's parents were solidly upper middle class, and his mother lived in New York, where he had been born, while his father lived in Santa Monica, so it was easy enough for him to enjoy the free and easy existence he obviously preferred. That he could drag Perry, who was at sixteen years older, into this lifestyle is more difficult to understand. Equally difficult to understand is how Perry, who, though he could be lazy, never was lacking in devotion to his work or ambitions, could put up with Beau's frequent disappearances.

Whatever the reasons, their relationship wasn't solely one of days at the beach. Perry, who liked to involve everyone he was close to in his work, used Tropper as a model—he was actually the first man to come down a runway in Perry's yet-to-be-produced men's line in the fall '78 "cheerleader" collection—and in that capacity he became more and more involved with the house.

It is difficult to gauge how much a relationship influences its participants, but it is quite possible that Tropper was the individual responsible for the dramatic change in Perry's appearance. It was, at any rate, around the time they met that

Perry started to grow his hair long and change his style of dress.

It was also around this time that Perry, though unwilling to publicly avow or allude to his homosexuality until after Laughlin Barker's death in 1986, became far more open about this side of his nature. Before Tropper entered his life, Perry kept his affairs very much to himself and his circle of closest friends; with Beau it was different. They were frequently seen in public and photographed together (Beau was one of the people photographed for John Duka's *New York Times* article), and it was an open secret in the business that they were lovers. Perry would also take Beau with him when he visited his parents at Christmas time.

Finally, it was also around this time that Perry began to spend his summers at Water Island, a community on Fire Island—a long, narrow sandbar of beach houses set in dunes, with no roads, about a mile off the southern shore of Long Island. Unlike the bigger Fire Island communities such as Ocean Beach (a family resort) or the Pines (predominantly gay and "in" with the fashion and performing arts crowd), Water Island has no direct ferry from the mainland and the small community of about thirty-six houses has no shops or restaurants. As a result there are no day-trippers to Water Island, as there are to the other communities on Fire Island, which made it an ideal getaway for someone as private as Perry. That summer he began to rent a small house, on the bay side of the island, that he was to eventually buy.

Although a part of Perry still desired isolation and complete privacy, he was definitely more social by then and not nearly so intimidated by crowds as he had once been. It was a change that cannot simply be put down to what was going on in his personal life. Surely as influential was the great change in his professional status. The fact that he was now being fêted, waited on, and fawned over had to affect his ego. Although he would never lose that shy, little-boy-lost quality, his ambition and ego were given free rein, and he could afford to be both more outgoing, as well as more demanding.

Yet, unlike many recently arrived stars, it is to Perry's credit that his head never became so swollen that he lost his graciousness, manners, or concern for the problems of others (except, perhaps, in some of his dealings with Manhattan Industries executives, where he could be as stubborn as a mule). His ego, more often than not, would manifest itself as quiet determination. He had matured far beyond the screaming-and-shouting stage of his Miller & Rhoads days, though there would always be a boisterous side to his nature that he would indulge when he felt safe and secure among friends or in the office.

The atmosphere in the Perry Ellis office at that time was, according to all accounts, quite extraordinary; there was a sense of excitement and dedication in the air. "There was something special," says Erwin Isman. "You found yourself wanting to associate with him and be associated with him. Our receptionist was the envy of every other receptionist on Seventh Avenue, and everyone from the lowliest messenger boy to Larry Leeds himself wanted to be a part of what was happening at Perry Ellis."

Much of the glamor was yet to come. The showroom was still under construction and by Christmas of 1978 there were only eight employees in the company. "We had our Christmas party at Raoul's [a popular French bistro in SoHo] and we had eleven people there, but three of them hadn't joined the company yet," remembers Isman. Most of the people in the company were young, in their twenties, with Jed Krascella the baby of the group. Perry, Isman, and Beste were the only ones over thirty.

By January, 575 Seventh Avenue was finished to the point where merchandising and sales people could move in, though Beste recalls that a lot of the furniture was still stored in their office and they had to work around stacked-up desks. The design studio wouldn't be ready until April or May, so

Perry, Patricia, Jed, and the design assistants remained at the loft on Thirty-seventh Street for the time being. Still, the company was organized enough for Perry to show a small summer collection for late delivery (June, July, and August) that he entitled "Indian Summer." It was presented at the beginning of February without all the fanfare of his semi-annual shows, and there was nothing remarkably special about it. It was simply a stopgap designed to keep the retailers happy; obviously, he was saving his best efforts for what would be his first complete collection under his own name.

The first showing of the Perry Ellis fall collection on April 30, 1979, was possibly the most eagerly awaited date on the fashion calendar that season. Rumors about the stupendous new showroom at 575 Seventh had been circulating for months, and every fashion editor and retailer in the country, if not the world, was anxious to see whether the Perry Ellis fashion statement would change now that he was on his own.

Perry didn't disappoint them.

It was a far cry from the collegiate atmosphere of his last Portfolio show. Classical music wafted from the loudspeakers, immediately establishing a more sophisticated ambience, to which the sparkling marble-and-sycamore banking hall lent added dignity. When the first models began to sashay down the runway an excitement spread through the audience. The clothes were shaped and tailored, and full of deep, rich color. It was a new, far more sophisticated Perry Ellis they were seeing. While still youthful-looking, these were clothes even ladies of "a certain age" could wear. The look was so different, in fact, that one could almost believe it wasn't the same designer. There was a maturity and facility of design in the clothes that, however good Perry had been before, he had not previously demonstrated.

Of course, the signature Ellis touches were there to let you know the same irreverent Perry was behind it all. The girls were adorned with pheasant feathers tucked into their hats, breast pockets, and sweaters, and many of the skirts were short and worn under long sweaters, as Perry had done before. Still, for the most part the skirts were completely new. Now they were pleated from the hip and tailored in a very flattering silhouette, or beautifully constructed circle skirts. The trousers were also cut to define the hips, with pleats perfectly placed to keep the silhouette slim, a line that was accentuated by the high "Hollywood" waistlines. Equally impressive were the hand-knit sweaters. But most important of all was the new silhouette of the jackets, which were most significantly shown in a cropped version that ended about three inches below the belt, just at the point of the hip. Broad shoulders still characterized Perry's new tailored silhouette, but in themselves were completely new with what Perry called his "dimple" shoulder (a forward-facing pleat that became the most recognizable Ellis signature). This construction lent a rounded shape to the silhouette, which was carried through in the narrow tailored waistline and the broad sleeves that narrowed just below the elbow. In addition, not only were these jackets shown with Perry's new skirt silhouettes, but also with a new trouser silhouette that looked like jodhpurs only with a long inverted pleat on the side.

Just as much of a shock was the use of color and the combinations of color within the same outfit. Lilac was shown with purple, or three tones of pink all together, or blue, bronze, and brown together. And these were themselves combined with some of the richest gabardines, tweeds, and plaids money could buy.

The collection demonstrated an expertise and understanding of fashion that Perry had never shown before. Not only was the show itself beautifully accessorized—including Barry Kieselstein-Cord's sterling silver and gold belts—but Perry's showmanship and feeling for theater came into its own. At the finale, for instance, the runway was festooned with tiny multicolored feathers in keeping with his theme for the season.

It was also the first collection where he had concentrated on sophisticated tailoring and shape, and he managed to do it in a way that was uniquely his own. It was still lighthearted and whimsical enough to show his aversion to stolid, serious fashion, while handled expertly enough to show that he knew how and where to break the rules. (For instance, there were still no buttons on the jackets.) There was a fluidity to the clothes that took them away from traditional tailored ensembles and made them younger-looking. This ease and use of drape was even more prominent in the coats, which were generally belted and shorter than even the short skirts.

Perry's fur coats for Alixandre, shown with the collection, were equally irreverent. While tailored, he used skins such as chinchilla, skunk, and beaver in totally amusing ways, almost making fun of them. And they were shown with the dimple shoulder as well.

Perry also showed men's wear pieces to complement his women's collection, but again they would not be produced.

The press had much to be ecstatic about, and retailers were equally happy. "I think it was a milestone in his career as a designer," Bloomingdale's Kal Ruttenstein later told *Women's Wear Daily*. "It was fabulous. He's one of our most talented designers," added Barbara LaMonica of Bergdorf Goodman. Mimi Liebeskind of Ann Taylor was just as enthusiastic. "It's important because it's the first time we've seen a collection that was totally related to the American contemporary woman. He's brilliant." *Women's Wear* itself gave the ultimate imprimatur: "It was Ellis at his best—a major influence on American sportswear."

The collection, to no one's surprise, earned Perry a third nomination for the "Winnie," the Coty Award for the outstanding women's designer of the year.

In January, Perry had also been named by the prestigious Texas store Neiman Marcus as one of five recipients of its Award for Distinguished Service in the Field of Fashion (along with designers Mary McFadden and Giorgio Armani, photographer Richard Avedon, and the artisans of the glass company Baccarat). The awards were presented at a black-tie dinner for a thousand at the Beverly Wilshire Hotel on Friday, May 11. Perry dressed with his usual disregard for convention in an unpressed colored shirt and a patterned tie, although for once he sported a dark jacket.

If these honors, as well as the thousands of words of press coverage (including such mass-circulation publications as *People* magazine), weren't enough to let the general public know that Perry was *the* rising star in the Seventh Avenue firmament, then his new status in the stores would certainly do the job. The space that a retailer gives a designer is vitally important to how well that designer's clothes will actually sell— space, after all, demands attention, and attention in retailing is tantamount to sales dollars.

In Perry's case, it is easiest to see how the retailers perceived him by examining his positioning in Bloomingdale's flagship store in Manhattan. Kal Ruttenstein, who had been one of his strongest supporters from the beginning, moved Perry into their Young East Sider Shop when he joined the store in 1978. This was Bloomingdale's name for the category called "contemporary" in the fashion industry. Generally, it connotes youthful-looking, fashion-conscious clothes suitable for women in their early twenties and that don't necessarily have a designer name on them. When Perry was given his own collection in 1979, he was moved into a separate space next to their Paradox shop, which also housed Kenzo, his French counterpart. (Interestingly, Kal Ruttenstein told *The New York Times Magazine* that Perry actually fought to stay in the contemporary shop, whereas most designers would have tried to get out. "His position," Ruttenstein said, "was that he was different from all the other designers in the designer departments. He was not making clothes for the crepe de chine woman.") By the end of 1980, however, his prices had risen and his reputation was such that he was given pride of place on Bloomingdale's designer floor, with Calvin Klein to his left and Giorgio Armani to his right. It was Bloomingdale's way of stating that he had arrived.

All this makes it easy to understand why there was such an air of excitement in the Perry Ellis offices that first year. Every member of the staff *knew* that they were working for the most important American designer to come along since Calvin Klein and Ralph Lauren had first made their marks in the early '70s. There was a tremendous camaraderie and sense of fun in the office, and Perry was genuinely loved by his staff. As Judy Beste recalls, "The people that worked for him so loved him that the first year, and for several years after that, there was a cutout of Perry's face with a halo over it at the top of our office Christmas tree." Perry obviously enjoyed the informal atmosphere, and it was certainly he who instigated the office tradition of giving everyone campy nicknames. Whether this informality was a ploy on his part is difficult to judge, but given the fact that he never did anything in business without thinking about it carefully, one can assume that even though it was his nature to kid around, he also used humor as part of a calculated management strategy.

The camaraderie in the office did not extend to the Manhattan Industries management, however, where there was continual worry about Perry's spending. "I don't think he cared about the business side of it at all," says Isman. "Perry never really involved himself in operations and the day-to-day running of the business. To him the product was everything. He used to say, 'If we don't have the design, we have nothing.'"

For Perry, the starting point and much of the inspiration for his designs came from fabric, and as early as 1979 Manhattan Industries became so worried about his spending in this area that Isman decided to send Judy Beste with him on his November buying trip. After initially balking at the idea (which was not without its own irony, since Perry had insisted on going on such trips when *he* was a merchandiser), Perry and Judy, along with Jed Krascella, left for London just after the spring show in the middle of the month and stayed at the Savoy. From London they went to Frankfurt for the big fabric show, Interstoff, where they stayed at the Frankfurterhoff and entertained some of Europe's best fabric designers and mill owners at a little restaurant Perry loved called the Zur Mullerin. The next stop after Frankfurt was Paris, where they stayed at the Lancaster, a small but exclusive hotel just off the Champs Elysées under the same management as the Connaught in London. Judy was amazed by the lifestyle she had suddenly been thrust into, staying in some of Europe's best hotels and eating at its finest restaurants with Perry, who certainly wasn't about to economize on necessities such as living and eating. They spent the weekend of the twenty-fourth in Paris, and since they couldn't work Perry ordered a car and driver to take them to see the cathedral at Chartres. At one point, Judy tried to take a picture of him on the steps of the cathedral and Perry tried to stop her, saying, "No, you could use that as blackmail on me!" (She took the picture anyway, but strangely enough that one frame from the whole role came out blank.)

After Paris they were due to go to Scotland to work on developing some Shetland sweaters for the new collection, and Judy's account of one incident illustrates why so many legends grew up around Perry's European trips. "We got to Orly airport and I had this large fuchsia canvas bag I had bought at Brown's in London that was filled with Shetland sweaters I had bought as presents for back home. I was also carrying my briefcase and Perry said, 'Let me take one of those for you, dear.'

"I thought he would take my briefcase, but no, he takes this big pink bag! So there we were in line to go through these little booths they had in Paris to search you before boarding the plane. We had no idea what they were or whether they would frisk us or what. Perry said, 'You go first, you go first!' and added, 'Laugh if it feels good!'

"I didn't want to go in first, but Perry pushed me, so there I was with this man in a very official uniform with a gun. All he did was run a metal detector over me and then let me go. So I was sitting in the waiting lounge trying to get all the papers and fabric orders in my briefcase together, and I could tell that Perry was in the booth now, since I could see the bottom of his chinos and his Topsiders. Suddenly, I heard the alarm go off and in an awful moment I remembered that in the middle of all the sweaters was a music box I had bought in Paris as a gift.

"By this time there was a big fuss and I could hear Perry saying, 'It's madame's bag!' and then he whipped open the curtain to point at me. The security guard quickly shut it again, but not before I saw he had got his gun out. At that moment I thought, 'Well, here goes my job.'

"I could hear Perry trying to talk to the guard in English, who, of course, could only speak French, so I yelled, 'Perry, it's the music box!' and Perry tried to convey this to the guard by humming and miming a music box.

"As if that wasn't enough, we didn't get to Scotland until really late, landing at Edinburgh [Turnhouse] airport at about ten o'clock that night. There were no taxis and we had no money: we had changed all our currency in France . . . so we were virtually stuck. Eventually, someone called for a taxi and after waiting and waiting it finally arrived. We explained to the driver our position, and, luckily, he agreed to take us to the hotel, which we hoped would pay the fare."

The hotel they were booked into was the Hotel Roxburghe, one of those hotels one can find anywhere in the hinterlands of the British Isles, a Victorian neo-Gothic pile that can best be described as "quaint."

"When we arrived at the hotel they didn't have a cashier to change traveler's checks," says Beste, "but by rummaging around in drawers they were finally able to come up with the fare. By this time it was after ten-thirty and we were starving. One of the girls at the reception desk dug into her handbag and said, 'Och, I canna give y' anymore. Will this be enough for y', fer yer supper?' And then she gave us instructions to one of the two restaurants that might be open at that hour. The choice was Chinese or Italian. We decided, without much hesitation, that Scots Italian would be better than Scots Chinese, and though we didn't understand a word she was saying in her broad accent, we set off down the dark streets to find the elusive restaurant.

"You have to picture the situation: there was Jed, as dramatic as ever, in a flowing black cape, Perry in his hat and favorite jacket at that time—one of his down jackets that made him look like the Michelin man—and myself looking like Miss Priss. Finally, we see an establishment that's open, and Perry said, 'This is the place. This is the place!'

"'I don't think so,' remarked Jed dubiously.

Anyone who knows Edinburgh can picture this rather dramatic trio stumbling upon a Scottish workingman's bar. The air was thick with smoke and in came these three outlandish tourists, obviously American, surrounded by dour Scots.

"The three of us blew in," says Beste, "and it was like one of those scenes in the movies where everyone just stops what they're doing and stares. 'Well . . .' said Perry. 'I don't think *this* is the place, but maybe we'd just better go to the bar and have a drink.'

"In unison, Jed and I replied, 'Let's get out of here!'

"So the three of us, as graciously as we could, walked out of the door, laughing hysterically!"

A short while later they did find an Italian restaurant that was still open.

"Don't ever try an Italian restaurant in Scotland," says Beste ruefully. "We ordered pasta and it came out in these great big bowls. Perry stuck his fork into his and the whole mess came up in one great lump: it looked like porridge! We decided to give the pasta a miss after that and settled on pizza and salad. We only just got out of the place with our very last coin, because we'd had to order so much!"

It's easy to see why, with wonderful memories like these, Perry was so beloved by his staff and anyone else who spent time with him; it was quite typical of the funny and sometimes outrageous way Perry would behave with people he was close to.

Meanwhile, back in the public eye, earlier that September, Perry had finally won his first Coty Award. Unlike his private demeanor, however, he chose to play the star in the public's eye that year, and his behavior is more difficult to understand. . . .

He simply didn't turn up to receive his award.

Perry had told several people he wasn't going to show because he didn't believe in what he felt was Coty's policy of using the awards to promote their own products. But if that was the case, why didn't he just refuse the nomination as Calvin Klein had that year when he was nominated for the Coty Men's Award? Even Isman, whom Perry had asked not to attend the awards' ceremony, says, "Perry never did explain it to my satisfaction."

According to Rea Lubar, whose job it was to oversee his press relations, "Perry was always very ambivalent about the Cotys. . . . He wanted to get it, he wanted to take it, he wanted the recognition . . . and yet he didn't want it. He didn't really believe in the way it was done."

It is more likely that he simply didn't want to go through the ordeal of sitting through the ceremony a third time with the chance that he wouldn't win, which is what he told one of his closest intimates of that period, the designer Abbijane. But in the opinion of some of the people present at the ceremony, it was more a case of Perry trying to emulate Klein's stand against the Cotys (though Klein undoubtedly handled the affair with more finesse and politesse). Whatever the reason, it revealed a lack of manners on Perry's part that was uncharacteristic but nonetheless reprehensible. (It should be noted that Perry was always present after this for the other seven Coty Awards he would receive.)

Perry asked Abbijane to go in his place and "take care of things" for him, even though Rea Lubar would have been the more logical choice and had been asked by Shirley Goodman of F.I.T. (the Fashion Institute of Technology, where the ceremony was held) to accept the award for Perry. (It was an open secret that he would get it that year.) Abbijane recalls the evening being "a horror story."

"First of all, I'd asked Perry if I could wear something of his since I was representing him, but he said, 'No, wear something of yours.' So I turned up in a turquoise velvet minidress with a hat I had made to match, and the first thing everyone asked was if it was Perry's. I would say, 'No, it's Abbijane.' So they'd ask, 'Who's Abbijane?' We were seated in the tent they did that year at F.I.T., and I had gone with Bonnie West, the photographer from the *Times,* and the next thing I know the press is asking if she's my girlfriend, because she's wearing a tuxedo!

"In the meantime Bernadine [Morris, of the *Times*] had taken me aside and said you have to do something because he's going to win. So, there we were, seated at this table with Geoffrey Beene [who was cited for a special award that season], his mother, and Bernadine and Nina Hyde [the influential fashion editor of *The Washington Post*]. At the next table was that newscaster who was always drunk making rude comments about me all evening to Andy Warhol, who was at his table. I didn't know what to do, and when Perry's name was finally called out after that endless awful meal I ran up and received the award, which weighs five hundred pounds, from Dina Merrill and her husband [Cliff Robertson] and made the shortest speech I could: 'Right On!'"

Abbijane then tried to push her way through the audience to call Perry, by which time she was crying and her mascara streaming down her face. Sobbing into the phone, she said, "Hi—"

Perry cut her off. "You've got to hold on, I'm making eggs!"

"Perry, you won," Abbijane got in before he rushed back to the kitchen to turn his omelette over.

Finally, back on the other end of the line, Perry said sarcastically, "Bring that *thing* . . ." and then went on to ask about the limited-edition book of sketches of all the nominated designers' clothes that Coty had commissioned by the late, brilliant fashion illustrator Antonio. Still, his last remark to Abbijane was more in keeping with his usual self: "Would you do me a favor, would you wash your face!"

Rea Lubar, who was one of Perry's greatest supporters throughout his career, agrees that the way Perry behaved with respect to the 1979 Coty Awards ceremony was out of character and adds that Geoffrey Beene got in the last word when he said, "I've always hated a party pooper!"

It's all to easy to suggest that Perry's rising stardom was changing his personality by citing an example like this, but it was only one incident. In private, as well as generally in his public life, he continued to remain a polite, thoughtful, gentle man. Still, he was undoubtedly changing, becoming more aware of his power and celebrity than he had ever been, and definitely having legitimate cause to believe that all his ambitions were about to be realized.

The month before, he had finalized a licensing agreement that would put him into the international arena. The agreement was with the Japanese trading company Yagi Tsusho Kaisha, Ltd., of Osaka, to manufacture and market his women's line in Japan. At the time of the announcement, the manufacturer hadn't been settled on, but they were in fact negotiating with Renown, Japan's largest apparel manufacturer to produce the Perry Ellis line as a sublicensee.

The Japanese line would be more of a merchandising situation, since they were simply copying Perry's original designs (which they did perfectly) and rescaling them to the Japanese market, so much of the responsibility for the arrangement fell into Judy Beste's lap.

As she describes it, she was in her office one day when Perry called her and asked her to come to the conference room. "When Perry called," she says, "it was a *command!* I went to the conference room and there were at least ten Japanese gentlemen and interpreters there. They were the group from Renown and Yagi. And Perry said to me, 'Now, Judy, these gentlemen are going to be doing my Japanese line and they have some questions I know you can answer better than anyone regarding scheduling and everything.'

"So I sat down and, after the introductions, which gave me ten business cards of names I couldn't pronounce anyway, the questions started to flow. After several minutes of them, Perry stood up and said, 'Well, gentlemen, excuse me, I'm leaving you in good hands and Judy can answer anything you want to know.' An hour and a half later I came out banging my head against the wall, and from then on Perry regarded me as the in-house Japanese expert!"

Perry ended the decade of the seventies with a new spring collection, which was shown in November. While the looks were still youthful, he obviously felt the mood of the eighties would be different and showed his most "dressed up" collection to date.* The colorations were pale, soft, and sophisticated—pearl gray, seashell pink, shy blue, and tea rose—and executed in such luxurious fabrics as sheer linen and glazed silk organza. It was a simple, romantic collection that *WWD* likened to a Botticelli painting. The silhouette was definitely curved and emphasized the hips with a new shirt shape Perry had taken from Elizabethan times, the farthingale. These were shown with rounded versions of the short jacket he had presented the season before, and Perry was right on in calling it "the most feminine collection I've done to date."

Not content with merely showing one new silhouette, Perry also showed an elongated jacket that dipped down at the front and curved up over the hips, as well as miniskirts and dirndl shorts. Although the press wasn't quite as excited as it had been in previous seasons, retailers loved the collection and especially praised the sweaters, which were shown in many

---

* *Women's Wear Daily*, November 6, 1979.

versions that were to become Ellis hallmarks, including the single cable stitch down the front and strapless, elongated, and back-buttoned models. In addition, the tailoring in the new collection had progressed to the point where Perry was showing asymmetrically draped tops. Still, although the signature looks were there and it was typically irreverent Perry Ellis sportswear, it was obvious that he was becoming much more interested in a high-fashion look—the look of the eighties.

7

PUCK: *"I'll put a girdle about the earth*
In forty minutes."

—William Shakespeare
A Midsummer Night's Dream
(Act II, Scene II)

On the morning of January 20, 1981, Washington, D.C., looked as good as its French planner, Pierre Charles L'Enfant, could have envisaged it. The sky was blue, and in the clarity of the weak winter sunlight every overstated monument in this most monumental of cities was a tribute to the Republic.

It was a historic day: the inauguration of the country's fortieth president, an event newsworthy for many reasons, not least of which was the fact that the president-elect was the oldest man to enter the Oval office. That his major claim to fame was his past career as a B-picture movie star didn't seem to detract from the dignity of the occasion. Yet in world political terms he was viewed with a combination of fear and curiousity: Ronald Reagan was seen as a tough-talking hawk, and even the Politburo, ensconced behind the walls of the Kremlin, viewed the day's events with resigned trepidation, waiting to see if the old actor would come out shooting, as he had in his cowboy movies.

It was also a day of rejoicing, for precisely at noon what might be considered the most ignominious chapter in the country's history since the summer of 1814, when British General Robert Ross had captured Washington and burned the White House, would be brought to a close. Despite his pathological hatred of America, the Ayatollah Khomeini had grudgingly decided to set free the remaining fifty-two hostages from the American embassy in Teheran.

As a sidelight to these weightier political matters there was the personal style of the president's wife. For the first time since Jackie Kennedy, America had a fashion maven as First Lady. Nancy's clothes had almost become the raison d'être of that self-appointed manual of style, "W" magazine, and it was obvious to most observers that glamor was back in at the White House with a vengeance. Yet even in her ultra-chic "Reagan red" Adolfo outfit, Nancy found herself upstaged on the steps of the Capitol by her rather effete son, Ron Jr., and his rather purposeful new bride, Doria, who were both dressed head to foot in Perry Ellis. Ironically, Perry had arrived in conjunction with the dawning of the new age of political conservatism.

The election year, the first year of the new decade, had been almost as busy for Perry as it had for the candidates. He had finally launched his men's wear and Japanese collections had visited Japan twice, signed up two new licensees (one for legwear and one for shearling coats); made personal appearances in stores, and, of course, designed and presented two major collections, as well as making his usual European buying trips. He had also been seen hobnobbing with political figures in Washington, including the wife of the vice president, Joan Mondale. It was almost as if he were running his own campaign to become America's top designer and, in so doing, further enhanced his reputation.

It was also a profoundly emotional year for Perry. That summer he would meet the great love of his life, a young lawyer named Laughlin Barker. And in December his father, whom he so loved and admired, would die of cancer. Still, at the beginning of the new decade Perry had nearly achieved, or at least set in motion, everything he had wanted from his career and life. Conversely, all the elements that would eventually lead to his own tragic death were also in place. For a biographer, it is both a convenient and significant moment to step back and take stock of the life of Perry Ellis.

Most dramatic, of course, was the fame and fortune he had achieved in his career. In a little over five years Perry had grown from being the stylist of a rather third-rate sportswear line into one of the foremost designers in the country. His name was internationally recognized and he was counted as possibly America's most important and innovative designer for the younger generation. His years of working in the wings of the fashion industry had paid off and he was nearly at the point where he could take his bows center stage.

His show for the fall 1980 season was one of his most successful to date, and led *Women's Wear Daily,* as astute as ever about the current social and political climate (the Fairchild "rag trade" papers are read as avidly in the White House as *The New York Times* and *The Washington Post*), to run the headline MR. POP AND MR. GLAMOR in the April 29 edition. The article went on to compare and praise the diametrically opposed styles of what it obviously considered the two best American collections of the season—Perry's ("Mr. Pop") and Bill Blass's ("Mr. Glamor"). The extent of Perry's *pop*ularity at this stage of his career is captured tellingly in an excerpt of the article by Carolyn Gottfried and Ben Brantley (another *WWD* fashion editor): "True to his name, Mr. Pop came through with a full-fledged media event of a collection. There were enough photographers, buyers, foreign press and Fashion Groupies to rival a European collection."

Not surprisingly, with this collection Perry gained in stature and sophistication, even though he didn't radically change his shapes and silhouettes. Still, there was enough richness in the fabrics, colors, and textures, as well as in Perry's multiple choices of length and style, for *Women's Wear* to say, "Retailers indeed seemed to have dollar signs in their eyes after the show." Certainly the retailers were effusive in their praise, and for the first time a foreign store had entered the picture. The exclusive London boutique of Brown's had bought Perry's previous collection and would be buying this one as well.

From a design perspective, the most important new element in the fall collection was Perry's reintroduction of the capelet, which he showed on coats, jackets, shirts, and even on his hand-knit sweaters. It was often paired with back-swing skirts for a fuller, rounder silhouette, especially when seen in profile. At times, it almost looked like an Edwardian silhouette.

His favorite yarn for the collection was mohair, which he showed both woven and knitted, in sweaters and short fluffy jackets, as well as skirts. He also brought back one of his early favorites, corduroy, but it was his hand-knit sweaters that were most interesting commercially. In his own way, Perry had made his sweaters a signature statement with simple but amazingly influential styling details such as a single cable-stitch down the front that might be plain, bi-colored, or multicolored. In the estimation of many fashion editors, it was his sweaters that helped put Perry at the forefront of fashion design in this country, and certainly he did much to revive the economically depressed hand-knitting industry. (According to one journalist, however, this was not done without recourse to non-union labor and virtually "sweatshop" wages.)

Of less immediate fashion value, but perhaps equally important as a trend, was his gray flannel suit for women, shown with the baggy pants silhouette he favored that season. For the next three years the women's fashion scene would be dominated by what was called "man tailoring." Italian designers like Giorgio Armani and Valentino, Paris greats like Yves Saint Laurent and Emmanuel Ungaro, and American establishment designers including Bill Blass and Adolfo would dress women in clothes inspired by men's wear. Perry's gray flannel suit that year was one of the first, though one of the least severe, indicators of this important fashion movement of the early eighties.

Perry Ellis never really "invented" a new design; his

unique talent lay in reinterpreting diverse style elements and mixing them to create a signature look all his own. His inspiration could come from anywhere—a book he had read, a play, something he'd seen on his various travels, or even something as mundane as a delivery boy's coat. But his vision was always so acute, especially for America, that he quickly became *the* fashion leader in this country.

It was not mere coincidence that that season Perry was able to take the most common of men's wear fabrics, gray flannel, and, in his wonderfully witty fashion, turn it into something completely different for women. The fall 1980 show also marked the first season Perry came up with a full men's collection that was made available to the general public. As *Daily News Record* fashion editor Melissa Drier said of this first men's collection: "The clothes—fun, comfortable and slightly rebellious—are definitely not for the average men's wear customer. . . . But for the customer with a secure fashion identity and a taste for adventure, the collection offers some of the most refreshing new looks to emerge in a long while." In fact, Perry did show quite a few of his women's design elements in this collection, including rounded jackets, jackets without collars and jackets without buttons, and big baggy trousers, which partially explains why Drier considered the collection of somewhat limited appeal.

That Perry had waited all this time to produce his men's collection and then chose to make a purely individual fashion statement with it shows how much he had matured in the last five years. He was by then both personally and financially secure enough to insist that there be no compromise in his statement, even to the detriment of sales. Though this attitude would be a continuing worry for Manhattan Industries, Perry was now important enough to make his demands stand. The new men's collection, though manufactured and marketed by a Manhattan Industries company, Perry Ellis Sportswear, Ltd., was produced under a totally different deal than the women's collection. In effect, it was a licensing agreement between

Manhattan and Perry Ellis International, from which Perry would receive a percentage of the sales rather than a salary (as he did from Manhattan for the women's line)—a much more advantageous deal for him. That Larry Leeds would go this far with Perry, when Manhattan had yet to make a profit from the women's collections, is ample evidence of both Manhattan's and Perry's confidence in his marketability.

Perry was undoubtedly in control of most aspects of his professional and personal life at this point, but in the case of his men's wear agreement with Manhattan, he obviously benefited from being in the right place at the right time. Popular culture in America was in the grip of the designer-as-star syndrome, and Perry was canny enough to play it to the hilt, at the same time furthering his own professional needs. His women's collections had caught the imagination of the consumer with their freshness and ebullience, and only now, when he was a star, was he willing to introduce his long-awaited men's collection.

In the latter seventies to have a gimmick in the fashion business was almost a license to print money. All that three Israeli brothers named Nakash had to do to strike it big was get several thousand dollars together and make a television commercial with a Jerry Hall look-alike model to announce their new line of jeans. They had no production or design—except for the pair of Levi 501s they used in the ad—but with the tremendous response they received as a result of their TV campaign they were *then* able to go to Bank Leumi and borrow the capital needed to produce their wares—Jordache Jeans. It's no wonder, therefore, that establishment names like Bill Blass, Calvin Klein, and Ralph Lauren were making fortunes, and, with the sophisticated backup of their companies and powerful advertising, could draw large crowds at department stores when they made public appearances. Descriptions of the mob scenes that took place across the country are hardly exaggerations. And someone as handsome and beguiling as Perry, with all that press machinery behind him, could guarantee at least a crowd of a couple of thousand people when he visited a store. As Carolyn Gottfried puts it, "It was easy to promote anyone in those days. It wasn't just that Perry was right, but the whole industry was right."

All of Perry's close friends categorically state that he hated these appearances, which is in keeping with the notion of him being a solitary, shy man, but somehow it doesn't quite gel. Undoubtedly he didn't relish these "p.a.'s" (as they're called in the business), but one can be certain that he never turned one down if it would add to his stature and the sales of his creations. Perry was more than promotable, and he made the most of the exposure the press and retailers gave him.

Still, given the fashion hype and hysteria of those years, what is fascinating about Perry is how much he downplayed his own name. While everyone from Calvin Klein to little Gloria "Happy at Last" Vanderbilt was putting their name on the asses of the masses with "designer" jeans, Perry steadfastly refused to have a signature logo on any of his clothes during that period (even though Ralph Lauren had his polo player, Calvin Klein embossed his signature on the waistband of his underwear, and Giorgio Armani flew his eagle on the left pectoral muscle of his shirts, T-shirts, and leather jackets). He, alone, seemed secure enough in the knowledge that his design elements, like the "dimple" shoulder, were sufficient to make a statement people would notice. It says a tremendous amount about the individuality of Perry's styling, because his clothes *were* instantly recognizable among the cognoscenti without any overt form of signature identification.

At the same time, Perry had become a bona fide media star, and was meeting the likes of Joan Mondale, the vice president's wife, as well as other officials of the Carter administration at luncheons and political parties. Such social gatherings were symptomatic of a new, more public phase in Perry's life: he was actively courting the powerful and celebrated. He was also finding himself constantly courted by the media, and by this stage of his career there had been feature articles about him in many of the world's leading publications. It couldn't help but change him. Rea Lubar, who possibly knew him as well as anyone, suggests that success did change him. "I think it did. One can't be the greatest sportswear designer and not change, just as I think success has changed Calvin and Ralph. I think Perry wanted to be with more important people, which is perfectly natural, because often important people tend to be more interesting."

(A telling example of the extent of his popularity at this time was a personal appearance he made at Bloomingdale's White Plains store in conjunction with a show of his clothes. After the show, a woman who had bought one of his $8,500 Alixandre fur coats came backstage to ask him to autograph it. Perry graciously, though one imagines somewhat bashfully, acquiesced and discreetly signed the lining of one of the sleeves. Later, he admitted, "It was a nice feeling to be signing something you've designed."* And, according to Bloomingdale's Kal Ruttenstein, he then personally sold this customer a matching mink caplet for $1,300. Such was his allure and endemic star quality.)

Which is not to say Perry believed all that was written about him. Privately, he would remain the gracious, thoughtful person he had always been, but there was an undoubted shift in his priorities around this time, which resulted in his becoming more inaccessible to some of his oldest friends.

Still, there was never any doubt that however distant he might become or however much he utilized the power his unique talent had given him, if any one, close friend or otherwise, was in need and asked for help, Perry would be there without question.

Perry's generosity was legendary and totally without guile, and there are numerous examples of this wonderfully giving side of his nature. For instance, when James Terrell was starting up his own company Perry lent him a sum well into

---

* *Women's Wear Daily*, August 21, 1980, the "Eye" column.

five figures. Granted, Terrell's was a special case, but there was no denying that Perry had a sense of that old-fashioned virtue called charity, one he would exhibit in many small ways. Once when Melissa Drier was sick with the flu after her critique of his latest collection had come out in *DNR*, he called her up to thank her personally (as he did with many editors). "I was sick at home," she recalls, "and Perry found out my home number and called me to thank me for my review of the collection, but we spent the time discussing the merits of one of the Seventh Avenue deli's chicken soups. The next thing I knew, a delivery person was at my door—way downtown in Tribeca—with a Mason jar of 'Jewish penicillin!'"

Perry's help was extended to many people, most of whom never knew he had intervened on their behalf. In many ways, the fashion community is a small village, and his advice was constantly sought. There are more than a few people in the industry who owe their careers to him.

One such person was Jane Woolrich, now fashion editor of *The Miami Herald*, whom Perry first met when she was studying English history at Duke University. Woolrich had put together a one-day fashion seminar and was working with one of the best fashion journalists in the country, Nine Hyde of *The Washington Post* (who has connections with Duke). Nina, in turn, brought in Perry and Phil Miller, who was then president of Neiman Marcus (and one of Perry's great retail supporters from the very beginning). "This was at the beginning of 1980," Woolrich recalls, "and at that time Perry wasn't too well known outside New York—certainly not in North Carolina—so I had to ask Nina what he looked like, since I was picking him and Mr. Miller up at the airport. I hadn't been exposed to fashion designers then and I was rather in awe of these famous people flying in for my seminar.

"Nina said, 'Oh, that's easy. You'll be able to recognize him because he always wears the same thing: khakis and a blue cotton Oxford-cloth shirt, Topsiders with no socks, and his hair in a ponytail.'"

Perry was as natural as his attire and casually remarked to her after the seminar that if she ever came to New York he would be happy to help her. Still, she was more than surprised, when she finally did arrive, that he not only remembered her but also helped her get a job on *The New York Times*. His interest in his protégé didn't stop there, however, and he not only became close to her family, but helped her later when she encountered some personal problems.

In time, with his ever greater success, and as he became more reclusive due to his own problems, Perry wouldn't spend as much time lending a hand to others. However, he would continue to be drawn to students and young people, and would try to help where he could. His work with the students of the Parsons School of Design and the Fashion Institute of Technology (the two most important fashion schools in New York) is one of his greatest legacies, as is the endowment he set up at his own alma mater, the College of William and Mary.

The introduction of his men's wear collection at the fall 1980 show revealed another important aspect of Perry's character. Ever the showman, he was the only American designer to show his men's and women's collections together in one gigantic, lavish presentation. Before then, men's wear collections had generally been shown three to four months before the women's selling seasons—in January for the fall season and as early as July for the next summer season. Although Perry's men's collections continued to be shown privately to the press and buyers at these times, the most "forward" and crucial part of his men's collections would from now on make its debut at his women's shows in April and November. This meant that any store wishing to buy the collection would have to keep money aside out of its buying appropriation simply for Perry, which could be a strain on a store's budget, especially if it had overspent in Europe (where the season starts) and whose designers offered merchandise of equivalent fashion caliber and price point (since Perry's prices were rapidly increasing to the same level as the world's most expensive designers). This, in turn, put a strain on the company's marketing and selling staff, since they had to keep their major accounts interested long after the usual men's wear buying season was over. Yet, in a sense it was a brilliant marketing ploy, since it made Perry's men's collections that much more exclusive, and it quickly became part of the Perry Ellis mystique. Even today no other major American designer shows this way. (And in Europe, where the practice was common, the collections are now separated due to the different schedules of the men's and women's seasons.)

Why did he do it? Was it simply to satisfy his ego by having the showiest fashion presentation in town, one that would guarantee the most eager audience? Or was it a shrewd marketing strategy? Complex as Perry Ellis was, it was probably a mixture of both. Certainly, it made for great fashion theater.

His two collections for 1980 were again recognized by the fashion press, and Perry was nominated for the Coty Return Award (a second "Winnie") later that year. He won again, and this time he deigned to grace the awards ceremony with his presence, and in the company of a large entourage of friends and company employees.

One of Perry's more astute realizations was that *his* clothes, like all fashion, needed to be dressed up. Even the great Chanel had realized the value of accessories and styled her deceptively simple suits with bijoux and bagatelles. Perry knew that styling would add a crucial element to his sportswear while dramatically enhancing his fashion statement.

With his persuasive personality he was able to recruit some of the top talents on the international fashion scene to work with him. Not only did he use Patricia Underwood for his hats, but also Barry Kieselstein-Cord, one of the world's gifted jewelry designers, for precious-metal belts that were expressly commissioned to complement the collections, and the

French designer Jean-Charles Brosseau, creator of the world's most expensive perfume, Ombre Rose, to supply knitted accessories such as hats, gloves, scarves, and legwear.

Perry's first encounters with these last two designers were almost matters of chance. Kieselstein-Cord, already one of America's most renowned jewelry designers, was introduced to Perry by Jade Hobson, one of *Vogue*'s fashion editors, who persuaded Barry that he should meet Perry—"that chap with the long hair," as Barry called him. He was, however, already interested in Perry as a result of a photograph of the designer taken on the pier at Water Island that he had seen (probably in *The New York Times*). They got in touch, and Barry went over to Perry's studio (the loft, before he'd moved into 575 Seventh) with his wife CeCe. As Barry remembers it, "We met this good-looking man with laughing eyes who came over and said, 'Hi, I'm Perry!'" There was an instant rapport between the two that would last through many years.

Perry met Jean-Charles Brosseau in the simplest way—he walked into Brosseau's boutique on the Place des Victoires—a beautiful seventeenth-century circus in the heart of Paris that now houses some of the most exclusive fashion boutiques in the French capital—in 1978. Perry was there to check out the latest clothes of his favorite designer, Kenzo, with Patricia and Jed. As M. Brosseau describes their first meeting, "Perry came into my shop out of curiosity and admired my hats very much. Very simply, he asked me if I would do all his accessories, and we worked together for three years. . . ."

Brosseau and Perry worked on these accessories in a variety of ways. More often than not, Perry would tell Brosseau the concept of the collection and the Frenchman would work from Perry's description to execute the design. Their initial meetings in Paris would be followed up by subsequent ones in New York to finalize their ideas. It proved to be one of Perry's most successful collaborations and, though less publicized than his working relationship with Barry Kieselstein-Cord, laid the foundation for several of Perry's knit licenses.

Among the interesting aspects of the Ellis–Brosseau relationship is the fact that Brosseau hadn't heard of Perry before they first met, and his agreeing to work for Perry is all the more unusual because of this. "He was so sympathetic," says Brosseau. "He was so charming, and that's the only reason I decided to work with him, since I didn't know anything about him or his design at that time."

Brosseau would also give Perry considerable advice on the latter's twice-yearly visits to Paris as to where to find fabrics, wools for his sweaters, and shoes to accessorize the collections. All things considered, it turned out to be a remarkably beneficial chance meeting for Perry and was quite influential in his development as a designer.

Perry was also clever enough to bring together a stable of some of the top fashion talent in New York to make his shows and presentations the media events they became. Some of the best models, hair stylists, and music people, as well as his own highly talented design staff, all contributed greatly to what became known as "the Perry Ellis look." One of his great talents was recognizing ability in others and making it work for him, and inevitably these people came to love him personally and respect him professionally, despite his sometimes impossible demands.

Personally, the year was a profound one for him. It had become fairly obvious by this time that Perry was more attracted to men (though he would always be drawn to women and most likely wanted to lead a "normal" life, as evidenced by his later desperate need to father a child). Certainly, to use a common expression, he had "come out of the closet," and his homosexuality was an open secret in the fashion world. But it's simply too trite and dismissive to categorize Perry as "one of those fag designers." He was a sensitive man who led a sybaritic existence, but he was never effeminate (though he did indulge himself in "camp" humor among his intimates).

June of 1980 was probably the last time he was seen with his lover of four years, Beau Tropper, when they both traveled to Japan to launch the collection by Renown, his Japanese sublicensee. True to his extravagant style, Perry flew to Japan an entourage that included Patricia Pastor, Jed Krascella, and Judy Beste from the office, as well as a number of top New York models, including Beau for the men's clothes. Although apparently quite disorganized on the Japanese end, Perry succeeded in putting on a show that, to quote *WWD*, "garnered spontaneous, sustained applause"—the first American designer to do so in that country.

The collection opened on June 20, and the Ellis entourage was entertained royally. Judy Beste remembers being taken to a Japanese men's club that she normally wouldn't have been allowed to visit. The next day she was honored by the *mama-san* of the establishment, who sent her a couple of bottles of homemade saki. On their last night, the whole Perry Ellis brigade was entertained at one of Tokyo's finest French restaurants. Perry, who was sitting in the middle surrounded by Jed, Patricia, and Horoshi Motomora (who then worked for Renown and now works for Perry Ellis International in Japan), asked Judy to demonstrate her ability to count to ten in Japanese. Judy proudly obliged, and then Perry, with that certain glint in his eye, asked Horoshi to teach her a dirty word in Japanese. Beste demured, Perry insisted, and soon Jed was called in to the language lesson. Jed, never a shrinking violet, caught Perry's enthusiasm, and eventually the more delicately mannered Horoshi was persuaded to teach him how to say *shit* in Japanese, which he did very quietly. The sound of the word in Japanese is very guttural, and Jed, having finally got the right intonation, declaimed it rather loudly, goaded on by a boisterous Perry. The whole restaurant became deathly quiet . . . and Perry thought it was wonderful, finding the whole episode hilarious.

That there was still an immature side to Perry that could delight in this kind of scatological schoolboy humor, even when informally representing his country at a highly formal dinner, while perhaps reprehensible, was nevertheless endearing.

There is no doubt that several of Perry's friends, especially his old lover, Robert McDonald, did not approve of his relationship with Beau, and they expended a lot of energy trying to break up something they saw as potentially harmful to Perry. They very well might have been right in their assessment, since Beau's hedonistic lifestyle, with its continual comings and goings, was causing Perry anguish. Yet Beau obviously adored Perry and was well liked by the designer's inner working circle. As Judy Beste remembers, Perry had nicknamed her "Herr" because of the efficient way she dealt with the fabric people in Germany. That spring, when they all went to Frankfurt for the Interstoff fabric fair, Beau went with them. He left the group early, however, to go on a bicycling tour of Europe and wrote Judy a beautiful farewell note that began "Dear Hair . . ."

Who it was who introduced Perry to Laughlin Barker that summer, no one can remember, but everyone agrees that he fit in perfectly with the new image Perry was cultivating. At any rate, the attraction between them was immediate and powerful, and Beau was quietly dropped from Perry's life.

Although the decision ultimately was Perry's alone, and, as we shall see, his feelings for Barker were more important to him than life itself, the undeniable fact remains that Perry was having to be more careful. He could no longer afford to run off to Santa Barbara and sit with Beau at the back of the classroom. The pressure on him as a public personality by then was simply too great.

It was, perhaps, an indication of how afraid Perry was of "being exposed," and one reason why there has been so much controversy over his death. At the same time, the fact remains that there was a dichotomy between how much Perry allowed the world, or at least the people he trusted, to know about him, and how much the people surrounding him tried to pro-

tect him from what they felt might be threatening to his reputation.

For his spring/summer 1981 collection, presented at the
end of October, *Woman's Wear Daily* gave Perry what was for
it a gushing review. Under the headline ELLIS: THE IMAG-
INATIVE AND THE SALABLE IN BALANCE, the column began
in characteristically caustic Fairchild style:

> NEW YORK—The high-school gymnasium bleachers
> were set up, the usherettes in pixie hats and capelet
> sweaters stood guard, and very of-the-moment music
> like "It's My Turn" swelled syrupily in the back-
> ground. All the Pop accouterments. But in his up-
> beat, diverse show on Wednesday morning, Perry
> Ellis went way beyond cheerleader cuteness in his
> most sophisticated, grown-up collection to date.

Retailers as well were ecstatic. To quote Henri Bendel's president, Geraldine Stutz: "I think he is becoming our contemporary Claire McCardell. His signature is that strong. . . ." Other
accolades ranged from "the best he's ever done" to "every card
he played was a winner" to "spectacular."

Perry showed more silhouettes and more new shapes than
ever before, from long thigh-covering jackets over new
cropped pants to fitted jackets to camisoles and blouses with
full-flaired skirts both long and short. *Women's Wear Daily*
came to the conclusion that it was Perry's sense of proportion
that made this collection more sophisticated then previous
ones and singled out the mix of his tops with his new bloom-
ers, culottes, and "square-dance frontier skirts, often layered
over petticoats." In fact, Perry's sense of proportion had been
his saving grace throughout his career, often hiding or at least
disguising some of his more obvious stylistic gaffes. It was
only now, however, with his increasing maturity, that his
strongest design talent was becoming so apparent.

His men's collection, on the other hand, was more critically received, even though Perry used many of the same fabrics and some of the same silhouettes. The *Daily News Record* did not totally agree with all of his choices, including his Liberty prints and his Mandarin collar cadet jackets, although they did say, "Still, the collection succeeded as often as it faltered."

The more than favorable review of this collection by *WWD* was the end of the honeymoon, however, between Fairchild and Ellis.

At the beginning of December, *WWD* in Japan, the Japanese government, the Japanese newspaper *Asahi Shimbun*, the Shiseido cosmetics company, and a group of Japanese textile and trade associations selected the "Best Five" designers in the world to present a fashion extravaganza. The five were Perry Ellis of America, Zandra Rhodes of Great Britain, Karl Lagerfeld of France, Giorgio Armani of Italy, and Hanai Mori of Japan. (The resulting line, while distinguished by five of the world's great designers, was somewhat biased, as can be seen by the fact that Hanai Mori has a controlling interest in the Japanese *WWD*.)

Woman's Wear's article, under their infamous pseudonym "Louise J. Esterhazy" (a fictitious, deposed Hungarian countess), which was often written by John Fairchild himself and always in the bitchiest and most scurrilous of styles, began:

TOKYO—The Chinese may think their Gang of Four are exciting, but last week I was more interested in observing the hijinks of Tokyo's Gang of Five—Peevish Perry Ellis, Gentile Giorgio Armani, Katty Karl Lagerfeld, Zapped-out Zandra Rhodes and Modest Hanae Mori.

Imagine, if you will, my excitement at seeing these Shoguns of Style on the same runway. And imagine, if you can, the absolute ecstasy I felt at finding four of the five on the same floor of the Hotel Okura, draped around my luxurious suite like so many Savage Samurai. Before the week was out, fashion rudeness would be raised to an art form, and the intrigue that ensued put my old cronies in the Hungarian court to shame.

From "Mr. Pop" and being the darling of *WWD,* Perry had become "Peevish Perry" and was criticized mercilessly. Maybe he *was* demanding in the amount of time he kept models for show rehearsals (to the detriment of the other world-class designers) as was reported, but that was in character and Fairchild knew all about Perry's perfectionism. What was not in character, and the reason why Perry earned the sobriquet "Peevish," was simply because he isolated himself from the media circus for virtually all of the overly hyped trip. As he privately told Karl Lagerfeld, one of the few designers he admired, in one of their infrequent meetings during the trip, his father was dying and he was so upset he couldn't speak to anyone. Fairchild, one of his friends, should have known this, and if he didn't, at least he should have made an effort to find out why Perry was so uncooperative, ill-mannered, and obviously out of sorts.

Unfortunately, as a result of this story, Perry became known as a "difficult" personality. In fact, Perry fulfilled *all* of his professional obligations in Japan and only then did he fly directly back to Portsmouth, Virginia, where he was able to spend the last few hours of his father's life at his hospital bedside.

Journalistically, it was a mistake on Fairchild's part, and it wounded Perry deeply. However, it seems fairly certain that John Fairchild was not aware of the personal tragedy unfolding in the designer's life. Though friends with Fairchild, Perry was such a private person when it came to his family that he hadn't told the publishing magnate. In fact, as soon as Fairchild found out he offered Perry the use of his house in Provence so that the designer could recuperate quietly in the sun away from prying eyes, and it was there that Perry recovered from the painful blow of his father's death.

It should be noted that Perry and John Fairchild remained friends, despite what *Women's Wear Daily* or any of the other Fairchild publications had to say about him—and they would say far worse things than this, especially in 1984. The Fairchilds would continue to have Perry to dinner at their apartment on Gracie Square, and Perry would reciprocate by inviting them over to his town house.

It should also be noted that the old publicity saw "It doesn't matter what they say as long as they talk about you" was especially valid in this case. Despite the negative comments, the inclusion of Perry among the "Best Five" on this trip elevated him to the ranks of a "world-class" designer. Obviously, there were several American designers that could have been chosen, including more established names like Blass, Klein, or Lauren, all of whom had Japanese licensees, but Perry was the more newsworthy at the moment.

It *is* fair to say that the story made him an international star. It was covered widely in the press, and, as a result, in the minds of many people outside the fashion industry Perry became one of the top five designers in the world, however inaccuarate that might have been.

It was also recognition that was important for him at that point, because although Perry was still ostensibly a sportswear designer, his prices had already escalated to what would eventually become extraordinary levels. Just two years before his retail prices were between $36 and $100; certainly affordable. By 1980, however, they had at least doubled and within a couple of years they would quadruple. Which is not to say that the content and quality of his merchandise were overpriced—it is more a reflection of how much Ellis was costing Manhattan Industries at every level of his business, as well as how much more sophisticated his clothes were becoming.

Although he was now firmly established as one of the aristocrats of Seventh Avenue, Perry remained aloof from the business. There was undoubtedly a snobbish side to his character, and, as Erwin Isman puts it, "Perry's irreverence for the apparel business was incredible." Yet it was this same aloofness that was at the root of his sense of humor and enabled him to maintain a healthy perspective on his own abilities. In Isman's assessment, "He knew he could not change the world and therefore he knew it wasn't that important."

Certainly, when Perry was being candid, he would say that clothes should not be overemphasized and reiterated several times that love was the most important thing in life. Although it sounds simplistic, even in light of Perry's romantic side, the fact remains that the more caustic side of his nature simply didn't like "the business." He could be very vicious about people in the industry who took the whole game too seriously, and as Isman matter-of-factly states, "Perry had real difficulty with the 'garmento' types. He thought anyone who took the business too seriously was comical and he always made up nicknames for them. The only thing he respected was the quality of the clothing."

Perry's attitude was more akin to that of eighteenth- or nineteenth-century amateurism; despite his business background at college, he wasn't interested in the "trade" side of the business. It was almost as though he considered it beneath him. As president of the company, Isman understood this. "Perry always thought the design end of the business was the be-all and end-all. The business end of the business was necessary but not desirable."

In its own way, it's an understandable quality for a designer to possess. Most great designers have had a Svengali-like figure behind them to operate and manipulate their business affairs—Yves Saint Laurent has Pierre Berge, Calvin Klein has Barry Schwartz, and Giorgio Armani's empire was built by the late Sergio Galeotti—just as Perry would come to rely on Laughlin Barker.

While Isman was president of Perry Ellis Sportswear, Inc., it was his job to exert control over the creative and extravagant side of Perry. "It was a balancing act. If Perry asked for this, this, this, and this, then I only gave him the first of the four, which would keep him quiet for a while. All the time I was trying to keep him profitable.

"Constantly, whenever we had an overhead dispute, I would go in and say, 'Good morning, Perry. We're spending too much money and we've got to watch where we're spending the money.' But he would never, never cut back on the design room, nor assistants, nor sample lengths, nor people with taste."

Isman recalls one season when they had excess inventory and had to dump it at one of the discounters. (This happens often in the fashion industry and is why consumers are able to buy designer clothes at below normal prices from well-known retail chains across the country.) Perry's response to Isman's informing him of the fact was, "Why don't you sell it to Puerto Rico?"

Isman replied, "Perry, nobody in Puerto Rico is going to pay these prices; they don't have the market for designer clothing down there. You just picked a place where you don't care whether your clothes are dumped or not."

Isman suggests that Perry never understood that a manufacturer has to dispose of his inventory. "All he wanted was to protect the image of his line, and he would tell me in his usual way when he didn't want to be bothered with a problem, 'You figure it out somehow.'" Isman goes on to state categorically: "Perry was not controllable, much as I loved him. Perry would respond if he agreed. The only one he would take direction from, and then only if he agreed with the direction, was Larry [Leeds]."

Perry's outrageous spending to satisfy his personal standards and what he perceived as the image associated with the line was costing Manhattan Industries millions of dollars a year. Despite the critical success of Perry Ellis Sportswear, Inc., the company only broke even for the first time in 1980, two years after it was formed (and this on wholesale sales of about $20 million a year!). A good example of how such a state of affairs could exist can be seen in the way he handled sample fabrics.

"The situation was out of hand until Judy Beste took over," says Isman. "Judy is a very fine merchant, and eventually Perry developed great confidence in her ability.

"Up to that point, Perry would come back from a buying trip and I would say, 'Perry, how much did you buy?' 'Not much,' he would reply, and he would have spent hundreds of thousands of dollars' worth of fabrics! Perry bought beauty, and until Judy went along he would gad around buying everything and we wouldn't know what was coming in. With Judy there I knew we would at least have purchase orders to cover the sample fabrics we were buying, so that I could edit down to what we needed for the line and still have some economy."

It's clear that Perry's sample buying was almost profligate. Often, if he liked a fabric he would order it in fifteen to twenty colorways, even if he might only be interested in one or two colors for the collection. One year they had to lease extra space at 575 Seventh just for piece goods (cloth samples) storage!

The economics of just this one facet of Perry's business are extraordinary. Perry would buy hundreds of yards of fabric at $40 or $50 a yard that would never be used. Isman would have to turn around and sell it off at probably ten cents on the dollar to a fabric retail outlet. It may not sound like much, but when one considers the fact that in a year Perry would spend nearly a million dollars on sample fabric alone, it quickly adds up.

Similar money worries would continue to be the darker side of what was on the surface one of the most successful fashion stories in history. In a way, they lent a tragic quality to Perry's life. As Racine might have portrayed him in the retelling of a Greek tragedy, he was favored by the gods but flawed and fated.

Although perhaps biased, Erwin Isman's assessment of

Perry's contribution to fashion in this country is not without merit in trying to evaluate how much Perry influenced the American fashion scene in the latter half of this century: "Perry changed the way the game was played. Perry changed the way designers were perceived. Perry didn't design couture, Perry designed sportswear, and he was uniquely American: he didn't try to emulate Paris or Milan. He was what he was, and he had enough talent to change fashion in this country, in the same way that Julius Erving changed the way basketball was played, or Babe Ruth changed the way baseball was played, or Mohammed Ali changed boxing—that's how you measure the man.

"Perry's effect on his time was unique and powerful."

8

"Ladies and Gentlemen,
The Crystal Room is proud to present the club debut of
America's new recording stars . . . The Dreams."
"Every man has his own special dream
And your dream's about to come true.
Life's not as bad as it may seem
If you open you eyes to what's in front of you.
We are dreamgirls . . .
Boys, we make you happy."

—Tom Eyen,
Dreamgirls

It is eleven o'clock on the morning of Tuesday, April 20, 1982, and the old banking hall at 575 Seventh Avenue, renovated by James Terrell into the most luxurious fashion showroom in the world outside of Milan, is packed to the rafters.

The atmosphere in the room is electric: everyone who is anyone in the fashion business is there—if they have been lucky enough to get one of the hottest invitations on Seventh Avenue. Celebrities like the late Ann Baxter and Andy Warhol, Tina Chow, Phyllis George, Lauren Hutton, Cheryl Tiegs, and the French designer Sonia Rykiel (a great compliment; she's one of the most intellectual designers in the world) are forced to squash themselves next to mere mortals on the groaning bleachers of the Perry Ellis showroom. The scene outside is later described by *DNR* as reminiscent of a scene from John Schlesinger's film *Day of the Locust,* such is the pandemonium. With scores of photographers pushing and shoving to get enough elbow room to click their shutters, and with more press present than at a presidential press conference, it is obviously a major media event.

The Hollywood-like atmosphere of anticipation is brought to a climax by the drumroll and opening chords of Henry Krieger's music for the title song of the Broadway show *Dreamgirls*. The overture is enough to let even the dimmest journalist know that he or she is about to witness the latest offerings from America's newest fashion star: Perry Ellis.

His dream has come true: he's the hottest ticket in town.

Down the runway walk Perry's always stellar models, in tailored peplum jackets and tight skirts. While the fashion groupies scream and applaud, the fashion press sits astounded: Where are the eagerly awaited layered sportswear outfits? This is tailored couture! These are clothes for the Reagan set . . . ladies who lunch! What's going on here?

Perry Ellis has grown up.

Mind you, Ellis hasn't grown up completely. The suits—entitled "For lunching at La Grenouille"—are far too fitted for any of the matrons and established media stars who normally patronize the chic, elegant, and expensive restaurant on Fifty-third Street in Manhattan that attracts the fashion elite with its haute cuisine and exclusiveness. Perry, with his usual dry, almost cynical humor, is poking fun at the pretentiousness of the fashion establishment. He has always maintained that clothes should be fun, and in this show they are.

The previous year had gone well for Perry. Both of his women's collections had been acclaimed by the fashion press and retailers, and Perry Ellis Sportswear, Inc., the women's clothing company owned by Manhattan Industries, had finally made a profit—about $1.4 million on sales of $20 to $24 million, according to Erwin Isman, then president of the company.

The men's collections were also growing after the poor initial response from some of the country's top retailers, and Edward M. Jones, one of the best men's wear executives in the country, had been hired away from Calvin Klein Menswear,

Inc., to join Manhattan Industries as president of Perry Ellis
Sportswear, Ltd., on July 1.

When Perry had first decided to do a men's collection and
licensed his name to Manhattan Industries the year before, the
project was begun in a small way. Perry had only wanted to
sell the collection to a few of the best specialty stores in each of
the major cities in the country and his first account was with
Henri Bendel. Geraldine Stutz, the brilliant president of
Bendel at that time, and a close friend of Perry's, had negotiated to acquire his new men's collection on an exclusive basis
in New York. Bendel was basically a women's fashion store,
and Perry's men's collection was only their second men's boutique (the first being Peter Barton's Closet). The agreement
also meant that Perry was the first designer to have two
"shops" (specific areas devoted exclusively to a single designer's clothes) in the store.

However, Larry Crysler, who was the second retailer in
the country to pick up Perry's men's collection while he was at
Jerry Magnin, the exclusive Beverly Hills boutique on Rodeo
Drive, insists that Perry was having great difficulty in finding
any retailers to carry the line.

"I was on vacation and Jerry Magnin called me and asked
me if I would mind going over to see Perry's new men's collection," remembers Crysler. "Perry was apparently at the Beverly
Hills Hotel showing the collection and had called Jerry. I said,
'Would I mind?!' and rushed over, since Perry was already
such a big name.

"I don't know what I expected—not many women's designers know how to do men's wear—so I went with an open
mind. When I got there, there was Perry in the bungalow and
he was showing the collection himself. I had expected assistants, salespeople, and everything that goes along with a big
women's fashion designer, but it was only Perry, with Beau
modeling these slouchy, rumpled, wonderful clothes.

"His clothes were charismatic. Hundreds of people make
clothes, but somehow only certain designers design clothes

that have . . . soul, a soul of their own. It's hard to describe, but only a very few have it, like Giorgio Armani. It's interesting that Giorgio's clothes are similar to Perry's in the way that they're not forced. Their clothes are so natural, and that's unique.

"Even with the bad fit, and they didn't fit at the beginning, Perry's clothes were so natural. And with his off colors and those beautiful hand-knit sweaters, there was something about them."

On the other hand, Crysler never liked Perry's suits and feels it was because, at that time, Perry never wore suits himself. "It wasn't his lifestyle; since he didn't wear suits, how could he tell what suits were all about? I don't think he understood that side of the market; he was strictly a sportswear designer."

Still, Crysler was definitely impressed with the new collection and went back to Magnin having ordered a substantial part of it. He was planning on doing a big launch in the store, and had already asked Perry to send some of his signature shirts with the wide collar and pleated shoulder so that the salespeople could be wearing them when the collection made its debut. He also had Perry's publicity photograph blown up and made into masks, which were then put on all the mannequins in the store window.

Happily for Perry as well as Crysler, the collection sold extremely well, which makes it even more difficult to understand why Perry had such a hard time placing it at first in other stores. "I know that Perry had been to many other stores before he came to us," insists Crysler. "He had approached all the top stores, and I was one of the last ones he wanted to sell. In Los Angeles he had been to Maxfield Blue [now Maxfield's] and Tommy Perse [the owner] had, quote, unquote, laughed in his face. Apparently, Wilkes Bashford didn't want it, and neither did people like Jon Weiser [of Charivari in New York] and John Jones [of Ultimo in Chicago], so it was just Jean

Rosenberg [of Bendel] and myself who believed in him at the beginning."

In fact, Wilkes Bashford, the proprietor of the beautiful store of the same name on Stutter Street in San Francisco, one of the best specialty stores in America, bought the collection the next season and became one of Perry's major supporters in men's wear, as he had been from the beginning with Perry's women's wear.

"I think he was one of the few people in America to make a statement as a designer," says Bashford. "His men's and women's clothes were American in spirit and reflected the way we live in this country, though that's truer about his men's clothes. He caught on to what people wanted and made clothes real when many designers at the time were not. Along with Ralph Lauren and Calvin Klein, he made a strong, uniquely American statement that made this country important in world fashion."

With a nucleus of these three retailers, the men's wear began to take off, which was when Perry brought in Ed Jones to head the rapidly expanding company.

In addition, his women's collections of 1981 had been two of the best in his career up until that time. The fall show, presented on April 21, was a giant step forward for him. His most romantic and biggest collection to date, in it he showed a tremendous variety of looks, from Sherwood Forest in England to Irish peasants and fishermen, to Russian cossacks and Hungarian gypsies, all the way to North Africa for Berbers. It was a tour de force, and his use of fabric, with mixes of up to six or seven different fabrics, patterns, and colors in one outfit, was outstanding.

He also outdid himself in his production values for the show, using long bows and archery accessories as well as two Irish setters for his "Queen of the Hunt" finale, the fur-cloaked model in white looking like a Russian ice princess. *Women's Wear*, ever quick with new sobriquets, dubbed him "the

Archer" (quite a change from "Peevish Perry" just four months before!) and ran the headline ELLIS HITS THE MARK WITH ROMANTIC TRAVELOG. It was obvious long before the finale, however, that the press and retailers loved the theatrical show and, more important, that underneath all the hype and glitz the clothes themselves were brilliant. Anita Gallo of B. Altman was quoted in *WWD* as saying, "He's the best we have in this country." Bernadine Morris, in *The New York Times,* went even further; she compared him to the great Chanel. (For this collection, as well as the one immediately preceding it, Perry entered the Coty Hall of Fame with his third "Winnie" for women's clothes. He also won his first men's award.)

One of the most remarkable aspects of Perry Ellis's career was how rapidly he and his design team matured. From one season to the next his vocabulary and facility with design grew noticeably better, and though he would occasionally come up with a collection that didn't work at all, his continual progress as a designer makes his early death all the more tragic.

The extent of fall '81 collection was all the more remarkable in light of the fact that Perry was quite sick in the months before the collection was presented. He had been admitted to New York Hospital on February 7 and, though discharged on the eleventh, was apparently not able to work at full strength for quite a while afterward. Although friends disagree on what was wrong with him at the time, the general consensus seems to be that he had hepatitis. Barry Kieselstein-Cord says that Perry was taken ill just after he came back from a safari trip to Africa with Laughlin Barker, and that it was after this that their health gradually became more fragile. Other friends also remember Perry and Laughlin becoming more and more concerned about their health after this, and that at times Perry was even loath to be in a room with someone who had a cold. However, at this point hardly anyone had even heard of Acquired Immune Deficiency Syndrome, and Perry's future looked as rosy as ever.

In June 1981, the Council of Fashion Designers of America, under its president Bill Blass, announced the first CFDA fashion awards. For the Designer of the Year award in women's fashion, the fifteen-member panel of journalists and retailers nominated Geoffrey Beene, Calvin Klein, and Perry Ellis. The award ceremony was scheduled to be nationally televised that September, a development that would obviously damage the reputation of the Coty Awards. As Bill Blass told *WWD*, "What was needed in the industry was a national award on the scale of the Academy Awards." (As it happened, the CFDA awards would not be televised, but the CFDA itself would become vitally important to Perry personally in the last two years of his life.)

At about the same time, unbeknownst to most of America, a little-publicized English film had just been released in Europe. Almost immediately, however, it became recognized as one of those rare cinematic exceptions that's both a work of art and wonderful, moving entertainment. Fairchild's *Menswear* (now *"M"* magazine) did the first cover story in America on what would prove to be a surprisingly influential film, and predicted it would have a great impact on the fashion world. When Vangelis's now-famous theme music for *Chariots of Fire* opened Perry's spring '82 collection, shown at the end of October, *Menswear* was proven right. Milena Cannonera's Oscar-winning costumes for the film had indeed acted as a fashion catalyst.

It quickly became apparent that Perry had produced one of the most sublimely simple collections of his career. Inspired by the way clothes were draped in long, lean silhouettes in the thirties, he had made a breakthrough. Although the shoulders of his jackets were very broad, their just-below-the-hip length and sleeves that came to just below the fingertips made their proportions perfectly correct. Shown over long pleated skirts or wide-cut trousers in the crispest linen, they were reminiscent of the romance of Ascot garden parties in that halcyon period between the two world wars. His simple cotton knitwear with straight sweaters falling to just below the hip, worn

with long straight knit skirts or baggy knit pants and accessorized with Argyle socks, sandals, and floppy brimmed
hats, looked as if they had come off an English croquet lawn.
But they were not just a pastiche of a Noel Coward play. Perry
had made the look all his own with broad horizontal or vertical stripes (and with Perry broad meant broad; they could be
as wide as a foot). The most predominant color in the collection was white, with shadow stripes of gray, or pastel, or navy
blue. When he did use color it was in dark regimental strips, in
keeping with the Oxford theme.

The collection was a departure for Perry, and though he
showed short, alternative shapes and layers, it was a new,
pared-down, elemental Perry the audience was seeing. (And,
in fact, the long, lean silhouette would crop up in nearly every
collection he designed after this.) *Women's Wear*, with its cus-
tomary reservations, raved about the collection in its most po-
etic style, and other important fashion writers were equally
effusive. Bloomingdale's Kal Ruttenstein called it "the most
important statement to be made on both sides of the Atlantic."

That same year also saw Perry gain yet another licensee—
for children's wear. It had been announced at the beginning of
the year that he would do a line of girls' sportswear for Norstan Industries, but that had fallen through when Norstan
went into bankruptcy. By the end of the year, however, Perry
Ellis International had announced it would license the line to
Pelican Industries. Pelican also happened to be a subsidiary of
Manhattan Industries, so, as was the case with the men's wear
and, later, the scarves (licensed to Vera), both he and Manhattan would have a percentage of the sales, Manhattan making it
off its own subsidiary. Such was the tangled financial web that
Perry was weaving about himself.

The companies were growing so fast that by now the
headquarters of Perry Ellis Sportswear, Inc., Perry Ellis
Sportswear, Ltd., and Perry Ellis International, all housed in
575 Seventh Avenue, needed to be expanded. The number of
employees had grown from the original five to seventy-five,

and even Perry wasn't sure what they all did, as he told John Duka in *The New York Times*. "Sometimes people come up to me in the showroom and I don't know who they are or what they want." Perry had James Terrell draw up plans for a new reception area and men's wear and public relations offices on the mezzanine floor, moving the design, fabric, and sample studios, as well as the corporate offices, up to the second and third floors, which Manhattan Industries had leased.

The renovation would increase the space by about 30,000 square feet, and Terrell's plans for the project, under Perry's orders, called for the same high-quality material and standards that had so distinguished the showroom. Eventually, it would cost Manhattan Industries about $4.5 million, according to one Perry Ellis Sportswear, Inc., officer. This incredibly high figure is borne out by one of Hambrecht Terrell's assistant architects at the time, who states that the new offices and showrooms cost about $140 per square foot. It was an outrageous figure, however prestigious the company, for any kind of office space, but that was Perry.

All the design elements Terrell had originally created for the showroom were incorporated into the new two-story men's wear showroom, the design rooms, the offices, and even the hallways, passages, and toilet facilities (though the look was updated with a glossy, perfectly finished, soft beige paint in the upstairs reception area).

Richard Banks, who worked with Terrell on the project, says categorically, "The cost escalated simply because of Perry. He was exacting and consumed by every last detail. The drawings were racking to produce because everything had to be letter-perfect, even though the vocabulary [design] had been established with the first state of the showroom by Jim almost single-handedly. But that had to be translated into the very different circumstances of the second half. And because Perry was obsessed with the minutiae, it took forever because every last detail had to be anticipated."

Banks also recalls that even though the large space had

been partially leased for corporate offices, nothing really had been planned in regard to the needs of the executives of the companies who would occupy it and how this might affect the layout of their offices. This is in keeping with Erwin Isman's assessment of Perry's disregard for the more practical side of the business, his you-take-care-of-it attitude, and in and of itself is revealing of Perry's overall attitude by then: he was beginning to expect people to "pick up after him" without hesitation. In other words, he was becoming a "star" in the more unsavory connotations of the word.

It is interesting to note that around this time (though the showroom would not be started until the beginning of the next year), in February and March of 1981, Perry Ellis Sportswear, Inc., was restructured at its upper management level, with Erwin Isman being named president of the company, succeeding Perry, who became chairman, and three vice presidencies being created—Patricia Pastor in design, Steve Braverman in finance, and Judy Beste in merchandising. The more defined delineation of responsibilities and the six-fold increase in staff in two years should have released Perry from the more mundane matters of the business, enabling him to concentrate exclusively on the design of his collections, but this new Perry, even though demanding of others, was, conversely, passionately interested in everything and anything that had to do with the image side of the company.

Just as he would spend hours in fittings to make sure that every last detail of a garment was perfect, so too did he feel that even the smallest detail affecting "the Perry Ellis look" was of vital importance and would follow it up personally.

Amanda Manogue, who now heads public relations for Perry Ellis, told a wonderfully illustrative story to Patricia Morrisroe for the latter's article on Perry in *New York* magazine that appeared just after the designer's death. Apparently, Perry had wanted a special stamp for the invitations to one spring fashion show and finally settled on an orchid stamp that was being issued at the time. "Unfortunately, it was sold out,"

Manogue told Morrisroe. "Perry made me call every post office in the city. Finally we located the stamps in Red Bank, New Jersey, and we sent somebody out there to buy seven hundred and fifty of them. We had to get twice as many as we needed because Perry only liked two out of the four orchids in every packet."

Excessive, maybe, but it was by demanding perfection that Perry created the image for his clothes and company that he wanted. His obsession with making everything "just right" was an integral part of what made him such an important designer. And with his growing superstardom, the pressure on him became greater and greater. As a result, everyone in the company was made to share it.

"Even if you felt you had done the best you could, if it wasn't the best as far as he was concerned, he wouldn't accept it and you'd have to go back and do it again," says Beste. "Of course, that led to a lot of frustration."

It must have been the most frustrating for his design staff. There were numerous occasions when Perry threw out the whole collection days before the show because he wasn't satisfied with it. (Patricia and Jed used to call him Lizzie Borden because of all the last-minute changes he would make.) The extremes to which he could take his perfectionism were illustrated by an anecdote Morrisroe reported in her *New York* magazine article. "For one spring collection, Perry asked designer Patricia Underwood to create a hat with a 'very flat' brim. She made thirty of them; Ellis didn't like twenty-nine of them because they weren't quite 'flat enough.' Says Underwood, 'For Perry, the microscopic adjustment made all the difference.'"

While undoubtedly his prerogative as the designer and head of the house that bore his name, Perry's quest for perfection could and did drive his staff to tears on occasions. "He made everyone crazy with his changes before the show," says one designer who worked for him for a few years. "And although there would be a lot of screaming and shouting before the show, we did it because we knew he was right. It wasn't because he was being an obnoxious person, though at times it seemed like it. I don't believe he did anything on a whim, it was simply that he no longer liked what he saw in his designs. He'd say, 'I don't approve of that anymore,' and he'd have it changed to make it better."

If Perry's continual changes to the collections were difficult for the design staff, they were equally difficult for the people who ran the business side of his companies, and eventually would have extremely adverse affects on the profitability of Perry Ellis Sportswear, Inc.

"Sometimes it would drive me nuts," says Erwin Isman. "There were times when we would change the garments after we'd shown them to the buyers and the press. I would ask Perry why. 'I didn't like the way it looked,' he'd say without hesitation.

"'But that's what they bought!' I'd reply.

"'Deliver it, they'll never know,' he'd retort. Then he'd add, 'It will be better.'

"And, you know, it was."

Still, this inevitably meant that the samples would be late, which meant that deliveries would be late, which was ample cause for a store to return goods. So Isman would go back to Perry, who'd say, "Okay, no more changes." But then Perry would come in the next morning and want the collection changed yet again.

"You said no more changes," Isman would say, rushing into Perry's office at word of the latest delay.

Perry's reply would be, "But I *needed* this!"

"This happened all the time," says Isman, "and sometimes it wasn't commercially better. Certainly, it was never cheaper. After we had sold a garment at X dollars, it now cost me X dollars to make, so we would take an immediate loss on it."

Isman insists this was the rule, not the exception. "Just when the collection looked as though it was finalized, he would put his little twist into it. He would give it something special—sometimes it was humorous, sometimes beautiful, sometimes just a personal whim—but always something."

Part of the problem was that even though Perry was, and considered himself, a superstar, he never completely overcame his quiet-boy-from-Portsmouth insecurity. He was never content with the collection as it stood—or as it was recorded by the media on the runway. And despite all the acclaim he was ultimately given, in the final analysis it wasn't enough to appease the demons that ruled his psyche. He *had* to make his design statement as perfect as he could in *his* own mind. The result was constant alterations.

"In the early years that happened more than later on," says Judy Beste. "I'm not sure exactly why. Very often there were fittings—there were always ongoing fittings—and the clothes would look different then they had on the runway, or even in the showroom. His mind was continually jumping back and forth; it was difficult for him to just finish the collection and let it go. He would be still working on the old collection as his mind moved forward to the next."

In addition to Patricia Pastor and Jed Krascella, Perry's design staff would grow to include as many as eleven assistants over the next couple of years, especially when Perry Ellis International picked up licensees in home furnishings as well as the fashion categories for both the United States and Japan. The larger staff allowed Perry to concentrate on the conceptualization of the collections. As has already been mentioned, he was not a designer in the purest sense of the word, but his ideas and imagination were the basis for each design, which were then filled out and realized in sketch form by his design staff. These would be approved by Perry before they went to the next stage, the making of the toiles, or patterns, which would, in turn, be made up into original samples. Naturally, Perry would oversee every stage of this operation, but his most intensive contribution to the whole design process would come in the fittings. (Unlike many designers, however, Perry was candid and honest enough to recognize the importance of his designers in the evolution and realization of his collections. Patricia, Jed, and, later, Brian Bubb [the men's wear designer] would be brought out on stage by him after the shows in acknowledgment of their contribution.)

Perhaps Perry's greatest talent was his "eye," and though not technically proficient in many areas of design, he had an unerring sense of when something looked "right," as well as for proportion and color (though he would often take risks with these, which sometimes made his designs look heavy-handed). "There were constant fittings, especially when we were building up to a show," says Carol Lawler, who worked at 575 Seventh for a year and now designs the Greif Companies men's Portfolio line. "And though I was working in the merchandising area of the business as product manager of women's wear, Perry would get everyone involved in the fittings. We would be looking at a garment on a model and Perry would pick up on something that nobody else had noticed. Sometimes it would be a very minor change, but when Perry had indicated how he wanted it, it would be that that made it perfect."

It's fair to say that Perry designed more on instinct than anything else, a supposition that is supported by Judy Beste's comments on the inspiration for most of his clothes: fabric.

"He would shop the fabric market very quickly, because he knew immediately what he liked and what he didn't like. And this was very important to him, since his inspiration came from the fabrics themselves. He didn't work from a silhouette first, it was the reverse; the fabric stimulated him. Many things influenced him, but the beginning for a collection was always the fabrics and the color involved in the fabrics. The silhouette would be developed later."

As Carol Lawler puts it, "Nothing was really designed until the fabric came in. I'm sure there were some ideas in advance, but, especially in the women's wear, with say, the plaids, the size of the plaid would determine such things as where the pleats went, which in turn would determine the actual silhouette of the garment. That's backwards from the way everybody else works, but it was wonderful because the fabric became such an intrinsic part of the garment. It meant that the garment was conceived as a whole."

And in *The New York Times Magazine* piece by John Duka at the beginning of 1982, Perry probably explained the process of his design most succinctly:

> I start with the fabric; it is the inspiration. We select it four months before our show at places like the Interstoff Show in Frankfurt. Then we experiment with it when it arrives.
>
> It's a team effort. . . . We work off a backbone of ideas and designs that we have been kicking around. Then two months before our show, after I've digested the previous collection and I know what's selling, we sit and talk. We discuss what was successful the season before, we philosophize, we joke. It's an emotional process. We ask ourselves what we *feel* is interesting. Then we all sketch; we play with proportions. Out of that come four or five shapes, and then we narrow it down to two.

Another reminiscence of Judy Beste's provides a fascinating glimpse of just how collections could be inspired in Perry's mind by the right kind of fabric: "Perry was never known for his prints. In fact, print houses were always calling me and I would tell them that Perry doesn't do prints. It was just sort of a standard thing. And then one spring season he did a collection that included some Liberty prints and that was the beginning.

"We were shopping for the fall season immediately after that, and we were in Etro's [one of the best fabric designers in Milan]. We had been through all the beautiful plaids that Etro does so well and suddenly Perry came across this duck print. It was so un-Perry it was not to be believed. And I was sitting there writing the sample books and he started to throw on my lap one duck print after another, then quail prints, and then more ducks. In a few minutes, they were piled on my lap almost to my chin and I decided that he had finally lost his mind. I wasn't the only one, because Jed and Patricia were sitting there with their eyebrows raised and huge big eyes—they couldn't believe what he was doing. It turned out to be, when he finally pulled it together, in my opinion the best collection he ever did for fall.

"That's why I say fabric gave him inspiration. He saw something in that print that none of us saw, and then to combine the prints the way he did—the blues, the reds, the greens—that was what made him so special. Even Etro, who came in and saw the collection, was overwhelmed. He told us he thought it was the best creative use of his fabric he could have ever dreamt of. In fact, he agreed to pay for an advertisement in French *Vogue* of that particular silhouette because he was so proud of the way Perry had used his fabric."

Beste maintains that Perry actually relished the angst he caused. "The more of those duck fabrics he kept picking, the more we kept saying, 'Perry, stop!' But he just went his own way. He did it on purpose . . . especially to the design staff. Perry *enjoyed* rubbing them, because when they got angry he knew he had got to them—*then* he'd get the biggest grin on his face. *Then* he was stimulated."

Perry must have realized he was the most acclaimed designer in America by that time, and even in the snobbish European fashion community he was regarded as the most creative designer on the North American continent (though Norma Kamali was and still is very respected by the Europeans as one of the pathfinders of American fashion). Perhaps more importantly, considering the way he worked, he was tremendously respected by the fabric mills and top fabric designers, with the result that he was able to commission or obtain fabrics that no other designer in the country could get. In the last years of his life, as his designs became more sophisticated and therefore less revolutionary, the importance of this access manifested itself as his fabrics and yarns became integrally identified with his signature. "They wanted to work with someone they felt was very creative," says Judy Beste, "because they consider themselves very creative, and Perry was offering them the chance to show their fabrics as no other American designer was at that time." Perry probably spent more time (and more money) at the major European fabric fairs, Interstoff in Frankfurt and Idea Como and Idea Biella in Italy, than any other designer from the States, with the result that he personally got to know all the most important fabric people there.

The importance of these trips in Perry's mind is illustrated by a situation that arose one year when the dates of the New York designer collections were moved back to the beginning of May and November, with the result that Perry couldn't visit Interstoff. He went to Ruth Finlay, who runs *The Fashion Calendar,* a bimonthly newsletter that really controls the scheduling of the collections, as Finlay collates all the dates. With Ruth's help, Perry got together with some of the other Seventh Avenue designers and tried to change the dates of the New York collections, but ultimately wasn't able to get the cooperation of everyone he needed.

The idea of a single designer trying to change the whole New York fashion schedule to suit his own is actually quite preposterous. Although, according to Ruth Finlay, Perry was as quietly polite as ever about the whole thing, he was obviously determined to get his way. As Judy Beste puts it, "Perry would never take no for an answer." But in this case even his legendary stubbornness wasn't enough.

The incident also provides an insight into how Perry perceived himself by this time. That he had the effrontery, albeit for his own good reasons, to try to change a whole season's schedule for his own ends suggests that he had become a student of his own press clippings.

He was also becoming quite vain. Judy Beste tells a funny story that illustrates this. "When we first started working together I was about four years younger than Perry, but he would never admit to it and every year I would say, 'Happy Birthday, Perry, that makes you a year younger!' And he would laugh because at some point I turned forty before he did and that was the last birthday he acknowledged."

While just a personal quirk, it indicates that his public denials of his star status were more of a calculated stance than anything else. There was even a time when Perry's wish for a low profile actually backfired on him. He had been asked by Neiman Marcus president Phillip Miller to make a personal appearance, and for once he had agreed, since Miller was one of his best friends in the business. Still, Perry insisted on one condition. He called the Neiman Marcus president and said, "I don't want limousines or things like that taking me around." So Miller rented a recreational vehicle and picked him up at the Dallas/Fort Worth airport in a camper.

Perry's reaction was not available for the record.

However, Phil Miller *had* also laid on a helicopter to fly Perry and his entourage to the Johnson Space Center. "I'm planning to get him back for that!" Perry joked about the helicopter ride. "I told him I didn't want limousines, and I guess I got more than I bargained for."

That evening, Perry gave a formal showing of his spring 1983 collections to five hundred guests at Neiman Marcus's new Town and Country store. An innovation that Houston had certainly never seen, though Perry had used it at the Coty Awards ceremony before, was to dispense with the scrim and allow the audience to see the models changing (the models were wearing body suits). "There's so much chaos behind the scenes at a show, I thought it would be interesting to let people see it," was Perry's deadpan answer to whether he felt he had shocked the Houston elite.

Perry was also made an honorary admiral in the Texas navy by Richard Marcus at a dinner after the show. The evening was presented as a salute to the Houston Grand Opera and organized by Domaine Chandon, of Moet-Chandon wine fame, who had been working with Perry on several promotional projects.

Certainly, Perry's clothes and presentation left Houston somewhat stunned, but Perry was also stunned by Texan hospitality. (At one point he was even taken to Gilley's, the county-western bar made famous by the movie *Urban Cowboy,* but he declined to ride the mechanical bull with a firm, "No, thank you!") It was more like a royal tour than anything else, especially with the entire Ellis group, from Laughlin to Ed Jones to David Rosensweig, in attendance, but it was the sort of star treatment that Perry was growing used to wherever he made appearances across the nation.

Isman maintains that Perry was "very cool" about this aspect of his life. "To some extent he might have been embarrassed by it, but to a greater extent he loved it.

"I remember we went to one of the Coty Awards shows, and when we got out of the car the crowd started to scream and yell. He went through the barrage of students, press, cameras, and lights signing autographs, and he obviously enjoyed it. His face was beaming."

Ed Jones adds, "Perry did it in a very careful and subtle way, but he did enjoy it." Jones goes on to say, "He enjoyed being with stars. He enjoyed going out at night with people like Meryl Streep and Sigourney Weaver as his escorts, but it was more than just the fact they were celebrities; he liked them as people."

While it is true that Perry liked certain aspects of his celebrity and fame, he was also careful as to what functions he would or would not attend and only attended those that would enhance his career. The fact was, Perry was uneasy in the public gaze. Jim Terrell remembers that when they were out at restaurants and people would come up to Perry, he would quietly say, "Oh God, I can't stand this." Like many stars, Perry was a private person who didn't want the public to get too close. He was more at ease with the image of his popularity than the stark reality of what it meant in terms of his privacy.

When he wanted to get away from the pressures and trappings of stardom, Perry had his home on Water Island, which by then had become an enclave of two houses, one on the bay and a larger one on the beach, though both were simple frame structures and were never likely to be featured in the lifestyle pages of *Vogue* or *"W."* Still, Perry used his houses on Water Island like a summer White House; almost all his business during June, July and August was conducted from there and he was rarely seen in the sweltering heat of the city at 575 Seventh.

Perry would entertain quite lavishly when he was on the island. Richard Banks remembers being present at a dinner party held in the bigger house on the ocean. "There were about eight people there, most of whom were staying for the weekend. It was really the inner circle. Patricia was there, I don't think McDonald was, Lynn wasn't [Lynn Kolhman, one of Perry's good friends and a tenant of his at Sixty-ninth Street. One of the best models in the world, she was often photographed for his print ads at that time. She then turned her hand, very successfully, to photography and actually photographed some of his campaigns], but it was the usual entourage. Jim Terrell had brought me and it was the first time I had met Perry.

"He was very relaxed when he was there, unlike his public persona, and actually talked to me about his breakup with Beau and the anxiety it had caused him. It was a very intimate and unexpected conversation, especially as I had only met him that night."

In the summer of 1982 he even went so far as to buy his own Cessna 206 seaplane. Since a new Cessna costs about $160,000, it was quite a heavy purchase for him to make, in spite of the fact that his contract with Manhattan had come up for renewal and he had been given a very substantial raise, as well as more perks (one of which was a new Jaguar).

Perry Ellis as everyone remembers him. The charming, handsome world-famous designer in January 1982, when he received the Council of Fashion Designers of America Award as Outstanding Designer of the Year for 1981. *Tom Gates/Pictorial Parade*

FROM SCHOOLBOY
TO STAR

Perry at age 17.

Perry, voted "best dressed"
in his graduating class at
Woodrow Wilson High
School, Portsmouth,
Virginia, 1957.

Woodrow Wilson's Pan
American League. Perry is
third from the left in the
third row.

Perry and models relaxing just
before the breakthrough "Slouch"
collection for Portfolio in 1977. (At
the far left is Lynn Kolhman, one of
his favorite models and best
friends.) *Sal Traina/WWD,
Fairchild Publications*

Beau, Perry's lover of four years,
modeling the fall '79 collection in
the irreverent "skipping" style of
Perry's first shows. *Nick
Machalaba/DNR, Fairchild
Publications*

Perry in Tokyo with the executives of Yagi Tsusho Kaisha in 1979 to launch his Japanese collection. (To his left is Judy Beste, his vice president of merchandising.)

THE PUBLIC AND THE PRIVATE PERRY

Perry with Jed Krascella and Patricia Pastor, his two principal designers, in Tokyo. *Courtesy of Judy Beste*

Perry with a kimonoed Beau at the Japanese launch.

One of the many hand-written notes Perry sent to friends and colleagues expressing his appreciation and thanks. This one, written on his publicity photograph, is to Herr, his pet name for Judy Beste, and his favorite "pin figure" accompanies his signature. *Courtesy of Judy Beste*

A page from Jean-Charles Brosseau's guest book. *Courtesy of Jean-Charles Brosseau*

PERRY AT HOME

Perry in the dining room of his first town house at 57 West 69th Street, New York. Dressed in his personal uniform of a cotton oxford shirt, chinos, and topsiders, he is sitting at the specially commissioned table that he asked to have cut down after it had been painstakingly constructed, whether as a joke or part of his constant quest for perfection even his best friend James Terrell, the designer, doesn't know. *Courtesy of Barbara Walz*

Perry at his Water Island retreat, getting away from the constant pressure of Seventh Avenue. Two of his favorite pastimes were contemplatively watching the ocean and playing with his Brittany spaniel, Lily. *Courtesy of Barbara Walz*

The Perry Ellis showroom at 575 Seventh Avenue,
designed by James Terrell, which when finally
completed would cost Manhattan Industries in the
region of $6 million. *Courtesy of Hambrecht,
Terrell International*

Perry and Laughlin in the showroom in October 1982,
four months after Perry made Laughlin president of
Perry Ellis International, Inc. These were the happy
days (before Laughlin's health started to deteriorate),
and they felt they could conquer the fashion world.
Thomas Iannaccone/WWD, Fairchild Publications

Perry with Joan Mondale, the wife of the Vice President of the United States, at a Washington, D.C. luncheon held in his honor in June 1980. Despite the formal occasion, Perry is wearing his signature chinos, with no belt or jacket. *Guy Delort/WWD, Fairchild Publications*

THE TRAPPINGS OF STARDOM AND THE WORK BEHIND IT

In December, 1983 Perry escorts Mariel Hemingway to the opening of the Metropolitan Museum of Art's costume exhibit in honor of Yves Saint Laurent. *Tannenbaum/Sygma*

Perry's great talent was his sense of proportion. Here he is making final adjustments to an outfit from the Spring '83 collection. Jed Krascella, on the right, is assisting him. *Dustin Pittman/ WWD, Fairchild Publications*

Five seventy-five Seventh was run like a couture operation with many very talented people behind the scenes to provide the technical craftsmanship that Perry lacked. Here he is working on a toile. *Courtesy of Barbra Walz*

THE PERRY ELLIS
LOOK

Perry's first really sophisticated tailored
clothing collection, in the fall of 1982,
"For the Ladies who Lunch at La
Grenouille." The look cost Manhattan
Industries $9 million. *Thomas
Iannaccone/WWD, Fairchild Publications*

Perry's spring '85 "California" collection presented just before his daughter, Tyler, was born. Perry's designs in 1984 marked the peak of his career. (This collection is the author's favorite of all the Perry Ellis collections over ten years.) *George Chinsee/WWD, Fairchild Publications*

The quintessential Perry Ellis look—long and lean, with broad stripes—for the spring 1982 "Chariots of Fire" collection. *Dustin Pittman/WWD, Fairchild Publications*

**APPLAUSE
AND ACCOLADES**

Perry acknowledging the applause at the end of the fall '84 "Sonia Delauney" collection, which was viciously panned by *Women's Wear,* claiming that the collection was not well received. (To Perry's right is the final bridal gown from the collection.) *Rick Guidotti for DNR, Fairchild Publications*

Laughlin Barker at the launch of his greatest licensing coup for Perry, the Perry Ellis America/Levi Strauss collection, in September 1984. Already Laughlin is emaciated from AIDS, which would kill him just over a year later. *Roger Eller/DNR, Fairchild Publications*

Perry receiving the key to the city of Chicago from Mayor Harold Washington in March 1985 at the time of the international launch of his fragrance by Marshall Field's. On the extreme left is Robert McDonald, one of Perry's former lovers, who now runs the business and is one of Perry's heirs. Laughlin was in Chicago, but too ill to attend. *Bruce Paulson/WWD, Fairchild Publications*

The end is obviously near; Perry is only a shadow of his former self, his body devastated by AIDS. This photograph was taken at the Council of Fashion Designer's of America awards dinner in January 1986 two weeks after Laughlin's death. It would be Perry's third to last public appearance before his death on May 30 of the same year. *Ron Galella/Paparazzi*

With his salary, earnings from his licensees through Perry Ellis International, and a substantial legacy from his father, Perry was now a wealthy man. Winifred, his mother, however, would still be concerned about him, and send food parcels as well as gifts of money, despite the fact that he had given her his old Jaguar when he got a new one!

Undoubtedly, the seaplane was written off, since he used it to ferry his staff back and forth from the city for meetings in the summer, especially when he started to spend more time out there as Laughlin became sick. He also used it to transport the few favored members of the fashion press who were routinely invited out for weekends or interviews. (Carrie Donovan, a senior editor of *The New York Times Magazine,* would spend at least a couple of weeks at the house as his guest every summer.) These trips were a deductible expense as well, and, according to Bruce Dunham, who owns North American Flying Service, the outfit that operated the plane for him, Perry also leased the plane out on an hourly basis. Once the practice caused a rather embarrassing situation for one of his guests, Pamela Altman, then fashion features editor of *DNR,* who was spending the weekend with her brother.

"We had spent a wonderful day," she recalls, "laughing and laughing and laughing. At one point in the afternoon, my brother took Kate, Laughlin's daughter, out in the small sailboat, and Kate lost something overboard. I can't remember what it was, but it was practically floating away to China and my brother dove off the boat and swam out to rescue it. Needless to say they were late returning to the dock, by which time the seaplane had already arrived. However, Perry insisted that my brother go up to the house and take a shower and have a cup of coffee before we returned to the city, and we arrived at the dock about half an hour later.

"Perry and Laughlin walked down with us, and we found this woman sitting in the plane with a brand new baby. She was furious. As I got in I said, 'Oh, I'm sorry, I didn't know anyone was waiting,' trying to be polite. And she, who didn't know Perry Ellis from Perry Mason—at least to look at—replied, 'You're certainly very cavalier with my time.'

"Perry, in that quiet but very firm voice of his, replied, 'Madam, I own this plane.'

"That plane ride was the worst twenty-five minutes of our lives. . . . We sat there in absolute silence all the way back to New York . . . and we were still blushing half an hour later when we got back to my apartment!"

There is little doubt that Perry used his Water Island refuge to escape the pressures of his business, which had grown enormously complex, as is illustrated by the operation needed to manufacture the collections. "Initially, we made everything domestically," says Erwin Isman. "Then I took us into Hong Kong, essentially in the beginning for wool garments, because the way the duty laws worked wool *fabric* being brought into the country had a much higher duty levied on it than wool *garments* brought into the country. We figured out a way of using the lower-priced, highly skilled labor in Hong Kong to make the product to our standards, and the difference in duty more than paid for the extra cost of freight. It also broadened our production base. At one point all our skirts were made in Hong Kong. We manufactured quite a few garments offshore.

"Most of the fabrics and yarns would come from Europe. We also sourced [purchased] about ninety percent of our shirting fabrics from Japan—the silks came from Italy—and it was very easy for us to transport the fabric from Japan to Hong Kong and manufacture there." Although production was concentrated in the U.S. and Hong Kong, part of the collection was manufactured in Italy and some of the outerwear was made in Taiwan.

To design and sell fashion is far from a simple business; it literally requires a global operation when one is talking about the big designers with their sales in the tens of millions, and involves everything from arranging for the fabric to be delivered to the factories on time, to ensuring that the patterns are made correctly and then shipped back to the States, where the cost of customs and excise duties, freight, fabric, and fabrication all have to be taken into account in the final selling price of the goods. Then there are the deals that have to be made with the stores. A sale is never just a simple sale, and very often the fashion house has to make concessions on the advertising stores do, quite apart from the national advertising campaigns they might be doing themselves, as well as provide special prices for certain delivery and rejection clauses in the contracts in favor of the stores. As chairman of Perry Ellis Sportswear, Perry had to be cognizant of all of this.

"Sometimes Perry could be very sophisticated about the business, but sometimes he would be very naive and unaware," says Isman. "At one point he wanted to set up a quality control in the warehouse after all the goods had been brought in from all the factories. We did have a quality inspection in the warehouse but we did it statistically, and as the company grew bigger the statistical approach was absolutely necessary. Perry wanted everything inspected by hand, even though you simply couldn't physically inspect all the garments that came in.

"He insisted that he wanted every single garment looked at—it would have required an army of people. And I kept trying to tell him the place to catch these things was in the factory. We had inspectors going to every factory, we had in-process quality control, we had counter samples coming to be checked, we had offices overseas supervising the quality of goods made over there, and Perry refused to understand this."

Isman insists that Perry, although concerned with all sorts of practical problems, had no head for business. "I remember one occasion when he had been listening to friends who were telling him that his prices were beginning to get too high. So, Perry came into see me and said, 'Our prices are getting too high.'

"I said, 'Perry if you stop buying twenty-dollar-a-yard fabric I'll be able to keep the prices down, but if you insist on buying expensive fabric I have to price accordingly.'

"I think Patricia and Jed were in the room when that happened and they started to snicker, and Perry, slightly cross, said, 'I want the prices down.'

"'Perry,' I replied, 'these things are not unrelated.'

"'Well work on it,' he said, and left the room."

Similarly, for fittings he began to use his favorite model, Lise Ryall, who, at five-nine and very svelt, is not the size of the average American woman. And for the men's clothes he started to use Matt Norkland, who's about six-three and has a very slim waist. Not only was it extremely expensive for the company—star models like Ryall and Norklund earn about $2,500 a day—but soon problems with the fit of the clothes began to crop up. Isman recalls one occasion when they were getting a lot of complaints from stores about the fit of a pair pants for that particular season.

"It was a big selling item that season and it was not fitting well, so Perry called in Stephanie Robbins, our fitting model. Stephanie is probably the best fitting model in the industry. We put the pants on Stephanie [who is a *perfect* size eight] and they fit like a glove. I mean they were tight, but on Stephanie they looked great. Perry looked at them on her, turned back to the salesgirls, and said, 'They're all cows out there!'"

It seems a rather high-handed attitude for a designer to have when the fit of his clothes on the customer *should* be one of his primary aims. And, in fact, one of the most telling criticisms of Perry's fashion over the years was that it did not take into account the more normal proportions of the average woman. His clothes looked wonderful on the lean models who wore them on the runway, but for anyone with a more curvaceous figure, they could look dreadful—this despite the fact that Perry had gone on record saying he designed in the abstract, with no particular woman in mind. This seems doubtful—one has only to look at pictures of Lise Ryall to see what his ideal of a womanly figure was. In the rather scathing words of one major fashion editor, "Just like Giorgio [Armani], he designs for boys . . . not women who have breasts and hips."

Perry's sympathy for his customers, or lack thereof, was

not the only suspect side of his character that he began to reveal as his celebrity grew. Although he had been quoted in *Commonwealth* magazine in 1982 as saying about the South, "I was estranged for many years. That was during the Birminghams. I was highly embarrassed. I wouldn't tell people I was from the South. The whole racial situation—I just didn't feel good about it. I had to free myself," he may well have had racial prejudices himself.

One fashion editor from a major New York publication was doing a show in Florida and using local models. It soon came to the attention of a member of the Ellis staff that one of the models was black. The editor was taken aside and tactfully asked to take the black model out of the Perry Ellis section of the show. "It's not Perry Ellis's image, and Perry really doesn't want black people wearing his clothes," that person was told.

It is difficult to assess whether this was simply an aesthetic consideration or whether Perry was actually prejudiced in a way that he probably couldn't even admit to himself. The former would seem to be more in keeping with the generosity and kindness that made him such a marvelous person to know.

On the other hand, one of *the* most appealing things about Perry were his "old world" manners. Perry still adhered to that Jane Austen-like politesse of writing notes, no matter how busy he was, and he would take great pains over every word he wrote. Whether a "thank you" or "hello" or even a "wish you were here and I'm thinking about you," it was Perry's manners that distinguished him as one of the true gentlemen in his profession. As with his generosity, it was done without guile, although it did make him terribly endearing. It affected everyone who was on the receiving end, but he didn't just limit it to people he needed. Perry wrote from the bottom of his heart and because *he* felt he needed to.

What's especially fascinating is the fact that in his notes and letters he could be so personal, so giving, so unlike the individual who was so afraid of people getting too close to him. It's almost as if Perry felt himself to be inadequate, and therefore felt most comfortable when he was giving, not receiving. It was that that made him most secure.

Judging by many of his actions at this time, it's almost as though Perry was beginning to believe the image of himself that appeared in the magazines, rather than the reality of the fashion industry itself—which, after all, is a business. Not surprisingly, his obsession with image was, as has been noted, causing great concern at Manhattan Industries, where executives watched anxiously as their star designer, season after season, continued to spend a small fortune on fabrics, publicity, and the look of the showroom.

There have been many rumors about Perry's excesses, none more tossed about than the one concerning the flowers in the showroom. Though figures of an annual budget in excess of $50,000 have been bandied around, Ed Jones categorically denies it: "That's such a bunch of bull!"

"There was a time early on, when there was just the one showroom, when the flowers were probably done through a florist and it probably was an expense, but not a *big* expense at all. But as soon as we got to be big, and as soon as Manhattan started to clamp down on expenses, the way that was handled was very simple. Manhattan Industries gave us a budget, because Perry asked, 'If you have a problem with the amount we spend on flowers, give me a budget and that's what I'll live within.'

"So they gave us a budget, and Perry authorized it to Peggy Lee [Perry's long-suffering and faithful personal assistant], who went down to the corner every two or three days to purchase them herself, and she and a couple of the assistants personally did the arrangements for the showrooms, Perry's office, Laughlin's office, and my office. End of story."

Even so, it was during that year that Perry spent, according to Isman and other employees of the company at the time, in excess of $800,000 on sample fabrics alone. With the cost of the new showrooms that would be started at the end of the year, quite apart from the high operating costs incurred by the company, one can see that Manhattan had a right to be worried.

"I controlled him to the best degree he could be controlled at the time," says Isman. "The showroom was finished after I left and I'm not sure I could have kept it down below that six million total figure if I'd stayed, but I would have tried."

Isman was getting increasingly worried by the spending, as well as by Perry's attitude. "I always liked Perry, but it was getting to the point where he was not going to say, 'I made a mistake.'"

And that year Perry finally made a colossal mistake: the "Dreamgirls" collection flopped disastrously.

"The fall line of 1982 was an absolute disaster and the company was losing money," says Isman. "There was a lot of back and forth and more back and forth, and there *should* have been.

"I was as guilty of it as Perry, and a lot of people were pointing fingers. It became a very uncomfortable environment and the confidence level all around fell, so I elected to leave."

The troubles with this collection had been noted by the press. In fact, *Women's Wear Daily* was so aware of the rumored troubles at Perry Ellis that they decided to investigate. Under the headline NO CHANGE IN FALL LINE in their May 11 edition, Isman denied what *WWD* quoted as "persistent market reports that the line had been pulled back for revisions and had undergone substantial changes since it was formally shown to retailers and press last month." Isman was quoted as saying, "We haven't changed the line and we haven't pulled it back. That's ludicrous."

Although substantially true, the denials from Perry Ellis Sportswear, Inc., executives were not exactly as candid as they might have been. One retailer told *WWD* that "the line shown to buyers in the showroom had undergone 'considerable' change since its formal showing," and she further noted that some of the "La Grenouille" peplum suits had been eliminated. In fact, the main thrust of the collection had been a Scottish Highland theme, with some of the most beautifully treated tartans that had ever been translated into high fashion. But these tartans over tartans over tartans, very much in the Ellis style, were not enough to save the collection. The stores simply didn't like it, despite the great press reviews.

More importantly, there had been real growing pains at the Perry Ellis companies; not only on the new men's side, but also with the supposedly hugely successful women's company as well. "When it started to take off we had to spend a whole year repositioning and marketing the company to a new level," says Isman about the period between 1978 and 1981. And, according to the one-time Perry Ellis president, this growth was barely planned for. "It was more like trying to create a company that was as good as the talent that was coming out of the design room," he admits. "As we saw the product coming out, we began to recognize what was happening. There was some talk, but the planning was mostly in Perry's imagination."

Whether it was Perry's or Manhattan's fault, Perry Ellis Sportswear, Inc., was overextended by 1982 and in deep trouble. Not only was the showroom expansion going to cost Manhattan about $4.5 million, but in the year preceding Perry had spent nearly a million dollars in sample fabrics alone, and the failure of the fall collection would cost the company an additional $6 to $7 million.

Despite these tremendous financial problems, Perry had grown into his stardom. He continued to court the press and put on such a confident public face that even with the reports in the trade papers, and despite the individual knowledge of various retailers, very few people, even within the business, knew how close Perry Ellis Sportswear, Inc., had come to bankruptcy.

9

I touch your hand
and my arms grow strong,
like a pair of birds
that burst with song.
My eyes look down
on your lovely face,
and I hold the world
in my embrace.
Younger than springtime are you,
Softer than starlight are you.
Warmer than winds of June
Are the gentle lips you gave me.
Gayer than laughter are you.
Angel and lover,
heaven on earth are you to me.

—Richard Rogers & Oscar Hammerstein II
"Younger than Springtime" from *South Pacific*

"When he came on the scene is when it all came together for Perry; there's no question about it," is Ed Jones's appraisal of the importance of Laughlin Barker in Perry's private and professional life.

Without a doubt it was Laughlin's love, friendship, advice, and business acumen that propelled Perry from his position as one of America's foremost sportswear designers into the elite ranks of world-class designers. Barker was the catalyst, expanding Perry's vision and giving him the confidence to create a design statement that transcended national taste and made him one of those few designers whose influence is international.

With Barker masterminding Perry Ellis International, Perry's own company created to license his name and designs, in three and a half short years he was able to parlay the Perry Ellis name into a three-quarters-of-a-billion-dollar empire. In June 1982, when he joined as president of the company, Perry Ellis International had sixteen licensees earning it about $60 million annually wholesale.* At his death in January 1986, the company had twenty-three licensees and its revenue had been multiplied almost fivefold. (In the fashion industry retail prices are normally calculated at between twice to two-and-a-half times the wholesale cost.) It was a remarkable achievement by any business standard, yet this fiscal expansion was only a part of his worth to Perry's business.

Until 1981, Perry Ellis had been known primarily as one of America's most talented sportswear designers. But by the time Laughlin came on board, Perry was anxious to expand his design horizons. Social and political attitudes in America had retreated somewhat from the anything-goes liberalism of the late sixties and early seventies toward a "new" conservatism: among other things, style and high fashion were in again. Like all great designers, Perry was sensitive to the socio-political trends of the world around him and was beginning to feel the necessity of designing more serious and sophisticated tailored suits and evening clothes. The potential market in that direction had most likely been subliminally suggested by Ed Jones's concept calling for the expansion of the men's wear side of Perry Ellis Sportswear into "stratified" lines. With this concept, Perry saw a way to move toward the more serious side of fashion and it was up to Barker to implement it, both in respect to the agreements with Manhattan Industries as well as Ellis's other licensee arrangements.

As a result, by January 1984, Perry Ellis had six different

---

*November 10, 1982, *Women's Wear Daily* interview with Laughlin Barker.

fashion collections in this country alone. Though this expansion was not without real problems, as will be seen later, it was the single most important factor that made Perry Ellis a world-class designer.

Perry and Laughlin Barker probably met in the summer of 1980 on Water Island (even close friends cannot agree on the date), and it was love at first sight. "There was an instant attraction," says one of Laughlin's oldest friends. "For Laughlin everything about Perry would have made him interesting. Not only was he very intelligent and handsome, but he wore his hair long and lived in this exotic world of fashion—something Laughlin knew nothing about—which made him different from everyone he had ever met." For Perry the attraction was just as obvious: Laughlin was everything he had ever admired in a man, the ultimate WASP image. Not only was he incredibly cultivated, with a highly developed appreciation of the arts, he was also extraordinarily handsome, with an athletic body, blond hair, and striking blue eyes. Barker was also the antithesis of effeminacy; he had been married and from that union had a daughter.

Certainly, by September of 1980, Laughlin was enough a part of Perry's entourage to "officially" squire Patricia Pastor to the Coty Awards. Given the high profile these awards had at that point, it was quite a public statement on Perry's part to the effect that there was a new member of his "inner circle" who had also become his lover.

Yet their mutual attraction went far beyond sexual desire. As one of Perry's friends puts it, "Laughlin's great appeal was his mind; his looks weren't the primary factor. Laughlin was exceptionally well educated in the arts, and even at this stage Perry hadn't fully cultivated his own opinions about such things."

This statement reveals not only a great deal about Perry and Laughlin's relationship, but also about Perry's intellectual development to that point in his life. Though his intellect was patently manifest to anyone who met him, it was Laughlin who, in the last six years of their lives, expanded Perry's mind far beyond the formal strictures of his business and retail college degrees at William and Mary and New York University. Given Perry's thirst for knowledge and culture, Laughlin was the ideal partner to open his mind to a more intellectual appreciation of the arts and other cultures. This, in itself, was a major factor in the broadening of Perry's fashion horizons. Their relationship stimulated Perry to design from a broader cultural context, both historically as well as artistically.

Laughlin McClatchy Barker, Jr., was born in 1948, the oldest son of a prominent Santa Fe, New Mexico, family. His father still owns a large commercial and residential real estate company there and sits on the board of one of the city's big banks, and his mother is very active in the arts, an interest that Laughlin was to share. It was a large, happy, Roman Catholic family—Laughlin had four siblings: two sisters, Rosanne and Christine, and two brothers, John and David—that friends describe as "close-knit." Barker went to college at the University of Colorado in Boulder and then joined the Navy for four years, spending much of that time posted in Bologna, Italy, where he took advantage of the resources at one of the oldest universities in the world, and one that has specialized in law since the fourteenth century.

Upon his discharge from the Navy, Laughlin went to Jesuit-run Georgetown University to continue his law studies. It was around this time that he married, and the union produced a daughter, Katherine. After Georgetown, he clerked for a judge in Denver for a year, then moved to New York and joined the law offices of Patterson, Belknap, Webb and Tyler. It was while he was working at Patterson, Belknap that he met Perry, the "official" story being that they met when the designer sought legal advice on some personal matters. It's more likely, however, that they met socially on Water Island and, after they became involved, Perry went to Patterson, Belknap for his legal advice. In any case, their friendship resulted in Perry retaining the firm as corporate counsel to Perry Ellis International (a position they still hold, as well as acting as private counsel for the Perry Ellis Trust).

At the end of 1981, about eighteen months after they had first met, Perry asked Laughlin to leave Patterson, Belknap and take over Perry Ellis International as president and legal counsel. The responsibilities of the job had, up to that point, been handled by Perry himself, who was chairman of International, and members of his staff. In effect, it was a position created specifically for Laughlin by Perry. As one of Barker's friends, a lawyer himself, puts it, "It's not unknown in the legal business [for a lawyer to join a company he is retained by], since it solidifies contact between the law firm and the company. However, Laughlin was wary of making the move. He didn't know whether he should take the position, especially as he was Perry's lover, and he wasn't sure whether he wanted to work in what he called 'that fickle business'—the fashion industry."

"There was really no one in a business capacity that was controlling International," says Judy Beste. "What would happen was that Mort Kaplan [head of creative licensing and Perry's licensing agent] would bring people to Perry, and they would sit down and put the deals together, but from that point on no one was controlling the business. Obviously, Perry saw a definite need for that, as I did, since there were many business questions that the Japanese had to have answers to, and they would come to me and I would go to Perry and he would have to make the decision. No one was really there spearheading the International business."

Perry took Judy and Laughlin to a very expensive restaurant for dinner to discuss the matter. "It was La Grenouille I think. I remember I didn't eat too much because I was too nervous. But the food was excellent and for once Perry was on his best behavior," says Beste.

"Laughlin obviously came with great interest and great trepidation. Perry didn't say a word, except to coach me beforehand by telling me, 'I want Laughlin to run this business and I want you to tell him how much we need him.' I think that hearing the business needed him from someone who was already part of the company, was perhaps something that Laughlin wanted to hear. After that it was a fait accompli."

Whatever his misgivings, Barker went to work for Perry at the end of June 1982 and remained president of the company until his death on January 10, 1986. It was a relationship that never wavered, and, as Perry himself put it in an interview in *Women's Wear Daily* on April 9, 1986, just six weeks before his own death, "Laughlin was an extraordinary man and I loved him. We worked together twenty-four hours a day, and he brought genius and humor to this business. We were together five years, and there was never an argument or disagreement. I felt complete when he was here."

By all accounts it was an extraordinary relationship, and though some would find it offensive by its very nature, no one who came into contact with Perry and Laughlin during these years felt it was anything other than a true love affair and that there was something beautiful about it. As one of their closest girlfriends puts it, "They weren't just lovers, they were also the closest of friends.

"If you were allowed into the privacy of their bedroom it wasn't like any gay bedroom you would expect . . . I mean gay bedrooms always seem to be overdone, like Marie Antoinette or Louis the Thirteenth or something. Their bedroom had Laughlin's college pennants on the walls, there was a cheap stereo on the floor, and records everywhere. It was just like my brother's bedroom in college. They were like college buddies.

"It was only when you really got to know them that you realized how much they loved each other."

This aspect of their relationship was borne out by the fact that despite all the camp in the office and the nicknames that used to fly around, Perry and Laughlin would always address each other as "Barker" and "Ellis." Perry didn't even use the diminutive "Chico" that Laughlin's family called him.

Laughlin's influence on Perry was already becoming noticeable in subtle but profound ways by the middle of 1982. In

February or March of that year he had had himself shorn of his auburn tresses. The famous (or infamous, depending on the way you looked at it) ponytail was gone. Perry had suddenly gone corporate, and though he stated in an interview at the time that it "was attracting too much attention. I can go unnoticed with shortish hair. Long hair pulls you apart in a way, and recently I've been feeling like not being noticed so much," it is more likely that his decision was influenced by the establishment, corporate, WASPY image that Laughlin personified. While he undoubtedly enjoyed being regarded as an "enfant terrible" in public, it was time for him to accept the reality of his age, status, and celebrity. As James Terrell puts it, "One of the problems I had with Perry was how inappropriately he dressed for a while. It isn't like he grew up wearing that same old shirt. When he started [dressing down] it was appropriate, but when he grew so famous it started to border on the grossly tacky."

It should be noted that Perry grew his hair long for much of the same period, about 1977 to 1980, that he was involved with the hedonistic Beau Tropper, and was probably trying to emulate the carefree lifestyle of his youthful lover at that time.

Laughlin, the great love of his life, was more instrumental than anyone, however, in changing Perry. Not only did Perry begin to change certain aspects of his lifestyle, he also began to drop some of his oldest friends, including Jim Terrell, and surrounded himself with Laughlin's friends and family. The "inner circle" began to be composed of people such as Laughlin's sister Christine and his legal friends such as Richard Caples. However, the core of fashion industry friends such as Carrie Donovan, Lynn Kolhman, and Pamela Altman remained, as did the ever-faithful Robert McDonald.

It is also telling that Laughlin's influence over Perry coincided with the death of Perry's father. As fate would have it, just as Perry was losing the predominant male figure in his life, someone he had naturally turned to for love and advice, he developed a growing attraction to this young but steady and brilliant lawyer. It seems a logical assumption that some of the love, trust, and protection Perry had received from his father was soon expected of Laughlin, and it's probably why Laughlin became so much more important in Perry's life than any of his previous lovers had been. Although a strong and opinionated man himself, Perry's shyness and insecurity were always lurking somewhere in the background, and in Laughlin he found a partner and lover who was far from insecure.

Laughlin was much less inhibited than Perry, and it was very much due to him that their relationship became more public than Perry's earlier affairs. One American fashion editor recalls the time she organized a dinner for Perry and Laughlin at the famous La Bricola in Milan when they all happened to be in that Italian city at the same time. During dinner Laughlin took out some snapshots from his wallet, including some of a little girl. The editor asked, "Who's that?"

"My daughter, Kate," Laughlin replied.

Which evoked from the fashion crowd, who knew about Perry and Laughlin's relationship, the response, *"Excuse me!"*

Laughlin replied, "I have a daughter from a former lifestyle!" and the others at the table broke up.

There was definitely a collegiate quality to their relationship, and they were not above pulling pranks when they were supposed to be conducting business. Beste recalls a time when the whole Perry Ellis staff was at Interstoff. "Perry and Laughlin left us graciously at about seven o'clock," says Beste. "We had to continue working while they took someone out to dinner, but they were supposed to return later.

"About ten-thirty there was this noise, the door from the hallway crashed open, then the doors from the balcony were pulled open, and Laughlin jumped in from the balcony as Perry raced in from the hallway. They were both screaming their heads off. There were ten of us in this room, and by then all of us were screaming. Perry and Laughlin thought it was terrifically funny . . . they scared me to death!

"So then we asked if they were going to join us, and they

breezily replied, 'Well, we think it's a little late,' and said good night."

Their schoolboy pranks even reached the offices at 575 Seventh. "They were so mischievous," says Ed Jones. "Perry and Laughlin would be having lunch in the conference room just by Perry's corner office and, totally straight-faced, Perry would call in Peggy Lee and point to the truffles and tell her they were obviously shaved the wrong way. Peggy didn't know. And they would do a whole number for ten minutes right on her case. Perry would say, 'Couldn't you see when these arrived they were shaved wrong?' And then when she'd leave the room, practically in tears, he and Laughlin would break up laughing. Then they might tell her . . . sometimes they would, sometimes they wouldn't.

"They were bad boys, real bad boys!"

(Truffles were one of Perry's passions and he would order hundreds of dollars' worth from Balducci's, the expensive food emporium in Greenwich Village, just to put on the pasta that he'd have with a simple salad, fruit, cheese, and wine for lunch.)

Although Laughlin came from an affluent family, and must have been receiving a generous salary from his employer, Perry was by then a wealthy man and began to spend money on himself and his lover on a grand scale. The Cessna seaplane and the second house on Water Island were just two examples. Perry also enjoyed giving Laughlin expensive gifts, one of which was a beautiful mahogany sailboat, the *Ambiance,* which he gave Laughlin for one of his birthdays and which was moored at the dock at Water Island. And it was also around this time that Perry started to look for a new house in New York. Eventually he found it only a block away from his town house, at 39 West Seventieth Street. It was a five-story (including raised basement) brownstone, built in the latter half of the nineteenth century. Jim Terrell was again commissioned to draw up plans for the renovation, which would eventually take three and a half years and cost an inordinate amount of money before it was completed. By that time it would be too late for either Laughlin or Perry to enjoy it.

The new town house was reported to have cost Perry between a million and a million and a half dollars to buy, and rumors that he had borrowed the money from Manhattan Industries began to circulate—rumors that are denied by Ed Jones. "No way! The story is so misrepresentative. He would never go to Manhattan for anything like that. In fact, I don't know how valid it is, but he always liked for them to think he didn't need their money. Their money, meaning the salary they paid him. The money from the licensing was his, of course."

Since the Perry Ellis International licensees were earning a reported $60 million at wholesale, the company, owned by Perry, was grossing about $4.5 million, given the usual designer percentage of sales of seven and a half percent. Even with Manhattan's 25 percent of the net earnings and International's operating costs, this meant that Perry was taking home about $2.5 million on top of his salary from Manhattan for designing the women's collection. And he continued to pick up licensees. A children's line that had been announced at the end of December 1981 was quickly followed by a line of yarn kits for the spring season.

The home knitting kits were one of Perry's most original marketing ideas. The wool was sold in beautifully packaged clear plastic cylinders, and inside was enough wool or cotton to knit one of the sweaters from his collection. It was a brilliant move to create these kits for the woman who enjoyed knitting and didn't want to spend the $200 or so that a hand-knit Ellis sweater cost by then. The complete collection of home-knit sweaters was introduced in its own shop on the main floor of Bloomingdale's in March of 1982, and took off very well. (Unfortunately, the line was later discontinued.)

Although Laughlin joined Perry Ellis International in June, the two other licensees signed that year had been under negotiation for some time (though he may well have had a hand in closing the deals). In September it was announced that Perry had signed with Martex for a line of home furnishings to be introduced in May of the following year. Eventually, it was one of Perry's more successful licensee lines, and his sheets, pillowcases, and towels truly reflected the look of his collections from year to year. It's an important market for any designer, and Perry's were done better than anyone's (with the exception of Ralph Lauren's, which are much more extensive in scope).

At the beginning of November, Perry signed with one of the biggest men's apparel companies in the country, the Greif Companies, a division of Genesco, Inc., for a line of men's tailored clothing (suits and sportcoats). Rumors about the deal had been rampant since May, when Greif's head, Jimmy Wilson, was present at the "Dreamgirls" collection. Although Manhattan did make sportcoats for the Perry Ellis men's collection, Perry was able to pick up this category of tailored clothing (one of the most stable money-makers in the men's apparel business) because Manhattan was a sportswear company, not a tailored clothing company. While the difference might seem small to the public, there is a great technical division between the two categories within the men's fashion industry. Finally, a shoe line, to be produced by Michael G. Abrams, was also signed up in 1982.

Compared to many designers who have signed their name away for money and often to the detriment of their image (Pierre Cardin and Yves Saint Laurent come to mind), Perry was determined to keep absolute control over any product that came out under his name. Not surprisingly, given his mania for perfection, Perry was far more successful at this than most. For instance, even though the licensees were bound, contractually, to devote a certain percentage of their sales to advertising their Perry Ellis lines (which meant that Perry Ellis International didn't spend a penny on advertising any of its products), Perry was able to keep artistic and placement control over any product that bore his name. "In some cases we were guaranteed a dollar amount, quite separate from sales, which we would control," says Ed Jones. This is unusual in the industry, but Perry was so brilliant in the way he handled his advertising that it was to a licensee's best advantage. (Just how much control he had is illustrated by the fact that the model for his children's wear line was Kate, Laughlin's daughter.)

After June 1982, the person who had to deal with all of this was Laughlin Barker, who told *WWD* in an interview in November 1982: "We signed seven of our sixteen licensing arrangements in 1982. It's time for us to take a look at what we have before we get involved with any others." Barker's legal expertise helped him keep a tight rein on Perry's various collections, making sure they were produced to his employer's exacting standards, and though he may have initiated a retrenchment for the first few months of his tenure as president of Ellis International, he was soon on the lookout for new and more lucrative ways to use the Perry Ellis name.

The various collections were all designed in the main design room at 575 Seventh Avenue, and the team of eleven or so people under the direction of Perry, Patricia, and Jed worked on them simultaneously, including the Japanese collections, which included a number of categories such as umbrellas and handbags not found in the States. It's difficult to ascertain the financial details of the arrangement, but apparently the design staff was under salary to Manhattan Industries, while certain of his top designers—most prominently Patricia Pastor, Jed Krascella, and Brian Bubb—also received bonuses from Perry Ellis International. (Jed Krascella is reported to have said that Perry was very generous and that he never had to ask for a raise.)

In the meantime, fate again played into Perry's hands that year. It is doubtful, however much Larry Leeds needed the Perry Ellis name to add to the prestige of his company, that Manhattan would have absorbed the losses that Perry Ellis Sportswear, Inc., had incurred with the fall collection without the added income it was receiving from its percentage of Perry Ellis International's licensing agreements (which in 1982 would have been about $875,000). And with the additional licensees that International was picking up, Leeds knew the potential for profit was still very much there. He had also just signed Perry to a new two-year contract at considerable expense, and Leeds was not someone who would have risked losing face with his peers in the industry by admitting he had bought the fashion equivalent of an Edsel. Laughlin's appearance on the scene, in retrospect, was more than timely.

Laughlin now found himself in a position to act as a mediator between Perry and Manhattan in a way that no one else could. And the support he gave Perry enabled the designer to negotiate from a stronger stance. Ed Jones's opinion that, "Perry became a lot stronger. Laughlin gave a certain confidence to him," seems accurate. "Perry now had a partner who was there side by side with him, and that gave him strength. It allowed him to become a better designer because it allowed him to become a more assertive person in his point of view."

Although Perry might have been Laughlin's senior in years, was certainly more affluent, and was his employer, in Laughlin Perry had found an equal partner who would stick with him until the end. Perry now had a champion.

The Ellis publicity machine kept on rolling throughout the summer of 1982, and at the beginning of September Perry made a public appearance at Bloomingdale's in New York, where he drew such large crowds following a full-page ad in the previous Sunday's *New York Times* for his men's collection that the store was literally mobbed. (Fortunately, Perry and his staff were dressed in the basic Ellis uniform of blue Oxford-cloth shirt and khakis, so they were recognized.) At the end of the month he again presented his men's collection, this time at Louis, Boston, the city's best specialty shop (where he was photographed very neatly dressed in a jacket, shirt, and bow tie, exactly the same as Laughlin).

Although Perry had continued to maintain a hectic sched-

ule that summer, with the total absorption of Laughlin into
his personal and professional lives he began to want to spend
more and more of his time with his lover. From then on Perry
would concentrate on spending most of his time every summer
at Water Island.

The two beach houses (which Perry called "shacks") were
ideal for the laid-back, private existence Laughlin preferred.
Gone were the house parties of eight or ten people that used
to crowd into the main house and the "guest cottage." Now it
became much more of a private retreat for Perry, Laughlin,
and Laughlin's daughter Kate. Gone were the trips, entourage
in tow, to the weekend "tea dances" at the gay community of
The Pines further west along Fire Island, which were filled
with some of his fellow big-name designers. Unless Perry was
entertaining, he would spend most of his time there puttering
around the house, tending a small garden (of which he said, "I
think the deer get more enjoyment out of it than me"), sketching, or playing on the beach with Laughlin, Kate, and his remaining Brittany spaniel, Lily, who summered there with him
and wintered in Virginia with Perry's mother.

To watch Perry, Laughlin, and Kate together was quite
extraordinary. There was a special camaraderie between the
three that went far beyond any role playing. As Ed Jones, who
would visit with his wife on many occasions, says, "Laughlin
was an incredible, wonderful man. It was a marvelous experience to be there with them. To watch Katie and Perry doing
laps in the water and then running out and throwing themselves on the beach and putting bonnets on their heads, all
three of them splitting their sides—they were obviously so
happy."

Unlike the first couple of years of his celebrity, when
Perry had indulged somewhat in the "star" trip, under Laughlin's influence, he retreated into a shell. Granted, it was different from the cloak of insecurity he had pulled around him
when he was younger. Now he was less worried about people

knowing he was involved with another man, but he was still determined to make sure that that relationship was sacrosanct. With his growing involvement with Laughlin, and their soon-to-be-realized fears about their health, they began to retreat more and more to the sanctuary Perry had created thirty minutes by private plane from Seventh Avenue.

10

I don't really think I need the reasons why I won't succeed,
I have done . . .
And the money kept rolling in from every side,
When the money keeps rolling in you don't ask how.
And the money kept rolling out in all directions . . .
When the money keeps rolling out you don't keep books;
You can tell you've done well by the happy grateful looks.
Accountants only slow things down,
Figures get in the way . . .

—*Tim Rice*
"And the Money Kept Rolling In (And Out)" from *Evita*

By the middle of 1982, around the time Laughlin Barker took control of the business side of Perry Ellis's growing fashion empire, storm clouds were gathering on the horizon of Perry's relationship with his principal backer, Manhattan Industries. For four years Manhattan had poured money into Perry's bottomless pockets, and they were getting tired of waiting for a return. Finally, in 1981, they had realized a profit from his women's collection of about $1.4 million, but by that stage they were investing heavily in the new men's wear line. One can imagine that Larry Leeds and the board of Manhattan were at the very least expecting to break even in 1982 on the two companies, especially with sales of $30 million wholesale—$70 million retail—projected for the women's collections. In addition, they were well aware that Perry was negotiating with at least seven new licensees, which would eventually bring in revenue, and for which they had to do nothing except examine the sales receipts to verify their percentage.

But 1982's sales would confound everyone's revenue expectations and cast severe doubts on the wisdom of continuing the arrangement—at least from Manhattan's perspective.

"There was pressure from the very beginning," says Erwin Isman, "because Perry was building up this gigantic overhead—the overhead being the cost of the samples and the cost of the [original] showroom, and we had begun to hire a lot of people, so we were paying a lot in salaries as well as a high rent. We had a lot of depreciation on the showroom and the design offices we had built, so there was pressure from Manhattan for us to do enough volume to cover the overhead.

"Based on the experience we were having, we projected something like fifteen million dollars for that fall season [of 1982]. We thought it was going to be the most successful season we had ever had, but we only did nine million with it."

Isman is quite candid about how they used to calculate the breakdown of their sales. They figured on up-front sales (immediate orders from the stores during the "market week" selling period just after the show) of 60 to 70 percent of the total volume they would do in a season, a 20 to 30 percent reorder business from the stores at a later point, and closeout of the last 10 or—at worst—20 percent with the discount houses.

"That season our salespeople did a magnificent job," says Isman, "although they took a lot of flack for it—which was not right. They could only do nine to ten million dollars worth of goods up front, leaving us with a five to six million dollar inventory. Based on our normal experience with Perry's clothes, we would have reordered out another couple of million and closed out another million or so [wholesale figures].

"The line didn't sell [at retail], however. Not only did we not get reorders, which left us with that huge inventory of six million dollars, but we began to get 'returns' from the stores. They were constantly complaining about quality control or any of the other excuses that retailers give when they can't sell the goods. As you know, they can always find something wrong with the clothes.

"I don't think our quality control was any different that season than it was before. Quite simply, the clothes did not suit the marketplace, and so we got stuck with six million dollars' worth of clothes to closeout, plus about one million dollars' worth of clothes that had been returned. We took a bath."

This meant that for the fall season of 1982 alone, Perry Ellis Sportswear had to dispose of seven million dollars' worth of clothes—somewhere between $14 and $17 million at retail. It is unlikely they were able to pull it off. For one thing, in the village-like, rumor-mongering atmosphere of the fashion industry, *everyone* would have soon known that Ellis and Manhattan were in deep trouble.

Fortunately, this wasn't quite the case. "Our name was so good that the consumer never found out," says Isman. "The individual retailers knew, and we knew, but that's as far as it went." To this day, Isman firmly believes the fault lay in the collection itself. "It was the first time that the world—the real world of the customer, not the reviewers—didn't like Perry's designs," he says.

"Perry blamed everyone. He blamed me, he blamed the salespeople, but I think deep down he knew that the collection was not salable."

The collection should have worked. The Scottish tartans were handled with all the wit and sportswear appeal that Perry was known for, but the entire collection was overshadowed by his oh-too-fashionable fitted peplum suits. That was the image that reviewers and, especially, buyers were left with, because it was the first time that Perry had gone all out with a "high" fashion look. Not high in the sense of couture, but high in the sense of camp. In retrospect, it didn't work because it wasn't valid except for several hundred fashion victims in major urban areas of the country (which doesn't make for sales). To be valid, fashion has to sell; it has to be worn.

Although it may not be indicative of anything, it is interesting to note that 1982 was the first time in five years that Perry was not nominated for a Coty Award by the country's fashion critics.

His spring '83 collections, presented at the end of October, were not even as well received as the disastrous "Dreamgirls" collection. Although the production values were as lavish as ever and the audience consisted of the usual everyone-who's-anyone in the business (as well as the usual smattering of stars, including Tatum O'Neal and Bernadette Peters), what they saw were Perry's most exaggerated clothes to date paraded down the runway to music from the film *Diva*.

In a season that *WWD* had christened "FIT," Perry showed angular silhouettes with big tops and bottoms separated by three-inch "sailor belts" with silver buckles from Barry Kieselstein-Cord. There was much of the matelot about the collection, which was predominately white, but it failed to capture the romance of the "Chariots" collection from a year before: it was simply too aggressive.

As *Women's Wear* put it, "Perry Ellis' Wonderful World is a cartoon strip of larger-than-life shapes, sight-gag sweaters, vaudevillian accessories and can-you-top-this proportions." Although the collection was appreciated by some of the buyers, most agreed it was far from Perry's most successful collection. What is interesting is that it did fairly well at retail. Even though Perry had again gone for the exaggerated fit that had been so cooly received the season before, this was a younger look, and therefore more acceptable to Perry's fashion-oriented customers, even though the prices were just as high as the previous season's more sophisticated collection.

Whatever the root cause of the problems in 1982, Erwin Isman had decided to resign as president of Perry Ellis Sportswear, Inc., and Edward M. Jones III was named president and chief executive officer of the newly consolidated men's and women's apparel operations for Manhattan Industries at the beginning of March 1983. Even though Perry Ellis Sportswear, Inc., and Perry Ellis Men, Ltd. (the men's wear company had been renamed early in 1982 when two additional categories—dress shirts and neckwear—were added to it) were different in that the men's company was a licensee and therefore a joint venture between Perry Ellis International and Manhattan Industries, it was felt by upper management that the two "couture" operations should be under the leadership of one man, with the planned proliferation of Perry Ellis lines from Manhattan that would take place over the next couple of years.

It had been Perry's idea that Jones become president and CEO of both companies, even though Jones hadn't had experience on the women's side of the apparel business. But as Perry stated in a *WWD* article about Jones in February 1984: "He built my men's business in such a quiet, professional manner that when the women's post opened up, I thought we should get someone like Ed. Then I realized, we should just get Ed to do it." Perry's contract with Manhattan gave him the power to nominate the president of the Ellis Manhattan companies as chairman, even though he was also an employee of the apparel company.

When Ed Jones first joined Perry Ellis in 1981, one of the main reasons Manhattan Industries had wanted him was because he had been instrumental in building the Calvin Klein men's wear company into a fifty-million-dollar-a-year business (wholesale) in just four years. "Manhattan wanted a fifty-million business within two years," says Jones, "and when I first met with Perry that's what he told me. So I said, 'I don't want anything to do with you then. I loved meeting you but—' And he said, 'What do you mean?' And I said, 'That's not the way to go about it. You're not known in men's wear, okay? So what I would say is that we have to start at a very high price level, which is going to cost us two or three years of losing money, but it will establish you at the highest level with an image and a product that's the best in men's wear in America.'"

Jones's plan was to start the men's wear as virtually a "couture" operation, which would actually serve to complement the, by then, very high prices of Perry's women's collections, and later on to introduce a lower-priced line to achieve a market spread and capitalize on the name and exclusivity that the men's collections would have established by that time. Both Perry and Manhattan felt so strongly about this strategy that they were willing to take a loss on the men's company for the first two to three years. (Although Perry would not actually take a loss, since he was receiving a percentage of sales, regardless of profits.)

Jones says that Manhattan was very supportive. "For two and a half years we lost money before we got the men's business up to twenty million [wholesale]." But he maintains that the losses were minimal. "At that point in time it was the women's wear company that was making the big losses."

The idea of stratifying the Ellis collections into different price ranges obviously appealed to Manhattan Industries, which felt that with the lower-priced men's collection they could do the volume to make back the money they were losing every year on the "couture" collections.

Erwin Isman, on the other hand, feels that the proliferation of the collections was a mistake at that time. "At that point they were almost defensive measures trying to build volumes because of the overhead that was being created. The problem with that business, in hindsight, was that in order to cover the amount of money that was being spent—which was because of Perry—we would have had to do volume upon volume upon volume. If that business had been privately owned by Perry and myself, and we would have had to have funded it with our own capital, it would never have happened.

"It was the wrong thing for Perry at that point. It was obviously time to consolidate and reevaluate and instead we were pushed to continue the expansion to cover the overhead."

Whether Perry was pushed into what happened next or he

and Laughlin sincerely felt it was the right move is open to conjecture. Certainly it appeared the scheme would bring in more revenue for Perry Ellis International, so it is likely that Laughlin, not knowing the nuts and bolts of the fashion business, supported Manhattan's plan to multiply the lines.

Isman's assessment of Perry's business acumen, or lack thereof, is borne out by what happened between 1982 and 1984, even with Laughlin and Ed Jones trying to temper the designer's more extravagant inclinations (though Isman believes that Laughlin didn't do all he could to smooth out the corporate situation, simply because he was in Perry's court).

As it was, it was Laughlin who would have to negotiate with Manhattan Industries every time he wanted to create new license business. Ed Jones says that within the terms of the original contract between Perry and Manhattan, Manhattan retained the first option on any product license. "It was his obligation to go to them and say, 'I want to do shoes, may I proceed with negotiations or would you want to do shoes yourselves?'" However, Isman says it wasn't quite as cut-and-dried as this, since Manhattan only had the option on any category that they already manufactured. But the situation was more complex than that because the price of the product was also a factor. "If Perry wanted to do shirts in the hundred-and-fifty-dollar range, for example," says Isman, "he could because Manhattan did do shirts, but they didn't do them in that price range. There were a lot of gray areas and that gave Perry tremendous leverage."

Obviously, more moderately priced men's and women's sportswear was within Manhattan's sphere of operations and they took up their option, giving the new collections the Portfolio name. "When we were conceptualizing the new collections we spent a lot of time looking for a name," says Jones. "'America' was considered and dropped. 'Classification' was considered, but Ralph [Lauren] had that. And during the meetings Perry would keep penciling in the Portfolio logo. Finally, he and Laughlin went to Manhattan and the name

Portfolio was assigned to Perry Ellis International." This was necessary because even though Manhattan owned the name Portfolio and would be manufacturing the new collections, the men's Portfolio collection would be licensed from Perry Ellis International.

With the extraordinary costs of the expanded showroom mounting throughout 1983 and the losses of 1982, it was decided to create *two* new lower-priced collections. It is most likely that the decision was a compromise, since Perry wanted to do an even lower-priced casual line—but not with Manhattan. According to Isman, Perry and Leeds were already at odds by this point, but they had no choice except to work together. "There was certainly a divergence of views between Perry and Larry at that point," continues Isman.

"It was a very long and involved situation," says Ed Jones. "Perry was becoming more and more frustrated and disenchanted with Manhattan Industries for a lot of different reasons. They were fighting him on every little thing, the women's collections were losing money, and his personal relationship with Larry had deteriorated completely. As a result, he became more negative towards Manhattan at the same time as the whole concept of doing a casual line was being formulated. The idea had been first put to Perry by Michael Zelnick [then head of Bidermann Industries, U.S.A.], who came to visit sometime in 1982 and suggested that he wanted to market a casual line for Perry.

"The seed was planted then. Another big fashion corporation also approached him, which made him even more antagonistic towards Manhattan because they wouldn't agree to it. Manhattan was saying, 'Whenever anything like that needs to be done we will do it, and we certainly wouldn't allow Bidermann to do it.' That started a whole attitude in his own mind that really began to intensify, and it was the beginning of the end of any sort of friendly relationship between Perry and Manhattan."

The situation was further complicated when Perry was approached by Levi Strauss and Company to do a casual line. It was obviously a terrific opportunity for Perry to be associated with the largest apparel company in the world, and Laughlin had soon begun the negotiations.

"It was the worst period of all, not only for the relationship between Perry and Manhattan, but also for me, until that last year [1985–86]," says Jones. "What it all came down to after many months of very, very nasty meetings and threats of legal suits by Perry and vice versa was that they were actually going to fire him! They wanted to do the lower-priced casual line with him, but he had refused, so they said, 'We'll fire you and we'll have Jed and Patricia do it.'"

As inconceivable as this might seem, Manhattan could have actually fired Perry, but only as the designer and chairman of Perry Ellis Sportswear, Inc., which was a wholly owned subsidiary of Manhattan Industries. All the other lines, including the men's sportswear manufactured by Manhattan and housed within the showroom at 575 Seventh, were simply licensee agreements, no more, and Perry would have retained all rights to the use of his name. If it had ever come to such a head, it would have been an extremely messy situation and more than likely involved a legal battle that would have gone on for years, probably destroying both Perry and Manhattan Industries in the process. In that slow Texas drawl of his, Ed Jones says simply, "It was a nasty pissing contest.

"Finally, a compromise was struck, which was how Portfolio women's came to be. He gave them that as a bone so he could do the casual line himself. As a result, he finally got them to assign a portion of the rights to the women's sportswear over to Perry Ellis International. It was Laughlin's first big deal."

It is interesting that Jones does not mention any trouble over the men's part of the new casual line within this context, since Manhattan did have the first option on men's sportswear. It just demonstrates how much Perry's contract was subject to interpretation and could be read to his advantage.

And though Erwin Isman claims that Perry wasn't much of a businessman, one thing he *could* do, especially now that he had Laughlin to back him up with moral support and legal advice, was negotiate. "Perry could really carry a meeting, even a serious business meeting, and pull it off well," says Ed Jones. "He prepared himself, got all the information before the meeting and consumed it, and would let into them. He would completely dominate the thing."

However, Jones adds that Perry had the advantage over Leeds in that Leeds wanted Perry more than Perry needed Leeds. "It was warm water with those two," he says. "That was an unfortunate relationship, because all Larry ever wanted, and probably a big reason why it was never profitable, was because Larry was trying to be Perry's best friend and therefore allowed him to do many things that, as a senior executive, he probably shouldn't have. What he wanted more than anything in the world was to be Perry's best friend and confidant and buddy. Let's face it, Manhattan Industries became a 'name' through Perry, and Larry loved it; it was an ego thing."

The rift between Leeds and Perry had widened so much by 1983 that they didn't bother to speak to each other for nearly a year, according to Jones, but the tension between them had been building for some time before that and had actually been brought to the attention of a member of the fashion press by Perry himself.

"You know how Perry just loved to do p.a.'s," Pamela Altman says jokingly. "He would only do them for his friends, and when the men's wear was first bought by Bloomingdale's he did one for Marvin Traub. It was an informal modeling show and I ran a picture in *DNR* with Larry Leeds, Perry, and Eddy [Jones] together. Later that day Peggy Lee called me up and said, 'Do you have time for lunch? It's in the showroom.' I said, 'Sure.' And you know how nice Peggy is . . . she added in a whisper, 'I'm not supposed to tell you this, but he doesn't like his picture taken with Larry and please don't do it again.'

"So I went up to the showroom and lunch was set in

Perry's corner office, which is James Terrell for ever with lots of lilies, and the whole table was covered with food. And lunch was for only me and him and Laughlin!

"There was Perry sitting down with that enigmatic expression on his face and he said to me in a small voice, 'You know how I feel, Pru . . .'

"'Yes,' I replied, 'So you don't want your picture taken with Larry Leeds anymore,' and his face fell! It was obviously very difficult for him to admit to it, so I looked at him and said, 'Eddie told me, Peggy Lee told me, and probably my cleaner will also tell me!'

"And there was Laughlin sitting back and loosening his tie—you remember how he used to do that—and he smiled and remarked, 'You've just ruined his whole game plan. He's wrestled with this the whole morning because you know how he hates to yell at anyone.'

"I think Perry was a little shocked, because he went on to explain, 'It's not just Larry Leeds; I don't even like the idea of *anything* being associated with Manhattan Industries.'"

It is obvious that the overall picture at Manhattan Industries and its Perry Ellis subsidiaries was very unclear during 1982 and 1983, and it's doubtful that even the principals involved knew what the end result would be, which partially explains why there was so much maneuvering going on. What *is* fairly certain is that however much they threatened, and were threatened in return, Manhattan was not anxious to totally destroy its relationship with Perry. According to Jim Thayer, the apparel market analyst for the firm of Bear Sterns, "Whatever the losses and troubles Manhattan had with Perry Ellis, you have to remember that they were buying several things with him. Although their biggest line, their biggest brand name, was John Henry [the shirt company], Perry was the icing on the cake. They were buying the identity of Perry Ellis, the fame of Perry Ellis, and the cachet of Perry Ellis, and they were also buying into the future, when eventually they hoped it would return a profitability not only on an operating basis but also be extremely profitable on a licensing basis.

"Also, I think Larry Leeds had a lot at stake personally, not from a financial point of view but from a corporate-strategy point of view. Perry provided him with the market spectrum to be able to ship to stores he wouldn't have been able to ship to with Manhattan's existing lines, so it was a relationship of symbiosis. In other words, Perry Ellis was providing something to Manhattan with the potentially large licensing revenues down the road, and Manhattan was certainly providing something to Ellis."

It was probably Laughlin's licensing program that saved the relationship between Perry and Manhattan as much as anything. In March 1983 an agreement was signed between Perry Ellis International and Visions Stern, a Paris-based perfume company, for the rights to Perry Ellis fragrances and cosmetics for men and women. Milton Stern, chairman of the company, was quoted as saying, "We hope to have a Perry Ellis fragrance line launched in 1985 with initial distribution in the United States and Canada, as well as selected markets in Europe and South America."

The agreement was the ultimate feather in Perry's cap. It is a fact of life in the fashion business that fragrance and cosmetics sales can keep a fashion company exceedingly profitable, even when the house under whose name the fragrance is marketed is running up a huge annual deficit on the collections. This is certainly true in the case of such Parisian couture houses like Chanel, Dior, and Patou. In many cases, even with such famous fashion names as Yves Saint Laurent and Valentino, it is the fragrance part of their operations that actually pays for the collections, which may lose money each year.

With this potential revenue in mind and—though he may not have liked it—the promise afforded by the tie-in with Levi Strauss, Leeds would have been foolish to have destroyed all he had built up with Perry Ellis. It is probably the reason he allowed the construction of the new showrooms, studios, and offices to continue, despite the soaring costs to the company. It should be noted that these costs were charged back to Perry Ellis Sportswear, Inc., and Perry Ellis Men's, Ltd., which is part of the reason those companies were continually in the red.

At the same time, says Ed Jones, "There were so many reasons [for the unprofitability]. The blame is equally Manhattan's as much as it was Perry's. Manhattan Industries is a corporation that does not have the mentality or the operational structure to operate a designer sportswear line. They're a dress-shirt company.

"A lot of the expenses that we had to incur internally at Perry Ellis as a company, we had to incur over and above certain corporate charges that we didn't use, or if we used, didn't apply—computer costs, warehousing, and so on. We were always the stepchild in the larger Manhattan scheme of things.

"It always cost us money, and it was always expensive. We were never able to go out and do our own warehousing, for example. I think if we had, we would have been cost-efficient, but we were always shoehorned into the Manhattan system and forced to make it work. And this meant we still had to go outside and buy smaller computer services for additional help to track our business."

Jones agrees, however, that Manhattan's corporate structure could not be blamed for everything. Certainly carrying the cost of the showroom over a ten-year period had a lot to do with it, as did Perry's flamboyant spending on the PR side." One should remember that the cost of the showrooms was Perry's sole responsibility, and he continued to spend large amounts of money on samples each season.

In fact, his spending and perfectionism were directly responsible for the failure of one of his licensees in 1983, the children's line produced by Pelican, a division of Manhattan Industries, which must have worried the parent corporation somewhat.

"It lasted only a couple of seasons because again they allowed Perry to do what he wanted," says Jones. "And, in Perry's words, 'It cost them a bloody fortune.' The clothes were beautiful, but with the price of the yarn and the fabrics and the cost of making them, they were expensive clothes for women to buy for little girls, and the business was tiny. The Pelican division lost a lot of money trying to do it his way, rather than trying to direct him and saying, 'This is the way we should do it, Perry, can you work within these limits,' which is what I did with the men's wear with him. We always worked well, because we came at him with a plan and said, 'I'm willing to give here, but I need you to give here.' That never happened in the Pelican relationship; therefore it failed."

While the failure of the children's line may have been worrying to Manhattan Industries, its upper management's attention was focused elsewhere at that point. With the two new Portfolio lines in the planning stage, they now found themselves with a new collection that they owned and a new one for men's wear that they were licensing from Perry. Taken together with Perry's proposed deal with Levi Strauss, it looked as if their premier designer was about to corner every segment of the apparel market. But that's not how it happened.

"I was ready to go ahead with the Portfolio men's division just about the same time as I took over the women's company. We had been planning for the launch ever since I first joined Perry Ellis back in 'eighty-one," says Jones. "Then Perry decided to postpone the men's Portfolio line, so that he could start the women's Portfolio collection first. When it came time to formalize an execution timetable for Portfolio for men, which we were going to do by category, he began to get difficult with me and all of a sudden he was incapable of understanding the Portfolio-for-men concept. His method of confronting it was saying, 'One more time explain to me how we're going to do it.'

"And I had a problem with that, because he'd understood from day one and now . . . I knew the roots of it, it was more to do with Manhattan. Still, all of a sudden I felt I was getting screwed, because Portfolio for men, which is what I came there with as an idea, was being pushed aside."

Perry was undoubtedly more interested in the new America sportswear line with Levi Strauss by then and wanted to push it forward as quickly as possible. He also needed to introduce the Portfolio women's line quickly to keep Manhattan happy, so that it would have its moderately priced women's line.

As president and CEO of the two Manhattan companies, Ed Jones agreed to the new timetable with what he says was "reluctance." He had already advised Perry to wait with the America line and stagger the launches of the two Portfolio lines. "It must have been the only thing we fought about," he says. "In the end we reached a compromise. Perry wanted the Portfolio men's line to be delayed for a year until after the Portfolio women's and America lines came out. We fought and argued, and I went back in one last-ditch effort to compromise with him and said, 'Okay, I don't totally agree with what you're saying about Portfolio Sportswear, but I can more easily accept it if you allow me to do the Portfolio men's dress shirts and neckwear for the holiday season so that we can get a jump on the America line. At least it will give us a foot in the door in that segment of the market, and they'll know we're doing this cheaper classification.'"

Perry finally agreed with Jones's suggestion, which was actually based on sound market policy and not pique that Perry had postponed his pet project. It takes at least a year and a half for the public to become fully aware of and identify with a new fashion collection or name. Perry and Laughlin's mistake was that they saturated the market with three different price levels of Perry Ellis merchandise for both men and women at the same time. The result was that the public became confused about what it was buying. Why, for instance, should the average man pay $100 or more for a Perry Ellis shirt when there was another Perry Ellis shirt next to it for only $50, especially when they were almost identical? The fact that the more expensive one was made out of an exclusive fabric and therefore couldn't be found just anywhere was beside the point; they were both made of 100 percent cotton, and the cheaper one looked equally well made.

It was a problem that came to affect all the new collections. Ed Jones's prior warnings about the dangers of launching the collections too closely together were realized. The Portfolio women's collection started off poorly, and the much heralded collaboration between Perry Ellis and Levi Strauss (both names were on the label), while predicted to do between $30 and $50 million in its first year and climb to $200 million shortly thereafter (wholesale figures), barely reached $20 million by the time of the designer's death two years later. (Ironically, the men's Portfolio collection did better than either of them and took off.)

Jones puts the blame for the relative failure of this grand diversification scheme squarely on the heads of Perry and Laughlin. "They were just too anxious. They desperately wanted this deal [the America collection] with the largest apparel company in the world. If they had been more patient and waited, spreading out the launch dates, the consumer would have had time to understand all the different collections. As it was, they were confused. When you come out with several new concepts in a row, you can't help but muddy the water, and that's what happened. Ultimately, that was why America never really got going."

It was probably the biggest mistake Laughlin ever made in his handling of Perry's affairs, though it should have been his greatest triumph. The potential not only for the more moderately priced Portfolio collections but especially for the Perry Ellis America/Levi Strauss collection was enormous. (A complete line of casual sportswear and jeans for men and women from a designer as popular and associated with sportswear as Perry *should* have taken off.) There were two problems with the line, however, that could be attributed to Perry and Laughlin. The first was the price of the clothes—$60 for a sweatshirt was outrageous, however well made it was. The second was the fact that Perry Ellis International insisted the collection could only be sold to existing Perry Ellis accounts for the first year. There were only about three hundred Perry Ellis accounts in the country at the time, which was not a large enough retail base to go mass market. In retrospect, it's difficult to understand how they expected to make money by keeping the line so exclusive.

Still, the deal was seen by the industry as a whole as a major move on Perry's part. *The New York Times* even ran a piece on the first page of its January 18, 1984, business section, with a large photograph of Perry and Robert Haas, president and CEO of Levi Strauss and Company, signing the contracts. (Haas actually tells a funny story about the occasion. They were both laughing into the camera, and he says it was because the photographer caught them just after he had said to Perry, "You know Perry, I haven't read a word of this!" To which Perry had replied, "I haven't either!")

It's a pity that the America collection didn't do better. Perry probably admired Robert Haas more than anyone else in the industry, not only for Haas's considerable intellect, but also for his exquisite manners and attitude toward life. It should have been an ideal partnership.

Haas recalls that when Perry and Laughlin flew out to San Francisco (where Levi Strauss is based) to meet with him for the first time in 1983 so that they could get to know one another while Laughlin and the Levi Strauss lawyers worked out the organizational details, he asked Perry, "How will you know if Perry Ellis America is successful five years from now?" Haas says that Perry began to talk about financial goals and business projections, at which point Haas interjected, "You know, I feel five years from now we'll know it's successful if we can get together in some lovely place in the Napa Valley over a bottle of wine." Haas then goes on to say that they shook hands and the deal was consummated.

Of course, Perry would not be around in five years, although Robert Haas was one of the last people he visited. Less than a month after Perry's death, Levi Strauss and Company gave up the Perry Ellis America name, which was then licensed by Robert McDonald, the new president of Perry Ellis International, to Manhattan Industries. In the end, Manhattan got what they'd wanted all along and had fought so bitterly about with Perry for nearly two years.

11

. . . The sun and wind dried him, little grains of salt lay on his skin
and hair. He felt too good to lie down on the sand so went walking
along the beach, just ankle deep in the glassy water, feeling it suck
away at his feet and then flood back in, watching the patterns dis-
appear and change, like abstract and instantaneous photographs,
compositions of water and foam and sand, fleeting, but sharp and
definite for their instance of coherence. He was glad to be here to see
them, for they would never recur.

—Frank O'Hara
"The Fourth of July"

In a rare interview about his personal life with the author in
1983, Perry Ellis said about his Water Island home: "There is
nothing to do here except look at the beauty of the place. You
can go to the ocean's edge and look out a thousand miles
across the water." It was a solitude that gave Perry what he
called "clarity."

It was an exceptionally metaphysical statement for a man
of forty-three, in the prime of his life, to make. But though
he was at the height of his fame and influence, Perry had
cause for worry. His relationship with Manhattan Industries
was at its lowest point; and of even greater concern to him
were the alarming symptoms of illness Laughlin was beginning to exhibit. It was almost as if there was a premoni-
tion of sadness and grief in that moment as he looked out
across the Atlantic that, in light of what happened later, could
well have been an acceptance of his mortality. Yet there was
also a calmness.

Still, the next two years saw a flurry of creative output

from Perry, the expansion of his business, more time spent working with fashion students, the assumption of a leadership role at the Council of Fashion Designers of America, the continuation of his relationship with Laughlin, and the fathering of a child. It is almost easy to say, in retrospect, that he knew his time was running out, but the almost frantic activity of his last two years would seem to suggest that he was determined to create a lasting legacy.

On the brighter side, despite the in-fighting at Manhattan, Perry's fashion star was in the ascendency again. His two collections shown in 1983 were received extremely well by the press and buyers, and sales began to climb again. Of the fall 1983 collection, shown at the end of April, *Women's Wear Daily* in its lead paragraph said:

NEW YORK—He may have had the longest adolescence in history, but Perry Ellis is definitely a big boy now. In the fall collection he showed Thursday, he abandoned all the cartoon-whimsy and juvenility of previous years for a smart, sophisticated adult look, aspects of which could be worn by women of any age. The result: four-star Perry Ellis—his best, most well-rounded collection ever and the most original looking of the season.

The audience, which included the usual coterie of stars, including Susan Sarandon, Sigourney Weaver, Mariel Hemingway, and Isabella Rossellini, as well as hockey players Barry Beck, Ron Greschner, and Eddie Meo, was treated to a new silhouette from Perry. The slim, elongated waist was still there, but he had cut down the proportions of his tops and combined these with full bias-cut skirts or even bell-bottoms for a distinctively matelot look. The jackets, some of which were much shorter, just coming to the midriff, were pleated at the back to fly away from the body. The tailoring throughout was exceptional, as were his by now famous sweaters, which were very short indeed, though their full dolman sleeves and overemphasized details kept them in proportion to the ankle-length skirts. Levity was also present in the collection in witty zebra- or tiger-striped sweaters. The main theme of the collection, however, was nautical, and his brass-buttoned pea jackets and cross-Channel steamer coats caught the imagination of many people there. In addition, for the first time, Perry's evening clothes were thoroughly appreciated by the majority of the press, though for some, his naval mess jackets for men were not intended to be taken too seriously.

Still, *Women's Wear*, never a paper to pass up a chance at a dig, brought the incisive pen of "Louise J. Esterhasy" to bear on Perry again in commenting on the collection. Having praised it first, they then used their "countess" to say, "After all a designer's runway appearance does leave the most lasting impression. Perry Ellis showed his most grown-up collection to date, then he nearly spoiled everything by doing his old skip-down-the-runway number."

The rest of the fashion press didn't seem to mind the familiar display, however, and with this collection, they nominated him for two more Coty Awards, for both his men's and women's collections. (He would win both: his first women's Citation an award for a multiple "Winnie" recipient and the men's Return Award. Also, in June of that year, he had won the Cutty Sark Men's Fashion Award as the Most Outstanding U.S. Designer. And, earlier still in the year, he had received the CFDA award for his men's wear. No other designer in the history of American fashion has ever won so many awards in a single year as Perry did in 1983.) After the negative criticism he had received for his last two collections, it was obvious from the tributes and accolades that Perry was back in top form.

At the end of April a licensee agreement with The Vera Companies to manufacture and distribute a collection of scarves, mufflers, and shawls was announced as well, proof that although Perry may not have been talking to Larry Leeds, there was certainly a dialogue going on between Perry Ellis International and Manhattan Industries.

In May, Perry made his first foray into theater costume design when he did the costumes for a production of Noel Coward's *Blithe Spirit* for the Santa Fe Festival Theatre, a project dear to his heart, since Laughlin was one of the founders of the theater and sat on its board of directors. The production starred Susan Sarandon, Amy Irving, and Madeline Kahn, and Perry's designs were quite understated for Coward's brilliantly witty, and bitchy, play about a dead wife who comes back to haunt her husband and his new wife. "They are not grand-entrance clothes," said Perry. "They're not for Elizabeth Taylor's version of Noel Coward." (A rather snide remark on Perry's part, referring to the revival of *Design for Living* that had just opened on Broadway with Taylor and the late Richard Burton.)

The production in Laughlin's home town was very successful, although Madeline Kahn did not like her costume at all! However, before the production she had co-hosted a benefit performance of Neil Simon's *Brighton Beach Memoirs* with Perry for the Santa Fe Festival Theatre. This was followed by dinner at Mr. Chow's, the exclusive Chinese restaurant on 57th Street, so she couldn't have been too upset about the redesign he did for her. Perry and Laughlin actually spent quite some time each year visiting Santa Fe, where Laughlin's family lived, but this was the only time Perry designed costumes.

In ninety-degree temperatures that July, Saks Fifth Avenue in New York devoted five of its windows to the fall Perry Ellis men's collection and officially launched the Greif Companies' licensed Perry Ellis tailored clothing collection. According to Bob Franceschini, a vice president of Saks Fifth Avenue at the time, the response to the new men's collection was "very positive," despite the heat wave. In addition, Saks would be selling the clothing collection in twenty-two of its thirty-six stores across the country, so yet another Perry Ellis collection was considered successfully launched. (Although it didn't do quite as well as expected, Perry's new suit business performed respectably and brought his name to the attention of the more conservative male fashion customer, whose biggest purchase each year is a business suit.

That summer Perry kept a low profile, spending most of his time out at the beach with Laughlin. (They'd flown in for the Saks opening with Perry looking fit and tanned, and wearing a jacket and tie!) They had taken to spending more and more time at Water Island each summer, especially as work on the new town house came closer to being finished (though it wouldn't be completed until the following summer), but, more importantly, because of Laughlin's health.

The ocean must have inspired Perry that summer, since in his collections for spring '84, one of the themes was the America's Cup (which had just been lost to Australia off the coast of Newport, Rhode Island). Perry took to the outback of Australia for one-half of the collection and again returned to a nautical theme for the more casual side of it. (Travelogue was "in" that spring season: while Perry had gone "down under," Ralph Lauren had been inspired by the African safari, though as *WWD* quite rightly put it, "Never mind that each collection is about as genuinely African or Australian as, say, the Empire State Building.") Perry's show had all the usual glittering stars in the audience, including a couple of new ones—Carol Channing (which was somewhat of a surprise), Terri Garr, and the Ron Reagan, Jrs.

His silhouettes were somewhat of an evolution of those from the preceding season, though the outback was evoked in some crisp linen dresses under what could have been called interpretations of the "driz-a-bone" (an Australian riding coat), as well as by jodhpurs for both men and women worn with straw fedoras with the brim turned down. It was in the burnt colors of the island continent, however, that Perry showed how he had matured as a designer over the years. As was the case with his first Portfolio collections, he showed a lot of earth tones, but here they were handled in an exquisitely subtle fashion, with tone upon tone upon tone. While the outback segment was reminiscent of the clothes Rachel Ward wore in the television adaptation of *The Thorn Birds*, Perry's nautical segment was a far cry from the rigors of twelve-meter-yacht racing. Here were striped blazers and polka dots in profusion. It really had more to do, especially the men's collection, with *Brideshead Revisited* and the banks of the Thames, than either Newport or Perth. Retailers, happily, went wild over the collection (and judging by all the polka-dot sweaters, jackets, and ties one saw the following summer on the street, their reactions were justified).

With the success of the spring collection and the plans for the two Portfolio collections and the America collection finalized—sufficient grounds for an uneasy truce to be called between Manhattan and its star designer—Perry should have felt excited about the prospects for 1984. There was only one cloud on the horizon—Laughlin's health. He was spending very little time in the office and, consequently, Perry was spending more and more time away from it as well. They were also taking frequent trips to England and Ireland, traveling around the countryside, which they loved, but also spending time with friends such as the late designer Laura Ashley, at her home in Powis, Wales. When in London they would spend much of their time buying antiques for the new town house.

As with the first town house on West Sixty-ninth Street, Perry had asked Jim Terrell to renovate the new building just one block north, even though they weren't as close as they had been in the past, because of Laughlin.

"The new house was meant to be a free adaptation of the old house, a renovation," says Terrell, "but Perry outlined the original project so briefly it turned into something completely different. . . . It was extremely frustrating.

"It was in the little details that Perry drove me crazy, for instance, the woodwork in the living room. When we first set out he just wanted us to clean it, then he wanted to take pieces of it out, then he wanted to completely change it. It was a late Victorian house built about a hundred years ago and it ended up looking like an English Georgian town house in the middle of Mayfair [one of the most exclusive areas of London].

"It just sort of evolved. It started when we had to renovate the back wing, which was being turned into a staircase. As it turned out the wing wasn't structurally sound, so it had to be taken down and rebuilt. It then became a very elaborate staircase with arched windows that were Georgian in style, which led to all the other windows being replaced, which led to the brickwork becoming Georgian, which led to seventeenth- and eighteenth-century fireplaces that he'd bought in London being installed. Every detail had to be perfect. In the end it became a museum piece."

The bathrooms were another example of Perry's perfectionism. He had bought a couple of the beautiful marble-and-glass Art Deco bathrooms from the Savoy Hotel in London when it was being renovated—they were about the only features of the house that weren't Georgian—and had had them shipped to New York. In transit they were broken, which meant they had to be rebuilt to their exact original specifications in order to satisfy Perry. Even the glass mirrors had to be specially made and recut to the exact sizes. With problems like these, the bathrooms alone took six months to install.

Ultimately, the renovation took three years. According to Richard Banks, who was still working for Terrell, "It went through such a series of revisions in style that Jim could have gutted the building and rebuilt the whole interior from scratch for what they spent on it. The detailing was quite incredible; for instance, we had to construct a wine cellar in one of the basements and Perry demanded that it should always be at the perfect temperature and humidity, so we had to import these Japanese river stones. And with all the revisions, we had to tear out some splendid Victorian architectural detailing . . . which was a great pity. Even the garden was revised several times."

Terrell doesn't know exactly how much the house finally cost Perry to renovate, because Perry used his own contractors, which was an unusual procedure for Hambrecht Terrell, and later brought in his own experts to continue the restoration. Overall, the work on the house took about three years, and according to informed sources cost between $3.5 and $4 million, a figure that does not take into account the money he lavished on antiques and furnishings to complete it.

One close friend suggests that Laughlin, in a way, was more responsible for such changes than Perry. Perry had bought the house for Laughlin and himself to live in, and allowed Laughlin to have a great deal of say about the interior and how it was planned (including a suite for his daughter Kate to stay in when she was in town). "There was a difference between the public rooms and the private quarters. Granted everything was decorated to the nth degree, but I believe Laughlin pushed Perry's pretentions to grandeur—which, as you know, were already there—to an extreme that Perry would not have gone to if he was doing it simply for himself," the friend says, without rancor.

Of course, the great tragedy about the house that Perry built was that he and Laughlin would only finally settle into it late in 1984, just over a year before Laughlin's death. Consequently, they never really had a chance to enjoy their palace.

January 1984 saw the announcement of Laughlin's much praised business triumph, the joint Perry Ellis/Levi Strauss deal. As has been noted, to all appearances it seemed like an ideal marriage between one of America's most exciting designers and the world's apparel giant. Also in the first six months of the year, Laughlin signed up two more licensees —a men's wear line in Japan that Yagi Tsusho had sublicensed to the giant Japanese apparel firm, Kashimyama (this was a relationship brought about by the refusal of

Renown, who had the women's license, and their men's subsidiary, D'Urban, to take on the license because of the high
royalties Perry was demanding on the line), and a new foot-
wear license for America with the venerable firm of Church's
English Shoes, Ltd.

In addition, in April Perry was elected president of the
Council of Fashion Designers of America for a one-year term,
which could be followed by a second, optional term with
board approval. It would prove to be one of the most important roles Perry was to play in his life. Founded in 1963, the
CFDA had been a loosely knit association of major designers
with little direction or organization until 1981, when its then
president, Bill Blass, announced CFDA awards in competition
with the Cotys. (Unfortunately, the plan to have the CFDA
awards be the first nationally televised fashion awards never
came to fruition.)

"Perry turned the whole CFDA around," says Blass. "He
had such enthusiasm and a great sense of leadership that I'd
never seen evident before. He was able to achieve things other
people wouldn't have even bothered to try." One such example of this was getting Katharine Hepburn to accept a lifetime
achievement award. But Perry did more than just arrange
glamorous and exciting awards ceremonies; he also managed
to get most of the Seventh Avenue designers together and
forged a bond between them that will last long after his death.
Perry didn't just care about his clothes; he cared about fashion
and wanted to build a solid foundation from which to further
the popularity of it in this country. According to nearly every
one of his peers, he laid that groundwork.

In other areas, too, Perry expended a tremendous amount
of energy and time in the service of fashion, and he was one of
the most active of all designers in his work with students, especially in conjunction with the Parsons School of Design. Each
year Parsons would ask a dozen of the top designers in the
country to work with a group of its seniors on a design project. The seniors would work up the preliminary sketches and

patterns, and then the designer would choose one of them to be made into a preliminary toile. The designer would come back again and do a fitting with the students on a professional model, and then fabrics would be chosen. After three weeks the designer would see the actual fabric basted on the model and there would be another fitting and discussion. Although the program only involved five days of the designer's time, there would be much back and forth between the students at Parsons and the designer's studio, so it was quite a commitment for the designer. Finally, at graduation, he or she would give a "golden thimble" award to the student he or she considered most deserving.

Perry contributed to the program nearly every year from 1978 until his death, and made an enormous contribution in terms of advice to the school. In 1982 he also gave a complete series of lectures there, and also lectured at the Fashion Institute of Technology on many occasions as well. The time he spent with students is ample evidence of how dedicated he was to helping young people.

Frank Rizzo, chairman of the fashion design department at Parsons, says, "I would say he was brilliant as an educator. He was very difficult to please, because he had very definite ideas about what fashion was about, but he didn't bring his own taste to the classroom; he helped the students to express themselves. He was very stern, but then these little one-liners would come out that took the students aback. He had a sparkling sense of humor.

"The students responded to his criticism. They all wanted to work with him: he made it a challenge for them. He liked strong students. He liked the students that would stand up to him and say, 'It's exactly what I want.' He hated wimps."

And, in fact, Perry chose almost his entire design staff from Parsons. "At least twenty students," according to Rizzo, "from Patricia Pastor onwards. He was a snob about talent. He loved to surround himself with talent, and he felt that if he was going to do a line he should get the best talent available.

In that way he was a modern designer, but he considered himself a merchant, too." Many of the fledgling designers Perry took under his wing are now working for some of the best houses on Seventh Avenue. Obviously, it was marvelous training for them.

One can see many parallels between the way Perry worked with his own design staff on the collections and the way he worked with students. "He dealt beautifully with concept," says Rizzo. "He wasn't a technician, he would say, 'That's not my bag.' But he could see the total picture. As soon as the garment came out, if it didn't speak to him, you could see it on his face and he'd say, 'Look, there's something wrong here, because the sketch is telling me something that the garment is not.' Then he would point out certain things that were wrong, the proportion or the fit or whatever, and he made them see it."

Another institution that Perry never forgot was his alma mater, William and Mary. On more than one occasion he hosted alumni parties at his showroom. Bob Andrialis, president of William and Mary's New York City alumni association, says, "I was really surprised. I didn't know Perry, but I rang up and left a message. I thought with him being this big designer he would get some secretary to call back, but very shortly there was Perry himself on the phone. He was most generous, providing everything for the reception as well as giving us a taste of his current collection. It was a very thoughtful thing for him to do."

Perry was also quite generous in monetary terms, and established a $100,000 endowment for William and Mary's humanities faculty. Dr. Thomas A. Graves, Jr., who was then president of the college and who used to lunch with Perry whenever he visited New York, says, "I think that he felt that through the humanities, and quite frankly, through the education he'd received, with an emphasis on the arts, the creativity of individuals could blossom. The kind of inner resources that young men and women have could lead to any career they decided to go into. We talked a lot about this and felt that no matter what kind of a career an individual was going into, whether it be engineering or business or publishing, if they got a sound education in the humanities, in the arts, that would stand them well throughout their lives."

There can be no doubt that Perry was deeply concerned about leaving a legacy for future generations, and at the beginning of 1984 he would take steps to make a member of that generation his own child.

Barbara Gallagher had been friends with Robert McDonald for many years, probably meeting as a result of their careers in film and television. McDonald had introduced her to Perry in the mid-seventies, and they took an immediate liking to each other. Soon, Barbara had become a member of the "inner circle."

Her own career progressed nicely, and she rose from being a receptionist for "The Ed Sullivan Show" to associate producer for "Saturday Night Live" and on to vice presidencies first at NBC and then ABC. She eventually left ABC to live in California and work as a free-lance film producer and screenwriter.

Perry, with his everlasting penchant for nicknames, used to call her Mary Tyler Moore because she had once worked as a writer for that show. "I remember the first time I met Barbara," says Jim Terrell. "Perry told me we were going to Mary Tyler Moore's for a birthday party . . . this was back in the 'Beau era.' We went and there was Woody Allen in the corner and all sorts of movie stars there and lots of other famous people, but I couldn't find Mary Tyler Moore. He had introduced me to Barbara when we arrived, and I never made the connection!

"They were wonderful friends," Terrell continues, "and they were always going out together. Barbara lived on Seventy-ninth Street, and [they] would eat at that 'hot' Italian restaurant on Lexington and Eightieth all the time. I had several meals with them there and she was just like an extension of him."

Perry had always wanted a child, and by 1984 it is quite possible that he knew his time might be limited. Barbara herself was nearing forty, so her childbearing years were running out. As Robert McDonald told the story to Patricia Morrisroe, they were at dinner one evening and talking about wanting to have children and Perry turned to Barbara and said, "So what about it?"

Friends are divided over how the child was conceived; most say that it was by artificial insemination. However, Jim Terrell (who probably knew him as well as anyone), when asked if he thinks that was the case, says, "I don't know, but I suspect not."

There are a number of reasons to suspect it might have been artificial insemination. The fact that one of the best hospitals for "in vitro" fertilization is the Eastern Virginia Medical School, located in Norfolk, Virginia, adds credence to the argument. But most important was the precarious state of Perry's health, which very well might have precluded natural conception (and which will be examined in greater depth in the next chapter).

Whatever the truth of the matter, it will probably never be known except to Barbara and Perry; the important thing was that they had a child they loved very much.

Working at a feverish pace, Perry put on two runway shows that spring. The first, given in March, was for the new Portfolio line and received good notices; the second was his usual extravagant production to introduce his men's and women's "couture" sportswear collections. The show, held on May 3, had all the superstar accoutrements one had come to expect from Ellis, and the anticipation built to a climax during the long seating period that habitually preceded Perry's shows. Then the mood changed and, to Vangelis's music for the movie *Antarctica,* out came a collection inspired by the work of the French artist Sonia Delauney, whose Art Deco abstract paintings and drawings Perry admired—he had three in his house.

The collection started off with severely tailored "Quai D'Orsay" suits that actually reminded one more of the forties than the thirties, and moved through various segments named after Paris landmarks to the "Luxembourg Cashmeres," which were some of the most beautiful sweaters and knit skirts, all colored in the Delauney palette and faithfully reproducing her designs, that Perry had ever come up with. Other highlights included black velvet evening dresses and suits "de L'Opera" and some outstanding men's evening suits "en Couleurs"— and in color they were (imagine, for a moment, a blueberry jacket worn with a magenta shirt, a hunter's green bow tie, and gray flannel trousers). The final tribute was to "Le Jazz" age, with beaded flapper sheath dresses in colors similar to the men's suits, and his finale was a long, straight, simple beaded wedding dress that could have rivaled the work of the artisans who create the work of the foremost Parisian couturiers. All in all, the collection was a tour de force, and the audience went wild, clapping and cheering as Perry came down the runway.

Quite out of the blue, however, *Women's Wear Daily* chose the next day to blast the collection in a piece that was so filled with hate and vitriol that it's worth quoting in full:

PERRY ELLIS—Perry Ellis tried to take a tour of Paris Thursday, but the poor thing got lost in the Metro.

Although each of his passages had titles such as the "Quai D'Orsay Suits," "Place de la Concorde Coats" and "Luxembourg Cashmeres," most of the clothes actually looked like the suburb of La Gout d'Or on a best-forgotten day, with dowdy shapes, pathetic hats and oh so sad colors—even if they were allegedly inspired by Sonia Delaunay. Simply put, this collection was not Perry at his peak.

But it wasn't that Ellis didn't try. In fact, the

problem may be that he tried too hard. Although he loves being touted as New York's trendiest designer, Ellis also wants to break out of the "Mr. Pop" mold and turn himself into a serious "creator" with the kind of cachet Yves Saint Laurent and Giorgio Armani have now. In a few cases, particularly in the country tweed and checks as well as the silk satin blouses, long skirts and velvet jackets that opened yesterday's show, he actually achieved it for one brief minute, but then he fell into a pretentious muddle that is neither him nor anyone else. It would have been a lot better if he had stayed on the BMT.

The languid, long lined suits that opened the show were shown in wan colors, such as teal with brown and purple, and made sadder still by the clothes the models wore. Ellis' ill-conceived attempt at gallic chic continued with long-skirted slim plaid suits, and segued into a series of swingy, back-tied "Pont Neuf" coats in overly subdued magenta or beige.

Next came the quaint Madeleine jumpers in prim wool plaids over silk shirts whose spiraling patterns and vibrant colors were based, in the loosest sense, on Delaunay's work. Looking very slouchy but a good deal livelier were the requisite cashmeres: sweaters over pants or skirts in warm color combinations that gave the collection some animation.

But what followed next was sadly disappointing. Ellis released onto the runway a non-stop parade of knits that should have been his showstoppers, but instead were merely jolting. These shapeless tunics over short or long skirts were candidly billed as the designers homage to Delauney, but were so overburdened with color and Art Deco pattern that they simply suggested overdecorated banners.

Ellis was far more successful when he returned to the classics, as in a single-button long checked jacket and matching pants. And, although he called them his Bois de Boulogne coats, his mannish plaids looked refreshing and briskly American. Ellis was clever to mix them with colorful argyle sweaters and confident-looking pants.

But he lost ground again with the evening offerings. These consisted, in the main, of graceless long silk crepe dresses, some of them bottom-heavy with Deco-ish bugle beading. Looking smarter, however, were the opera velvets, especially one long-stemmed beauty—an almost severely simple black velvet sheath.

Still, the applause was loud and long. There was the usual cast of upwardly mobile movie stars—Mariel Hemingway, John Shea, Glenn Close (who couldn't bring herself to take the sunglasses off)—as well as the cheerleaders packed in the bleachers. In fact, there were so many on them that the chairman of Bergdorf Goodman had to stand throughout the show.

Publicly, retailers said they liked the collection, praising its originality and color, especially the Delauney knits. But the same retailers, when speaking not for attribution, questioned whether they would be able to sell the collection and suggested the mood was too old-fashioned. "Like a bunch of old refugees getting off a boat," complained one store vice president.

The level of journalism in this piece can be gauged by the phrase "as well as the cheerleaders packed in the bleachers." These so-called cheerleaders were the world's most important fashion journalists and retailers—*Women's Wear*'s professional peers. Why they were attacked in this manner simply because they applauded the collection was incomprehensible and un-professional. The tone of the article might lead one to believe that the attack was more personally motivated than anything else. Still, it seems unlikely that John Fairchild himself, or Michael Coady, the editor of *WWD*, would have allowed the article to print unless they too felt the collection wasn't up to Perry's usual standards.

More is the pity that it was one of Perry's favorite collections. "He loved that collection," says Ed Jones, "every piece of it." Perry was always anxious about reviews, and if they turned out to be bad, he would say brightly to everyone in the office, "Darling, I loved it. I did it for me, not for them." But with the Delaunay collection Jones says he didn't say a word to anyone.

Whatever *WWD* thought of the collection, the nation's fashion critics disagreed with them, and Perry won his eighth and final Coty that year, a second citation for his women's wear. With it, he had received more awards than any other designer in the history of American fashion. (They were the last Cotys ever held and it seems somehow appropriate that Perry should have been so honored in that last year.)

In June, the new Portfolio women's collection for the early fall season, made its debut in the stores, and it was fascinating to see Perry return to some of his earliest looks in the new line. In addition, its price points were between 30 and 50 percent lower than the "couture" collection, and it was hoped this would enable young people to afford the new line. Perry himself told the author in an interview that he was happy to be designing unconstructed, unbuttoned clothes again and said, "I look on all these collections as different opportunities, and it all seems possible to me."

The first part of the men's Portfolio collection was launched the following month, to be made available to the stores in November, and there was very little difference between the "couture" shirts and ties and the new Portfolio ones except for the fact that some of the more advanced styling details, like Perry's famous one-button folded cuffs, had been done away with.

While all this was happening, Perry and Laughlin continued to make numerous trips to Europe, buying antiques in England and touring around the Irish countryside. On one of these trips Perry bought Laughlin a vintage Bentley for his birthday, which they then had painstakingly restored. As usual, Perry wanted the car to be perfect, and Ed Jones recalls that there was a steady correspondence between the office in New York and the craftsmen in England. Invariably, Perry would discover things on these trips that would somehow become part of the workload at the office. Judy Beste tells of one buying trip on which Perry discovered the wool of the Jacob sheep, one of the most expensive wools in the world (there are very few Jacob sheep around). The wool, which was multicolored, with a very soft but coarse fleece, was never dyed, and, naturally, Perry fell in love with it. But, after bringing some back to use in the collection, he discovered it was too expensive.

Perry, never daunted, soon had made it a major project for the office. Staff were ordered to research the sheep, which are, in fact, an obscure breed mostly found in the Scottish Hebrides. Perry decided that he wanted to import them and breed them here, and had soon persuaded Ed Jones to let him graze them on Jones's horse farm in upstate New York and ordered Judy Beste to write a purchase order for them. When he realized they would have to be quarantined for six months, however, the order was cancelled. Still, it's a marvelous example of what lengths Perry would go to to get what he wanted.

As summer neared, he began to make even more demands on his staff, especially since Laughlin's health had taken a turn for the worse and they'd already decided to spend the whole summer at Water Island. This meant that the staff had to shuttle back and forth to see Perry, since, no matter how good the design team was, Perry still made the final decisions.

"They decided to spend the whole summer out at the

beach because Laughlin was so sick," says Pamela Altman. "I
remember visiting them that summer and Laughlin couldn't
go out in the sun because he had shingles. With them being
out there, it meant that every meeting would have to be held
out there as well. Jed and Patricia would get on the plane in
the morning and fly back at four in the afternoon. Even Karen
[Fortier, then head of publicity] was spending two days a
week out at the island, flying back and forth. I don't know
how they worked, because when you're out there you're not
really in a mood to think anyway."

The frustration it ultimately caused Perry's staff is
summed up by one story of Altman's. She was making one of
her frequent visits to the Ellis offices one afternoon toward the
end of the summer and happened to be in Karen Fortier's office when she overheard the following telephone exchange:

"Gee, Perry, I don't think I need to come out there, since
I only need five minutes with you at the end of the day and
can take care of it myself."

"No, Karen, you should come out here and you can take
the one o'clock plane back with Jed and Patricia in the afternoon."

"But, Perry, I won't get back till after two-thirty and then
the whole day's shot."

"Karen, I really think you should take the ten o'clock
plane tomorrow and leave at lunchtime."

"But, Perry there's only a couple of things I have to go
over with with you."

"Karen, you'll *be* on the ten o'clock plane."

"Well, Perry . . . I *can* come out there."

As Altman tells it, you had to be there, Fortier with her
head tilted back and smoking one of her long brown ciga-
rettes, to appreciate the humor of the situation. Perry was so
persuasive that he finally made Karen feel it was her own decision. (For a long time after that, "Well, Perry . . . I *can* come
out there" was a standard joke around the office because of all
the time they were spending just meeting with Perry.)

At the same time, the enclave on Water Island became a major preoccupation of Perry's, and he began to think about rebuilding the bigger house on the beach so that Laughlin would have more privacy. He had also hired extra help for the summer, including a cook and people to work on the garden and around the house. In previous summers the atmosphere had been, as Pamela Altman so aptly puts it, "like a family," but now it had changed. Laughlin was rarely seen in public, and Perry had far fewer weekend visitors.

At the beginning of September, the eight-thousand-square-foot Perry Ellis America showroom was opened on the twenty-first floor of the building at 575 Seventh Avenue. For the opening, the showroom, complete with glassed-in terrace, was hung with the photographs Perry had commissioned from Bruce Webber, who had gained acclaim for the images he had created for Calvin Klein and Ralph Lauren, as well as for his astounding magazine editorial work. It was a beautiful evening, marred only by how thin and worn Laughlin looked.

The Webber photographs captured to perfection the mood Perry had wanted to convey with the America collection. Here were groups of those perfect young American men and women Webber is so famous for capturing, lounging around the edge of a lake or lolling in a hammock or just "hanging out," wearing the loose, easy sportswear of the kind Americans love and only American designers can do really well. What was especially surprising about the collection was how Perry it looked—even the jeans. It all had those special Perry touches—the pleated shoulder, the broad horizontal stripes in offbeat colors, the proportions, the silhouettes. It was a remarkable collection and was made to the high-quality standards Perry always insisted upon and Levi Strauss achieves in their denims and jeans. The only trouble was the price. It was *designer* sportswear, and therefore out of range for the kids at whom it was aimed.

Just a few days after this opening, *WWD*'s Eye column

announced that Perry was to be a father. The baby girl would be born in California in November.

California was also the theme of Perry's spring/summer '85 collection, which was shown to the press and buyers on November 8. In this author's opinion, it was the best collection Perry ever did, and was quite astounding in its simplicity, sophistication, and mastery of subtle color. After ten years of designing sportswear that was always exciting and always adventurous, but sometimes clumsy, it was as if Perry had emerged from a cocoon to cast away superfluous style and concentrate on the pure essentials.

The "California" collection had all the grace and style one associates with Grace Kelly, Katharine Hepburn, and Carole Lombard. These were simple, sensual clothes designed for the American woman. At the same time, it was a movie-star collection, with silk crepe cross-over blouses and fitted skirts in soft California colors of avocado, cream, blue, desert, terra-cotta, and, of course, tan. White lightweight duster coats were worn over some of the best-cut trousers and simple light sweaters or sensual blouses. The slim-fitting sun dresses reminded one of Hollywood style in the fifties, and there was often a hint of Marilyn Monroe lurking under the cool, Grace Kelly sophistication. Perry had not lost his mischevious humor!

The crowd, which was much smaller for this show—Perry had cut out a hundred and fifty seats and changed his usual U-shaped runway to a simple single platform—was, of course, waiting for his signature knits, and they weren't disappointed. Perry had figuratively crossed the border into Nevada and gone gambling in Las Vegas and his "playing-card" sweaters—faithful knit reproductions of the lower deck as well as the face cards—were quite extraordinary.

Perry had also reached back to the fifties with his floral prints, but for once he was restrained in his use of flowers, unlike his showroom or houses! Here, he just showed one or two blossoms on an entire dress; the effect was quite extraordinary.

Women's Wear was alone in its sarcastic criticism, starting their review with "Mr. Pop went back to Beverly Hills High . . ." The retailers, on the other hand, adored it, and so did most of the press.

Ten days after the collection Tyler Alexandra Gallagher Ellis was born, checking in at eight-and-a-half pounds and twenty-one inches, with blond hair and blue eyes. Perry was there for the delivery and totally ecstatic, and there couldn't have been a prouder father. He had bought Barbara and Tyler a large house in Brentwood that was hidden from the road behind a large garden; it was the perfect place for Barbara to bring up Perry's daughter and heir.

Becoming a father seemed to change Perry, as it does so many fathers. For a while he became more open with his staff and friends, and would talk incessantly about Tyler, claiming she was the most beautiful thing he had ever seen. Winifred was equally thrilled and would fly to California and stay for long periods with mother and daughter, as well as have them visit her in Richmond. It was a happy time for all the Ellises, though in retrospect it would prove to be only the quiet before the storm.

Despite the triumph of his designs that year, 1984 ended with a business setback for Perry when Ed Jones resigned as president and CEO of Manhattan's Perry Ellis group to start a business of his own. Not surprisingly, Perry had come to trust and completely rely on Jones to run that part of his fashion empire, and Jones had proved himself to be more than adroit at handling both Perry and his bosses at Manhattan. Much of what the group had become, in fact, was due to Jones, who had brought in many of the key personnel working in the huge offices and showrooms that now housed the operations for two women's lines and two men's lines (the men's business had grown to the point where it had had to be subdivided into four parts). And though the businesses were still not profitable and often had to deal with substantial returns, the future looked bright. In a word, it had become an organization that was organized. And it had to be, because Perry was spending less and less time in the office, not only visiting Tyler in California, but also spending the majority of his time with Laughlin, who was by then so sick that he was in and out of the hospital when he wasn't traveling to Paris with Perry.

12

He slept a summer by my side
He filled my days
With endless wonder
He took my childhood in his stride
But he was gone when autumn came.
And still I dream he'll come to me
That we will live the years together
But there are years that cannot be
And there are storms we cannot weather
I had a dream my life would be
So different from this hell I'm living
So different now from what it seemed
Now life has killed
The dream I dreamed . . .

—Herbert Kretmer "I Dreamed a Dream"
from *Les Misérables*

They had been together almost four and a half years, and though they had had their troubles and problems, as all couples do, they were still very much in love. Tragically, for the past two years something had been insidiously at work destroying Laughlin's health, reducing the brilliant and formerly effervescent attorney to an invalid.

By the beginning of 1985 his health had so deteriorated that he was spending as much time in the hospital as out, undergoing chemotherapy for Kaposi's sarcoma, a form of cancer that is nearly always fatal and, until recently, with the mutation of the virus, one of the primary manifestations of Acquired Immune Deficiency Syndrome. There seems to be no doubt that Laughlin was dying of AIDS (although his death, a year later, was announced as due to lung cancer). Rumors about the nature of his illness had been flying around the fashion industry for some time. What was not known was just how long he had been ill, or how ill Perry himself was by then.

According to one highly placed source who worked for Perry Ellis, Laughlin had begun to experience skin problems as early as 1983, long before his shingles—a form of herpes often related to AIDS—had developed. "We used to joke with him about the 'cigarette burns' on his face," says this source. "We didn't realize then what it was." In retrospect, it seems likely that they were the first signs of Kaposi's sarcoma. By early 1984 he had developed a full case of shingles across his chest, to the point where he couldn't bear to wear a shirt—a major reason why he began to spend increasing amounts of time away from the office.

Perry also began to spend time away from the office, not only during the summer, when he and Laughlin retreated to Water Island, but also to Europe on vacations with Laughlin. But there was something frenetic about their wanderlust by then, as well as the huge amounts of money they were spending on antiques for the house and presents like the Bentley. Sources close to him say that in the final two years of his life, Perry disposed of sums that went well into seven figures. One of their closest friends says, "Nothing that was done in those days had any logic. Everything that happened, the spending on the house, how the business was run . . . they're what I call 'AIDS decisions.' At the end, neither of them knew what was happening; they had lost their grasp of reality."

For much of these last two years there seemed to be a desperation about their lives. It was almost as if they were trying to live life to the fullest and do everything as though it were the last time they would experience it together.

Although the old Ellis magic seemed to be reasserting itself in the collections, the atmosphere around the offices had deteriorated as a result of Perry's and Laughlin's virtual disappearance. (This very well might have been a factor in Ed Jones's decision to leave, though he had wanted to start his own business and continued to act as a consultant to Perry Ellis International.) One of the salespeople has been quoted as saying, "You were feeling like you were on the *Titanic*. And Perry didn't help matters. He could have made an appearance. Sent us a note. Anything. But he didn't. It was like we were working for Howard Hughes."

For Perry to disregard the business so completely was disturbing in itself, and seems to indicate the fact he knew he was ill and had a limited amount of time left to attend to his other commitments and responsibilities.

One of these was the CFDA, of which he had been made president in 1984. He had soon taken complete charge of all the arrangements for the annual awards dinner, which was held every January, and was conferring with Robert Raymond, one of his oldest friends and the man he had made executive director of the council, on the phone several times a day. Perry was also on the phone to Bill Blass, Donna Karan, Calvin Klein, Mary McFaddon, and Oscar de la Renta, getting their support behind the gala event he was planning. For someone who had shunned most of Seventh Avenue for the better part of his career, it was quite a turnaround. Just like the old days at 575 Seventh, he was into everything, from deciding on the location—he moved the ceremony from the Temple of Dendur room in the Metropolitan Museum of Art to the Astor Hall of the New York Public Library on Fifth Avenue at Forty-second Street—to tasting every dish on the menu and approving the table settings that Glorious Food (*the* chic catering service in New York) had suggested. Every aspect of the event he could give that "Perry Ellis touch" to, he would.

Pamela Altman claims, however, that a lot of the work was actually done by Karen Fortier. "I used to jokingly call her the president of the CFDA because she would do everything. Perry took it on, but, as he was wont to do, he just handed it

to Karen. He would stroll in, make one of those majestic statements of his, and then he was gone again.")

All the major designers showed up for the CFDA awards
and dinner that January, and it was a triumph for Perry, who
acted as master of ceremonies. The awards had taken on added
meaning since the Cotys had been terminated, and Perry created new categories for people who had made a significant
contribution to the fashion industry, including Bruce Webber
for his fashion photographs, and Diana Vreeland, the doyenne
ex-editor-in-chief of *Vogue*, for her autobiography, *D.V.* (This
expansion of the scope of the CFDA awards gave them far
more prestige and set them on a path that could eventually
lead to them being televised, as Perry wished, if the momen-
tum is kept up.)

Although Perry may have been concentrating his energies
outside the office by this time, the one thing he couldn't afford
to do was neglect publicity, especially with the rumors about
Laughlin circulating within the industry. The show, as they
say, had to go on, especially for financial reasons.

The beginning of 1985 saw Perry involved with a full
promotional schedule. At the beginning of February he
launched the new America line at Bloomingdale's on a Monday, then flew directly to San Francisco to launch the line at
Macy's California the next day. He spent Wednesday in the
San Francisco store signing autographs and helping to sell the
merchandise, and flew directly back to New York for more
promotional appearances. The extent of this bi-costal launch
shows how much Perry, and Levi Strauss, were banking on
the success of the new sportswear line.

The end of March saw Perry in the middle of the country,
in Chicago, for the international launch of the new Perry Ellis
fragrances, hosted by Marshall Field and Co., whose new
chairman was Perry's old friend Phil Miller, from Neiman
Marcus. Miller was determined to do the whole thing properly; the fragrance launch would be the start of a Perry Ellis
Fortnight. The festivities opened in the afternoon, when Perry

was presented the keys to the city of Chicago by Mayor Harold Washington. That evening there was a gala to launch his men's and women's fragrances, and the following day a ceremony at the Chicago Art Institute, where Miller endowed a $50,000 scholarship in Perry's name. The next day Marshall Field's gave a black-tie dinner and presented him with their Distinction in Design award. For once Perry wore a tuxedo (with one of his polka-dot bow ties), no doubt in deference to Laughlin.

Pamela Altman flew in for the event as Perry's guest in a private plane Perry had chartered, and remembers that Laughlin was so sick by then that they weren't even sure he would be able to go, even though it was the launch of one of his biggest licensing coups. Ultimately, he managed to make it, but he was already so weak and in such pain that he could only walk with a cane, and then only with difficulty.

Perry made his next personal appearance at Saks Fifth Avenue in New York to promote the fragrances and then went on to Atlanta, Georgia, on April 1, to launch them at Rich's, one of the oldest and most prestigious department stores in the South. On the twelfth he was back on the West Coast for a visit to Bullock's in Beverly Hills.

The next big event in this hectic last year was Perry's show for his fall collections, which had been inspired by the plays of Shakespeare. Unfortunately, it wasn't well received at all. Obviously, Perry's attention was focused on other matters by then. Perhaps the best part of the collection were the signature sweaters with beautiful sixteenth-century tapestry designs as well as motifs lifted from some of the Bard's more famous plays.

To most industry insiders, it looked as though Perry and his team had been trying too hard, or else hadn't had any direction at all; there were parts of the collection that looked almost amateurish, especially the satin evening separates with bi-colored pant legs, which looked like badly executed hose for a summer-stock production of *Romeo and Juliet*. It was a great pity, and judging by the long faces afterward, the "house" knew it, though the worry could have been caused by Laughlin's appearance. Hardly anyone in the office had seen him for months, but he had come to the show, remaining backstage, and from his appearance it was obvious he was dying.

Still, despite Laughlin's illness, Perry Ellis International continued to expand into new areas of apparel, and in April it was announced (in Laughlin's name) that Jockey International had signed a license to manufacturer a line of men's underwear. Given the success of Calvin Klein's underwear, it seemed like another clever move on Laughlin's part. However, it was already apparent that he couldn't continue working for much longer, and in May Perry called Ed Jones while Ed was in Dallas and asked him to fly back for a meeting.

"He wanted me to come back to New York to discuss something with him and Laughlin at the house," says Jones. "I thought it was one of the projects I was working on for him at the time, but when I came back and saw them at the house, I realized just how sick Laughlin was. He could hardly walk and there was a wheelchair in the room. . . . I knew something was up. In fact, Laughlin had not been to the office for at least three months and things were really beginning to slow down."

Perry asked Ed at the meeting to come back to work for him on a full-time basis. "He wanted me to run International as managing director and to manage his personal business affairs as well. But he was very specific about the fact that I would be answering to Laughlin, not replacing him. He didn't want anyone to think that Laughlin wasn't still in charge—he made that very clear." Which is why Perry told Jones that he couldn't make him president of the company and asked if the title of managing director was all right. "That's fine with me," Jones replied.

He managed to wrap up his other business by the middle of June and rejoined Perry as quickly as he could. He was to remain managing director of Perry Ellis International until six weeks before Perry's death, but he never saw Laughlin again after that meeting. Although Perry had made it clear to Ed Jones that he was to report to Laughlin, in effect that never happened. "I never had a conversation with Laughlin again," says Jones. "Every time I would send a report to him it would be Perry that would go over it with me, though he would say, 'I spoke to Laughlin about this' or 'Laughlin thinks that' or something like that."

Jones says he found the situation extremely frustrating. Not only could he see problems with the merchandise that he wasn't allowed to correct, since Perry was having problems with Manhattan again, he was also frustrated by Perry's and Laughlin's inability to deal with everyday business.

"They [Perry and Laughlin] weren't answering the reports, and if I pushed to get an answer, the next few days would be spent with them trying to find it," says Jones. "So then I would send them another copy and it would be sent back to me with no answer or a scribbled note, 'Do what you think best.' There was a lot of that. The business just wasn't being addressed and it really bothered me."

In addition, Perry was hardly in the office during this period and Ed Jones was having to answer the worried questions of the licensees who had heard the rumors about Perry and Laughlin's health, having to deny them.

While Jones does say that Perry was still very much involved with the collections and would see Jed and Patricia all the time (though more often than not up at the house rather than in the office), the entire licensee business was beginning to fall by the wayside. Day by day it became more obvious that the Perry Ellis empire was sliding into an abyss. Whatever Jones did to keep the edifice from crumbling, he couldn't do anything without Perry or Laughlin's input and final approval. The licensees were seriously doubting their position with regard to Perry, as well as whether there would be any future collections. The $750,000,000 business (at retail) that Perry and Laughlin had built up looked to be in danger of collapse. And Perry didn't even seem to care.

Nearly all of Perry's energy at that point was directed toward Laughlin. His devotion to his lover was quite incredible and must have been dreadfully destructive to his own spirit, not to mention his health. The terminal stages of AIDS are possibly worse than those of a patient suffering from leukemia or cancer; the nearest analogy one can think of is suggested by the horrifying images of the victims of the Holocaust. At the end, an AIDS patient looks like one of those skeletal bodies, and the care he or she requires is just as wrenching.

The exercise room at the top of the town house had been turned into a sickroom for Laughlin, and Perry was with him night and day. Eventually a nurse had to be brought in and Perry asked Robert McDonald to move in and help with the dying Laughlin. McDonald agreed, left his job at NBC, and took over the running of the household and Perry's day-to-day financial needs. He also began to take an active role in the business, working with Ed Jones.

During this last dreadful year Perry found the strength to keep going by turning to his mother's church. Winifred had long been a member of Silent Unity and Perry began to derive great solace from the *Daily Word,* a prayer and thought for each day published by the church.

The only thing apart from the caring for Laughlin and the design of the collections that Perry did seem to care about by then were the upcoming CFDA awards—he had been elected for a second term as president by the board. Earlier that summer he had read a book about Katharine Hepburn. As a result, he called Robert Raymond and suggested that since she had been such a fashion inspiration to so many over the years— particularly in her popularization of pants for women—why not give her the CFDA Lifetime Achievement Award? Raymond, knowing that the great star was loath to appear in public, dubiously said to him, "Good luck."

Perry's stubbornness was aroused, and he wrote one of his wonderful notes to Hepburn, sending it with, inevitably, a beautiful floral arrangement. Hepburn refused the honor, but

Perry, as stubborn as she, continued writing and sending her flowers. Eventually, she like everyone else, succumbed to his charm and agreed to accept the award. Perry then asked his old friend Calvin Klein to interview her for the program, knowing of Klein's admiration for the actress. "He put all his energy into that last CFDA," says Raymond. "I think it kept him alive for an extra year. He would call me at least five times a day, more than he called Patricia and Jed. We even tasted four different menus before Perry decided which one he wanted. His attention to detail, even then, was incredible."

Raymond is one of the few people who will admit that Perry knew how sick he was. "He wanted to leave a legacy. It's telling that Perry started to campaign to become the president of the CFDA at about the same time as Tyler was conceived."

Rumors about the state of Perry's own health had begun to circulate within the industry with the growing knowledge of how gravely ill Laughlin was—rumors that were continually denied by anyone involved with the company, as they were to the moment of Perry's death, but the seriousness of the situation was not evident until the November show for the spring '86 collections.

The collections themselves were beautiful in many respects. Perry had not let his public down, and, outwardly at least, it looked as if he was in form again. The inspiration for the collections had come from the interior of the town house he was now spending nearly all his time in; the primary motifs were taken from the collection of Chinese and Wedgwood ceramics he had accumulated over the years. Some of the Chinese or willow pattern prints in the collection were quite astounding, especially when they were executed in the sweaters, while some of Perry's more Oriental silhouettes were not. Many aspects of the collection had gone too far East, though, to be accurate, they suggested more the costumes from *The Flower Drum Song* on Broadway. However, many of the colors he used—rose, emerald, and indigo, as well as black, white,

and china blue—made the body-conscious sheaths in silk wonderfully simple dresses for the summer. The less Oriental and
simpler the clothes in this collection, the better. Still, it was
not universally well received, and one editor, rather shaken by
some of the silhouettes and split skirts more reminiscent of a
Shanghai whorehouse, described it as "Susie Gone Wong!"

Far more painful than the few stylistic mistakes, however,
was Perry's appearance on the runway after the show to ac-
knowledge the applause. He was by then very gaunt, with
blotchy skin and receding hair that had gone gray, and was
wearing glasses and a big red sweater to hide how thin he had
become. After a moment of stunned silence there was an audi-
ble gasp from the audience, most of whom hadn't seen him for
at least six months—six months during which the ever-
youthful Perry had aged dramatically. Instead of looking as if
he was in his late thirties, he now looked as if he were in his
late fifties. One word, or at least the thought of it, spread
through audience with a kind of dread—*"AIDS."*

The Ellis people tried to pass off Perry's appearance as
nothing unusual, saying that he was tired and under a lot of
stress, or, to those they knew well, quietly mentioning Laughlin's illness. It wasn't quite enough, however. The damage had
been done. If the industry hadn't known it before, they did
now: Perry was also very sick.

So what was wrong with Perry and Laughlin? Was
Laughlin dying of AIDS, as seems so evident from his symptoms, and was Perry more than just sick with worry? Despite
the denials, the evidence would tend to suggest that Laughlin
was in fact in the grip of the last stages of this ravaging, un-
controllable virus, and that Perry was also probably afflicted by
it. However, since this has been denied publicly, one has to
examine the facts—as far as one can—carefully. To do so, it is
necessary to go back as far as the beginning of 1981. In January of that year Perry and Laughlin went to Africa on safari,
and soon after their return Perry came down with hepatitis
and was hospitalized in New York Hospital for several days

and was so sick he didn't go back to work for a couple of months after that. According to a couple of their close friends this was when their health problems started. As Barry Kieselstein-Cord says, "After this Perry didn't even want to be in the same room with you if you had a cold. He was frightened of catching anything from anyone."

Dr. Mathilde Krim, Ph.D., an early researcher into AIDS, has put forward a hypothesis that the gamma globulin treatment for hepatitis could have started the AIDS epidemic in this country.

[It is my personal opinion that] the HIV [AIDS] virus was imported into this country and the most likely explanation is that it came here through blood. The virus first occurred in Africa, where antibodies to the HIV virus have been identified in stored blood collected in Zaire in 1959.

It's true that AIDS first appeared in this country in the gay communities of New York and Los Angeles, but it's a multi-focal epidemic, so it could not have spread as fast as it did by sexual contact alone. Even with certain behavior patterns within that community, if one person had contracted the disease in Africa or Haiti we would have seen a pattern like this: one case one year, ten the next, twenty cases a year after that, and so forth—a slow buildup. In 1981 the first nine cases in New York and the first five cases in Los Angeles were identified and then we had *several hundred* cases that same year and *several thousand* the next year. There is absolutely no conceivable way the disease could have started from social contact because of these figures. The only answer is that many people must have become infected at the same time.

What I believe is that we [hospitals and physicians] gave it to the gay community in the first place. There was an epidemic of hepatitis in the late seventies and early eighties, especially among the gay community, and they got AIDS because they were innoculated with infected gamma globulin. Until 1984, when blood was first carefully screened in this country, gamma globulin and other blood products were made out of pooled blood that wasn't collected in this country. It was brought from overseas, from the Caribbean and Africa, and also from prisoners. It is possible that blood lots were purchased in which many individual blood donations were infected, and the infectious virus would be trapped in the concentrated form needed to manufacture gamma globulin. The purification procedure that is used to obtain gamma globulin is done under what they call 'mild' conditions—it will not kill the virus.

This certainly happened in the case of other blood products, such as Factor VIII, which is used with hemophiliacs, and we know it was the blood that infected them.

Dr. Krim's hypothesis naturally leads to a number of searching questions as to who was responsible for the spread of AIDS in this country. If gamma globulin was in fact a major contributing cause, then the nation's medical profession is in serious trouble. In West Germany, for instance, the huge Bayer pharmaceutical company is being sued for billions of dollars as being the cause of AIDS among a substantial percentage of the country's 3,000 hemophiliacs.

The Centers for Disease Control in a study published in April 1986 states that immune globulins produced by plasma fractional methods approved for use in the United States "carry no discernable risk of transmitting HTLV-III/LAV [the HIV virus]" while admitting that globulins produced before 1985 were positive for the HIV antibody. However their tests only commenced in 1983, so Krim's hypothesis could still hold true for people treated with gamma globulin in the late seventies.

Dr. Krim herself feels that in Perry and Laughlin's case gamma globulin was not the cause of their catching AIDS because of the time frame, and suggests that they might have got it in Africa where the virus is so prevalent. Certainly, with new information that the incubation period of AIDS can be as much as seven or even ten years, it is possible that Perry or Laughlin contracted the disease as early as 1975 or before. It's almost impossible to say for sure how or when they caught it, yet, circumstantially, the evidence points to early 1981. AIDS can appear far more quickly in someone whose immune system is depressed, and although Perry was rarely seriously ill before then he was not the most robust of people. As a child he was asthmatic, and even though he was active in sports at college and actually coached tennis as a youth, Troy Swindell claims, Perry had problems completing the rigors of the Coast Guard boot camp. As an adult, Perry rarely sought out strenuous exercise. At the height of his friendship with James Terrell they did go to exercise class, and they were even photographed for *People* magazine "working out" at a dance class given by a woman called Abigale, which they attended on a regular basis in 1976 and '77. As Terrell puts it, "It was about that time that everybody jogged. Perry pretended to jog, but he hated it, so we went to Abigale and did this exercise/stretch class for two hours a week."

Under Laughlin's influence Perry did become more physically active. Ed Jones has been quoted as saying, "You'd see them after playing squash, with their hair still wet and their faces flushed. And you'd say, 'God, they just look so healthy.'" And Perry and Laughlin were also abstemious. Perry was known to have used "recreational" drugs in the seventies on occasion, but probably far less than most people of his generation and milieu, and it's possible Laughlin did too, but after they met they basically lived quiet, sober lives. Neither really indulged in spirits, and though Perry was partial to wine, he gave it up when Laughlin stopped smoking around 1983. (Which meant that the wine cellar, constructed at great expense in the second town house, was never really used.)

Essentially, there was very little about their lives that was scandalous in any way. It is likely that they had affairs with others, but they were far from the stereotypical image of gay men that the public and media has latched onto and led a relatively circumspect life. Regardless of how or when they might have contracted the HIV virus, it seems certain that by the end of 1983 they were being treated for AIDS.

It is known that after May 1983, when the license arrangement with Visions Stern for the Perry Ellis fragrances was signed, Perry and Laughlin began to make frequent trips to Paris, ostensibly in order to test the fragrances that were being created for Perry. "They would go back and forth very often to visit the 'nose,'" says Ed Jones. "I couldn't quite buy that, because why didn't the Visions Stern people fly to see them here or send the vials by courier? But that was the reason they gave for their trips. It was thought that they went there for medical reasons."

It is almost a certainty that Perry and Laughlin were using the development of the fragrances as an excuse to visit the Pasteur Institute in Paris, according to a couple of close friends. The Pasteur Institute had been in the forefront of AIDS research, and the only reason they both could have had for going there would have been for AIDS treatment.

Other sources close to them also admit that they were on medication that could not be obtained in this country at the time. "I do know that through their connections they were able to acquire all the new drugs that were available in Paris," says one close friend. It is quite possible that they were using one of the experimental drugs that were being tried at the Institute on AIDS patients from all over the world, including such celebrities as Rock Hudson.

It is evident from this information that certainly Laughlin, and most probably Perry, knew they had AIDS as far back as 1983 or 1984, the denials by Perry Ellis spokespersons notwithstanding. It would seem to be fairly certain that Laughlin did. But in 1984 Perry did something that no person in their right mind with the virus would now do: he fathered a child. At that time it was *not* generally known that the AIDS virus could be transmitted through semen, so it is possible that he knew he had contracted the disease but was not aware of its ramifications, or, supposing that Tyler was conceived by artificial insemination or 'in vitro,' it was felt there would be little or no risk.

Even now, a leading pediatrician at the Albert Einstein College of Medicine of Yeshiva University in New York, which deals with many pediatric AIDS cases, says, "With 'in vitro' fertilization the chances of the mother, and therefore the child, contracting the HIV virus are almost nil, as we are dealing with pure sperm which had been extracted from the body fluids which carry the virus. Even with artificial insemination the chances haven't been determined . . . It is possible, but highly unlikely." (The AIDS virus is comparatively difficult to catch, and the limited exposure inherent in artificial insemination would not necessarily be enough for the mother to develop HIV antibodies during the nine months of pregnancy— the fetus only contracts AIDS through the placenta from the mother's blood, and therefore the mother would have to have been exposed to the HIV virus before conception or during conception in sufficient quantities.)

What *is* known is that Tyler was born healthy and until the present day has shown no sign of having HIV antibodies, as far as the author can determine. (Children who contract AIDS from their mothers generally show signs of the disease within six to fourteen months.)

By December 1985, a month after the fashion show, Perry was beginning to show disturbing symptoms. At the opening night of the Costume Institute of the Metropolitan Museum of Art he collapsed in the receiving line. The evening, which is probably the biggest fashion event of the year, is always held on the first or second Monday in December and most of the world's fashion luminaries fly in to be there. The press was also there in force, and Bernadine Morris of *The New York Times* reported the incident in her column that week. As a result, the rumors about the state of Perry's health gained credibility. (Perry had been standing between Bill Blass and Pat Buckley, the glamorous wife of William F. Buckley, Jr., when the incident happened, and Mrs. Buckley tried to make light of it, saying to Perry, "Don't worry, I've fallen in reception lines before. The only problem was nobody missed me!")

That December must have been horrible for him. Laughlin was in New York Hospital most of the time, and Perry, who loved Christmas, was hardly in a festive mood, despite having his mother up for the holidays. Still, he sent out gifts and hand-written cards to everyone on his special list as usual. Laughlin's name was always included, and one can only imagine how hard it must have been for him. There was something about his notes that year that made one realize he knew the end was near.

As Judy Beste recalls, "Each Christmas he would give me a book, and I guess I could forgive him a year for the inscription he would write in it! But that last year I had been away for Christmas and came back just before the first of the year and opened the book. In it Perry had inscribed, 'L and I both love you.' I closed my office door and cried my eyes out. It was then that I knew what I had been avoiding all along . . . that they were dying. I tried to accept it as best I could."

Laughlin was brought home over the Christmas holidays and died on January 2, 1986.

Perry was totally distraught. On the tenth a memorial service was held for Laughlin at the New York Public Library. Everyone from the staff was there and a chair was held for Perry, but he couldn't bring himself to attend. "We left Perry's chair empty," says Ed Jones. "We knew he was there."

Perry's third to last public appearance was on January 19, 1986—just over two weeks after Laughlin Barker's death—at the 1985 awards ceremony for the Council of Fashion Designers of America, held in the New York Public Library, where Laughlin's memorial service had just taken place. The official story of that CFDA evening has it that even though he was already very weak and Robert Raymond, the new permanent director of the organization, had arranged for a substitute master of ceremonies to fill in, Perry refused to be dissuaded from attending. Yet one of Perry's closest confidantes categorically maintains that Perry called Calvin Klein, Ralph Lauren, and Oscar de la Renta to tell them he couldn't go through with it and ask them whether they would consider filling in for him.

They either didn't return his calls or refused to stand in for him.

"You can't imagine what it was like," says Pamela Altman, who had flown back from the Italian men's collections that day to be a guest at Perry's table. "It was one of the worst nights of my life. Although I knew what to expect, I had been away since before Laughlin's death and I was shocked at his appearance. It was just awful . . . his cheeks were sunken in and his fingers were all clawed up. He was so sick that he couldn't eat anything or swallow and he could hardly speak. His speech was slurred because he was losing motor control. Yet he went up and did it."

At the table with Altman, who was sitting on Perry's right, were Robert McDonald on his left, Ed Jones, Robert Raymond, Kitty Hawks (who had recently been brought in as creative director of Perry Ellis), and her boyfriend Mitch Rosenthal from Phoenix House, and even though Perry had changed the seating so that Altman was sitting next to him, she recalls that he couldn't muster the strength to talk to her and really only talked to McDonald the whole night. But she *could* hear the whispers about Perry's appearance from the tables nearby.

The effort Perry was making was obvious to everyone as soon as he was helped up to the podium by McDonald and began to speak. In a very weak and hesitant voice he acknowledged the thunderous applause, shouts, and screams from this normally dignified audience that read like a *Who's Who* of the fashion world. Repeating "Thank you very much" twice, he went on to quietly say, "My name is Perry Ellis. I am president of the Council of Fashion Designers of America." It was almost as if he had to, he was so much a ghost of his former self. A jaunty red bow tie disguised the thinness of his neck, and his hair, which has been noticeably gray at the October show, was brown again—it had been dyed.

In retrospect, the evening was a macabre black comedy,

from Calvin Klein's opening joke, "This is the evening of the invalids!" (Klein, it should be said, was on crutches, having just broken his ankle skiing in Switzerland), to Katharine Hepburn's, "I have a skirt which I can wear at funerals, if I must!" to the very poignant salute and retrospective fashion show for designer Rudy Gernreich, who had died the year before. The event was painful for everyone who had spent $750 a ticket for the privilege of being there and the only relief from the tension came with a salute to the hit Broadway show, *Tango Argentino*.

The long evening was a tremendous strain on Perry, who by now couldn't stand without McDonald's support. McDonald got Perry out of the library immediately after the ceremonies, and he was whisked away in the back of his limousine through the cold rainy night to the town house without speaking to anyone. He was obviously aware of the impression his appearance had made and the next morning he called Altman at her Fairchild office four times within an hour. "He'd never called like that before. He was on the phone sobbing and saying, 'What an awful fool I've made of myself' and 'Everybody is going to know' and 'Why did I do it?'" Altman tried to reassure him by saying, "Perry, of the fourteen people who could hear you past the first four tables, they were all much more interested in Katharine Hepburn than you!" But even her levity failed to work.

Rea Lubar, who was there as press agent for Liz Claiborne (who was receiving an award) found the event heartbreaking. "I went over to see Perry and all he said was, 'Don't kiss me.' I asked why not and he replied that he had the flu. You know what? I thought he had the flu. I didn't know it was because he had AIDS and was very sick. Those were the only words he said and then he ran out. It was the last time I saw him."

Perry's actions during the period between February and April 1986 leave no doubt that he knew he was dying. He wrote numerous notes to the many friends who had sent their condolences over Laughlin's death; Perry's notes always seemed to have a sense of finality about them.

Pamela Altman was staying at Ed Jones's farm in upstate New York one weekend that February and answered the phone while Ed was out. "It was Perry, though I didn't recognize his voice at first. He said, 'Who's this?' And I replied, 'Pammy Sue,' and there was a silence. Then he said, 'Who? Who is it?' and then I recognized it was Perry, so I said, 'Prunella' [one of Perry's pet names for her].

"He tried to be friendly, but he couldn't. I realized later that he couldn't even think properly. I knew something was wrong so I told him Ed wasn't there and asked if I could leave a message. It sounded as though he was vomiting and he said, 'I'm having trouble swallowing, Prunella.' I said, 'You don't sound so good, is there anything I can do?' and he said, 'Yeah, make it quick.'"

He then hung up. One can only imagine the despair he must have been feeling to ask in this way that his death be hurried.

Ed Jones called Perry back, and Roland, Perry's houseboy, answered the phone and said that Perry would call him. When Perry called back, he said almost exactly the same thing to Ed that he had to Pamela, having already forgotten the earlier conversation. Perry called back four times that night.

It was around this time that Robert McDonald was named president of Perry Ellis International. It was the obvious move for Perry to make, especially since he had just made McDonald the executor of his estate in the will he had drawn up on January 27. McDonald was not only one of Perry's oldest friends, but he had been handling many of the designer's private affairs since the days when they were lovers, and Perry trusted him implicitly. (This trust has been borne out by the way that McDonald, who had no previous knowledge of the fashion business, has handled Perry's business interests since his death.)

At about the same time, Ed Jones went to see Perry at the

town house to hand in his resignation. The strain of the last few months had caught up with him and he felt he had to leave for his own good. "We met in the library. Perry was dressed in layers of clothing, with a sweater over a sweater over sweatshirt and pants, trying to stay warm, even though there was a large fire blazing in the fireplace," says Jones. "It was so touching. Perry was crying and kept saying how much he loved Laughlin." Jones explained the problems he was having in the business and how he wanted to get back to being more involved with the merchandise side of the industry. He also told Perry that he and his wife had decided to make a move back to Texas, but that he would continue to work for Perry as a consultant. "Perry was thrilled for us," says Jones, "and by that time Robert was taking over the day-to-day running of the business and doing it so well. He's a very intelligent man and a quick study, and the business was running smoothly."

Perry walked Jones to the door and Ed turned and said, "Perry, I would really love to hug you." Then he took Perry in his arms. "It was at that moment I realized. He was all skin and bones. All those layers of sweaters had hidden how thin he was." Ed Jones walked back to his own apartment completely sick at heart. It was the last time he ever saw Perry.

In March Perry seemed to get better. At least he was well enough to travel and took pains to see and visit all the people who had been especially helpful to him during his career. One of these was Bob Haas, the president of Levi Strauss and Company, a man he admired perhaps more than anyone in the apparel industry. Haas had heard that Perry was ill and, like all the licensees, was concerned about his health. But then he'd been told that Perry was back in the office and taking charge of things again. Perry called him and said he wanted to talk. "I think we were mutually disappointed about what had happened with Perry Ellis America," says Haas, "and we needed to re-commit each other to the future. My understanding was that he came out to talk about how we would proceed with the business and to give me his personal assurances that he was going to be more involved with all the businesses and at the same time would be more attuned to the things we had learned running the business. I realized subsequently that he was saying good-bye." Haas continues, "I felt it was a very beautiful thing for him to do."

After the meeting Haas, Perry, and McDonald (who had accompanied Perry) went to lunch and talked about some of the books they had read recently, Perry and Haas being voracious readers. Haas recommended that Perry read *West with the Night,* the story of Beryl Markham, an Englishwoman who was brought up in Kenya and became one of the first women bush pilots and eventually the first person to fly the Atlantic from east to west. Perry enjoyed the book so much that he gave, as Haas had done, copies to several of his best friends. It was the last time that Haas saw Perry, but their mutual admiration for the book made him feel a special link with Perry that transcended the designer's death.

After their visit to Haas in San Francisco, Perry and McDonald went to Los Angeles so that Perry could visit his daughter. Tyler was only a year and a half old, and for him to leave her, knowing he would never see her grow up and become the child of his dreams, must have been the hardest thing he ever did in his life.

Even though he knew he was dying, Perry still hadn't lost his sense of humor. One of the people he wrote to was his old colleague and friend Michael Black. Black, in an effort to cheer him up after Laughlin's death, had sent back to Perry in a very elaborate box an old tuxedo of Perry's that he had borrowed from him in Richmond during the sixties. Perry, in turn, wrote him a note saying, "Do you think this is going to start a new fashion trend?!"

Perry returned to New York, and, just a month after his forty-sixth birthday, gave *Women's Wear Daily* an exclusive interview that was almost incomprehensible in its lack of a sense of reality. Admittedly his disease seemed to be in remission, as often happens with the victims of AIDS. He had acquired a deep tan from his visit to California and gained about twelve pounds. But the interview reads like a wishful dream. In an article titled PERRY LOOKS AHEAD, he told *WWD* that he was healthy and looking forward to the future. He also maintained that "The life and soul of the company is still very much here and it's changed. I used to do such wild looks and now I want to be more serious about life and the quality of my life." He added, "When I started 100 years ago I had so much fire and ambition . . ." It was one of the few realistic remarks he made in this, his last interview.

But underlying all the bravura was a note of resignation and pathos. It was almost as though, with his optimistic outlook, he was trying to chart the future for his companies, not himself. The most personal part of the interview were his remarks about Laughlin. Susan Alai, who wrote the article, captured Perry's acceptance of his own future in her last quote: "There is a solitude and peace that encompasses life."

Women's Wear were exceptionally generous with this article. They must have known what the situation was and this is born out by their using an old photograph of Perry—where he looked wonderful—to illustrate the double-page spread. Certainly he wasn't as well as he made out in the article.

Soon after this Pamela Altman saw him for the last time. "Perry, Robert, and I went to see *The House of Blue Leaves*. Perry was fine for the first forty-five minutes and then he started to cry and couldn't stop. And Robert got really pissed off, so I said, 'You stay, I'll take him home.' Robert wouldn't allow me to go through that, so we all left the theater together and took him home," says Pamela, tears streaming down her face. "He was very, very sick by then."

Perry only made two more public appearances after that. For most of April he was bedridden, but on April 29 he made an exceptional effort to attend the huge AIDS benefit organized by the American Foundation for AIDS Research at the Jacob Javits Convention Center. The benefit was organized by

Karen Fortier, who had since left Perry Ellis, and was the first time the fashion industry had acknowledged the problem of AIDS, which had been decimating its ranks for the past four years. Still, she had little success getting support until Calvin Klein put his weight behind it. Klein's appearance, especially with the beautiful Elizabeth Taylor on his arm—Miss Taylor is the foundation's national chairperson, and has probably done as much to raise money for AIDS in this country as the government itself—ensured that the media would be there, and the benefit raised a considerable amount of money.

Perry insisted on going in spite of his terrible condition, and everyone who saw him there was shocked. He was accompanied by Robert McDonald and Robert Raymond, and, even in his weakened state, he insisted on posing for the AmFAR ad, which was photographed at the benefit. "He really wanted to be in that photograph," says Fortier, "even though he was so ill." Perry got his way and was photographed for the group shot of some of the top names in the fashion industry with his old friend Geraldine Stutz and just behind Klein and Taylor.

No one could understand why he'd made such a heroic effort to be there, but one of his oldest friends, Arlene Meyer, suggests that it was Perry's way of acknowledging he had AIDS. "I don't believe he avoided the issue," she says. "He stood up, desperately ill that night, and he didn't have to do it. He was making a statement by doing that. Knowing Perry, and knowing how scrupulous he was, that was his way of not denying the truth, and that's as good as an affirmation.

"There is no question in my mind that that's what Perry did that night. He was too private and had too much taste to make a public statement—'Laughlin died of AIDS and I have it, too.' That wasn't Perry's style. He made his statement his own way by being there."

Perry's fall show was scheduled for May 8, and despite his rapidly weakening condition he oversaw many of the details from his town house. As usual Michael Purri did the music and had chosen Gershwin's "'S Wonderful." But Perry had a song in the back of his mind and tried to hum it to Purri, who told Patricia Morrisroe, "He called me. His voice was really weak, and I could barely hear his voice, but he kept trying to hum the song. After he had finished, he said, 'So what is it?' And I told him I didn't know. He seemed disappointed: 'Well, I can hear it in my head.'"

Perry had also been after Amanda Manogue about some duck stamps he wanted as well as the seating arrangements for the show. He was making such an effort to make sure the collection was just right, in fact, that he would come down to the office for a few hours a week to oversee everything. Patricia Pastor is quoted as saying about these last few weeks, "He was driving everybody crazy again. We said, 'Well, he's back to being his bitchy old self.'"

The night before the show, Perry called Purri again about the music, but with the pressure of the encephalitis on his brain he couldn't even hear properly anymore. No one in the office thought he was strong enough to attend the show, but just before nine o'clock that morning they were told to prepare the freight elevator: Perry was coming up the back way so that the press wouldn't see him. Apparently, Jed and Patricia tried to lighten the mood of everyone present, from the staff to the dressers to the models, by joking, "Oh, no! It's Lizzie Borden." During the show Perry didn't make any of his usual last-minute adjustments to the clothes, and instead simply sat on a stool and watched through the two-way mirror he had had installed when the showroom was renovated to watch the reactions of important people in the industry. (Although, according to Brian Bubb, he took an interest in the male models' outfits and insisted they all wear hats, even though only a few had been made.)

Ironically, this last collection was one of Perry's greatest triumphs. The clothes were simple, clean, and lean—everything Perry had been trying to achieve for the last four years in his quest to become accepted as a designer of sophisticated day and evening clothes, not just sportswear. Of this fall '86 collection, much of the fashion press said he had achieved it more succinctly than ever before.

Perry, always the showman, knew his audience and had gauged their reaction to the show. There was nothing that was going to stop him from going out on the runway, despite his condition. He came out supported by Jed and Patricia and then moved just in front of them, alone. At first there was stunned silence, then the entire audience stood up and gave him a thunderous ovation. Perry basked triumphantly in the limelight of this, his final performance.

Right after the show, he was driven back home to the town house on Seventieth Street that he had lived in for such a short while. A small bag had already been packed for him, and Robert McDonald immediately took him to New York Hospital—Cornell Medical Center, where he was registered as Edwin Ellis, to avoid publicity.

Winifred had been at the show and stayed in New York to be by her son. Apart from immediate family, only a couple of close friends were allowed to see him. James Terrell was one of them, and was visiting when Carrie Donovan, Perry's close friend from *The New York Times,* called. Although Robert McDonald had told her how sick Perry was and said he didn't think it was worth her while to come by, Carrie, never a person to be daunted, said, "I'm coming right over." She sailed into Perry's room a half an hour later and looked around at all the flowers, which were everywhere—especially Perry's favorite Rubram lilies—on the shelves, the windowsill, the table, and the dresser. Carrie made one of her wonderfully imperious comments about the floral bedlam, and Perry, with a very weak smile, uttered one of his favorite sayings, which just as well could have been the motto for his life: *"Never enough!"*

They were the last words he spoke. Shortly after, he lapsed into a coma from which he never recovered. Perry Ellis died at 1:20 A.M. on the morning of May 30, 1986. He was forty-six years old.

Epilogue

He falls; but in falling
he is higher than those who
fly into the ordinary sun.

—Frank O'Hara
"Oedipus Rex"

"My dear, it's *never* enough!" This oft-spoken phrase of Perry's could have been his maxim. Although he wasn't born with the proverbial silver spoon in his mouth, his career and rise to eminence as one of the world's most renowned designers was certainly sugar-coated; he believed in, and demanded, the finest of everything, and that, in turn, influenced everything he did.

Without a doubt he milked and manipulated every professional situation in his life to his advantage, yet he was one of the most beloved figures in the fashion industry. To understand this seeming paradox one has to understand that first and foremost Perry Ellis was a compassionate, gentle, man. He felt for people. At the same time he was a rogue, with a sardonic, puckish sense of humor. He was also private and circumspect . . . even shy and self-effacing. In short, he was a man with a man's strengths and weaknesses. Undoubtedly, he was a man with a great talent.

And like every mortal he suffered. The pain and desperation he felt during his last couple of years as he watched first his lover and then himself die of AIDS must have been crushing, but he continued to act with the greatest dignity and love right up to the end. His is a tragic and controversial story that hasn't closed with his death.

Perry Ellis's death can hardly be said to have gone unnoticed. In fact, it was a major news item on every network evening news program in this country, and was remarked upon by many of the world's most prestigious broadcasting systems. Similarly, every influential newspaper and news periodical here and in Europe gave his demise prominence in its obituaries. Ironically, in death, Perry Ellis's name was more exposed to the general public than it ever was during his life.

The reason, of course, was the controversy over whether he had died of AIDS or not. In this country *The Washington Post, USA Today, Newsday, Newsweek,* and *The San Francisco Examiner,* as well as United Press International, felt bound to mention AIDS as the cause of the designer's death, while, conversely, such prestigious publications and news services as *The New York Times, The Los Angeles Times, The San Francisco Chronicle, Time,* and the Associated Press did not. It is a controversy that has yet to be resolved, and is due, in part, to the social stigma that is still associated with the disease.

Since Perry's death many other prominent figures have succumbed to AIDS, including a Congressman, a well-known sports personality, one of the most influential Broadway directors of the past twenty years, another fashion designer, and many, many talented and famous performers and artists in the creative arts, both here and in Europe. In addition, the latest, horrifying figures coming out of Africa chart the ravages of what one prominent doctor in this country calls "the worst threat to human life since the 'Black Death' [bubonic plague] decimated one-third of the world's known population," making AIDS one of the most discussed and debated subjects.

At first the general perception of the public was that AIDS was a disease limited to homosexuals and drug addicts, or, as one of the leaders of the "moral majority" in this country put it, "It's God's wrath on deserving sinners." But the social disgrace associated with the disease is slowly ebbing away as new figures become available. According to the most recent statistics, AIDS now poses an equal threat to the heterosexual population and is currently the single greatest cause of death of women between the ages of 24 and 36 in New York. AIDS has already reached pandemic proportions—the World Health Organization conservatively estimates that between five and ten million people in the world have already been infected by the HIV virus. In parts of Africa the estimation is as high as twelve percent of the population and it is believed that as many 1.5 million Americans are infected—a figure markedly higher than those given out by the govern-ment—and, according to Dr. Mathilde Krim, founding chair of the American Foundation for AIDS Research, "Twenty mil-lion Americans will be infected with it before the end of the century. And before we have found a way to destroy or immu-nize against the HIV virus it will have killed at least *two hun-dred million* people on earth," and adds that this figure could double.

Because Perry Ellis was one of the best-known figures in his profession, his death, and its cause, touched off far more speculation and editorial comment than perhaps the death of any other person in this country, with the obvious exceptions of Rock Hudson and Liberace. That AIDS was the cause of his death was denied vehemently by everyone involved in the Perry Ellis companies, who were scared simply for financial reasons. The rumor of AIDS would affect the sales of his mer-chandise, these people thought, and, in fact, one of the coun-try's major retailers (who prefers not to be identified) categorically states that the sales of Perry Ellis merchandise in the group of stores that that person represents did indeed suf-fer from the rumors surrounding his death, so there was justi-fiable cause for a cover-up.

Did Perry Ellis die of AIDS?

In the author's mind, given the facts surrounding his death and the nature of his and Laughlin's protracted illnesses, there can be no doubt that they were both tragically struck down by this dreadful virus. Laughlin was only thirty-seven when he died, and was suffering from Kaposi's sarcoma, one of the most common causes of death with AIDS patients. They both visited the Pasteur Institute in Paris, one of the foremost hospitals in the world for AIDS research and care, on numerous occasions. In addition, Perry, only forty-six, died of viral encephalitis, a virus that in normal circumstances a healthy person can fight off. In the words of one prominent physician who is also a teacher at one of New York's leading hospitals, "Encephalitis is one of the three most common causes of death in AIDS victims. AIDS totally destroys the immune system of the body and therefore the body can't even fight off the most common virus that attacks it, including one that causes inflammation of the brain [encephalitis]."

Although it is only one medical opinion, solid proof is provided by one senior member of the fashion establishment who told the author that Perry's personal physician, Dr. Denton Cox, in a very indiscreet moment, confirmed to that person during a social function in New York that "Perry died of AIDS." (The author has known this person for years and considers the source impeccable. Dr. Cox would not make further comment.)

To this day, the people at Perry Ellis International deny all rumors to that effect. It's understandable—they have a huge fashion empire to protect. Undoubtedly, the question will come up again if the rumors that three of the world's top designers are also suffering from AIDS prove to be true.

After May 30, 1986, the employees at 575 Seventh Avenue were in a state of shock. It couldn't have happened! The ever-youthful catalyst that had sparked and sparkled in their lives was gone. A three-quarter-of-a-billion-dollar-a-year company was like a ship becalmed.

Without a doubt it was the purposeful leadership of Robert McDonald that kept the company going during those weeks. In spite of his own personal grief, nothing was allowed to lag and new licensee agreements continued in negotiation. Certainly, Larry Leeds was determined that his position on Seventh Avenue would not collapse with the demise of his superstar, and his support and comments to the press contributed greatly to the picture of confidence that was presented to the industry and public.

"It's business as usual," said Zachary Solomon, Ed Jones's successor as president of the Perry Ellis group of companies at Manhattan Industries, in an interview with *Women's Wear Daily* on June 20, three weeks after Perry's death. And Leeds in the same article concurred. "The potential for success is as strong as it has ever been, and I have every reason to believe it will continue."

Yet these were simply placatory statements for public consumption, and it is safe to assume that McDonald and Leeds had to make some quick hard decisions to keep things operating along the lines they had before the designer's death.

Some of the decisions that had been made the year before by Perry were obviously detrimental to the companies' continued expansion and profile in the marketplace. "They were what I call AIDS decisions," says one close friend and a consultant for Perry Ellis International, and even though the end was becoming increasingly obvious to insiders, "Nobody was prepared for it. There were things that needed to be done, and Perry couldn't sign anything, he was in the hospital connected to a machine. The only provision that was made was for Robert to take responsibility for the business, the baby, Barbara, and the estate. Everything else was left open and undecided."

The first major decision facing McDonald and Leeds was who would design the collections, and whether anyone should actually be named to replace Perry. Patricia Pastor, who had worked with Perry for ten years, was the obvious choice and it was decided to give her overall control. She would continue as vice president of design, the position she had held for the past five years, but would now be responsible for the design of all the women's apparel—basically assuming Perry's responsibilities in that area. Jed Krascella, whose second love is acting, had already planned to take a leave of absence from the company that summer to attend a six-week drama course at Oxford University. But he agreed to return in September to work with Patricia designing the women's collection, as he had been doing with Perry and Patricia for the last nine years or so. Brian Bubb would retain his position as vice president for design for men's wear and be responsible for that part of the collections.

All in all, it was a side-stepping motion; the old team

would remain intact. The difficult question of "replacing" Perry was avoided and, basically, everything would remain as it had been. (This status quo remains in effect at the time of writing, almost a year and a half later, with the exception of Jed Krascella's resignation from Perry Ellis on May 15, 1987). Yet these precautionary measures, and even the signing of a new licensing agreement—with the Greif Companies for a new Portfolio tailored clothing collection—did not put a halt to the furor surrounding Perry Ellis's death. His was the first death of a major designer in this country due to AIDS, and the other licensees were indeed worried.

In 1985, according to one highly placed officer of Perry Ellis International, the twenty-three licensees and the Manhattan Industries Perry Ellis group of companies were generating about $265 million at wholesale (about $662 million retail), which can be broken down as follows—for women: $5 million for furs, $15 million for coats, $12 million for shoes, $6 million for legwear, $5 million for scarves, and $20 million for home furnishings; for men: $8 million for dress furnishings, $30 million for Portfolio, $10 million for the Greif clothing licensee, $3 million for hosiery, and $2 million for shoes. The men's "couture" sportswear collection was bringing in about $15 million and the Japanese licensees more than $11 million. The women's fragrance that year would sell about $12 million at wholesale and the women's "America" line about $15 million. The two lines that Manhattan owned, the women's "couture" collection and the women's Portfolio line, would bring in about $25 and $50 million respectively.

In 1986 these figures were expected to grow again, more than likely putting Perry's sales over the $300 million mark (wholesale) and making Perry Ellis International a $750,000,000-a-year company at retail at the time of the designer's death.

To use a cynical phrase, "Life goes on." There was now a serious question as to what would happen to the Perry Ellis empire. McDonald had already made the vital decision on who would design the collections, and only the success of the new collections for spring 1987 would prove whether he and Larry Leeds had been correct in their judgment that the Perry Ellis look could be carried on by Patricia Pastor, Jed Krascella, and Brian Bubb. (They did, in fact, do well at retail, even though they lacked that "Perry Ellis touch," in that they were very "safe" and therefore commercial.) In the meantime the country's retailers had to decide whether to continue backing and promoting the Perry Ellis label. Certainly, many of them were worried about the future of the company. Even though they knew how much the design team had contributed in the past to the whole Ellis look, there was still the worry that without Perry's guidance the collections would not be the same. In addition, like Ed Jones, some of the senior staff were leaving, including Judy Beste, who had been there from the start.

The lead on this front was taken by Marvin Traub, one of the country's most brilliant retailers and chairman of Bloomingdale's. Traub is one of the few people in the cut-throat fashion industry with the principles to support a friend, and he quickly made the decision to continue with a major Bloomingdale's advertising campaign that summer highlighting Perry Ellis merchandise. Bloomingdale's has been a leader in fashion retailing in this country for the past fifteen years, and many others followed suit. The support movement was also given impetus by many other powerful figures in the retail business, including Phil Miller of Marshall Field's, Ira Neimark of Bergdorf Goodman, Ellin Saltzman of Saks Fifth Avenue, and Geraldine Stutz of Henri Bendel. These retailers knew that rumors concerning Perry's untimely death could affect the sales of his merchandise, but their regard and loyalty for Perry went beyond mere financial concerns, and their continued support of the Perry Ellis companies must have been an important consideration for the board of Manhattan Industries when it decided to continue to back the Perry Ellis name.

This was all the more remarkable given Manhattan Industries' financial troubles at that time. In 1985 the corporation had lost $24,603,000, and the losses were continuing in the first quarter of 1986. In September, however, they announced they were back in the black for the second quarter, which had ended July 31, with a net income of $3,506,000, or 66 cents per share. So, to the general public it looked as though Perry's death hadn't hurt Manhattan Industries. Actually, they were only in the black *because* of Perry. It seems they had taken out a $5 million life insurance policy on him and this, plus another million dollars in pretax credit for the quarter, gave them pretax earnings of $2,406,000.

Perry Ellis International, on the other hand, was doing far better. With sales of the licensees over $200 million in 1986, given the average designer percentage of sales of seven and a half, the company's revenues for that year should have been approximately $15 million. After operating costs and the twenty-five percent due Manhattan Industries, their pretax earnings for the year would have been in the area of $10,500,000, which, in turn, was divided between Perry's heirs, as will International's earnings every year from then on.

Under the terms of the will Perry made on January 27, 1986, all the property and money left to Perry and his mother Winifred by his father Edwin Ellis would revert back to her. All Perry's other property and money would be divided among his three heirs—his daughter, Tyler Alexandra Gallagher Ellis, Winifred Ellis, and Robert McDonald. In addition, Robert McDonald was named executor and trustee of Perry's estate, and in his submission to the court a value was put on it in excess of $900,000—$400,000 in real property and $500,000 in personal property, including cash, bank deposits, securities, and personal effects.

However, considering that Perry left four houses—the town house in New York, the two houses on Water Island, and the house in Brentwood—there were still other assets involved. On November 19, 1985, Perry had set up the Perry

Ellis Revocable Trust, which he established between himself and Laughlin, with Perry as grantor and both of them as trustees. On Laughlin's death, Robert McDonald was made the other trustee and the trust was amended to this effect on January 27 at the same time Perry made out his will, which was witnessed by two of his employees, Margaret Lee and Catherine Burke Flannery, and his lawyer, Christopher C. Angell. According to Angell, a partner of Laughlin's old law firm of Patterson, Belknap, this is a blind trust and therefore its assets do not have to be disclosed; however, he did state that they were "substantial." All the houses and Perry's stock in Perry Ellis International, Inc., are included in the trust.

The main beneficiary of the trust is Tyler, though both Winifred and McDonald are also named as heirs. The houses on Water Island have been sold, for a reported $800,000, to James Terrell, and the town house, which McDonald continued to live in after the designer's death, has also been sold, for a reported $4.35 million.

To call assets such as these, as well as the continued income generated by Perry Ellis International, Inc., "substantial" is understating it. Perry died a wealthy man and left his heirs extremely well off, with a collective annual income well over $10 million.

Perry's personal philosophy of *"never enough"* had obviously paid off in financial terms, though this could not assuage the grief his family and everyone who had come to know him felt at his untimely death.

All his life Perry had been searching for an elusive "something"; probably the only peace he ever found was in the one great love of his life, Laughlin, whom he was to lose so tragically. And though the puckish side of his nature would have been amused at the furor surrounding his death, in those last months, despite public pronouncements, it was obvious to those who knew him well that he was resigned to, and even wished for, death. In death he found peace again.

Perry's mortal remains were interred in the family burial plot in Portsmouth, Virginia, in the presence of Winifred Ellis, Mr. Waldbauer (her second husband), Barbara Gallagher, and their daughter, Tyler Alexandra. It was a private ceremony far removed from the strained excess of the public memorial service.

Index

Abbijane (designer), 89–91
Abrams, Michael G., 155
Acquired Immune Deficiency Syndrome (AIDS), 122, 201–2, 208, 210–12, 213, 214–15, 218, 222–23, 229, 230–32, 234
Adolfo, 95, 97
Advertising, 36, 41, 99, 155–56
Alai, Susan, 222
Albert Einstein College of Medicine, 214–15
Alexander IV, pope, xix
Alixandre (fur company), 57, 71–72, 83, 101
Altman, Pamela, 137, 151, 169–70, 196–97, 203–4, 205, 217, 218, 219, 222
AMC (Associated Merchandising Corporation), 70
American Foundation for AIDS Research, 222–23, 231
Andrews, Frank, 48–49
Andrialis, Bob, 188
Angell, Christopher C., 237
Anilowski, Marge, 31
Antonio (fashion illustrator), 91
Armani, Giorgio, xxiii, 63, 83, 84, 97, 100, 110, 113, 120, 140, 192
Ashley, Jim, 29
Ashley, Laura, 183
Ashley, Pat, 40

Avedon, Richard, 83
Award for Distinguished Service in the Field of Fashion, 83–84

Ballantyne, 38
Banks, Richard, 125–26, 136, 184
Barker, Christine, 148, 151
Barker, David, 148
Barker, John, 148
Barker, Katherine (Kate), 137, 148, 152, 156, 158, 185
Barker, Laughlin McClatchy, Jr., 77, 95, 108, 113, 122, 135, 145–59, 160, 166–68, 169, 170, 171, 175–76, 179, 181, 185, 193–94, 195, 213–14, 220, 222; illness, death of, 79, 137, 178, 182, 183, 185, 195–96, 200, 201–2, 204, 205, 206–7, 208, 210, 215–16, 219, 223, 231, 236, 237
Barker, Rosanne, 148
Barth, Robert, 42
Bashford, Wilkes, 120, 121
Baxter, Ann, 117
Beck, Barry, 179
Beene, Geoffrey, xxii, 90, 91, 123
Bell, Katherine, 19–20, 21
Berge, Pierre, 113
Bertin, Mademoiselle, xix
Beste, Judy, 73, 80, 85–88, 91–92, 107, 108, 115, 126, 149, 195,

Beste, Judy (*cont.*)
   216; left PE business, 235; on
   PE, 129, 130, 131–32, 133–34,
   152–53
Beyermann, Hugo, 44
Black, Joanna, 25, 26, 43
Black, Michael, 25, 26, 28, 29, 43,
   221
Blass, Bill, xiv, xv, xxii, 48, 96, 97,
   99, 112, 123, 186, 203, 215
Blithe Spirit (play), 181
Bloomingdale's, 60, 70, 84, 101,
   154, 157, 169, 204, 235
Bonwit Teller, 55
Bottoms, David, Jr., 10, 11, 12–13
Bouet, Tibout, 54
Brantley, Ben, 96
Braverman, Steve, 73, 126
Breuer, Marcel, 47
Brighton Beach Memoirs (play), 181
Brousseau, Jean-Charles, 105–6
Brubach, Holly, 21
Brummel, Beau, xxi
Bubb, Brian, 130, 156, 224, 233,
   235
Buckley, Pat, 215
Buckley, William F., Jr., 215
Buonarroti, Michelangelo, xix
Burrows, Stephen, 58
Burton, Richard, 181
Butler, Michael, 78

Calvin Klein Menswear, Inc., 118–19
Caples, Richard, 151
Cardin, Pierre, 155
Catherine the Great, xix
Centers for Disease Control, 212
Chandon, Domaine, 134–35
Chanel, Gabrielle "Coco," xxi, xxii,
   34, 104, 122, 171
Channing, Carol, 182
Chariots of Fire (film), 123
Children's line, 154, 156, 172
Chow, Tina, 117
Church's English Shoes, Ltd., 186
Claiborne, Liz, 218

Cleary, Frances, 23, 24
Close, Glenn, 193
Coady, Michael, 194
Cohen, Arlene, 34–35, 36, 37, 38,
   41
Collections, 53–55, 57, 58, 59–60,
   95, 118–22, 128–29, 132, 147,
   156, 190–95, 202, 205–6, 207;
   1979, 81–83; *1980*, 96–98, 104;
   1981, 109–10, 121–22; *1982*,
   123–24; *1983*, 134, 179–80;
   1984, 182–83; accessories, 82,
   104–6; cheerleader show, 69–70,
   78; colors, palette, 3, 57, 59, 70,
   72, 81, 82, 92, 130, 182–83,
   191, 209–10; after death of PE,
   233–34, 235; "Dreamgirls,"
   143–44, 155, 163; failures,
   162–63; "Indian Summer," 81;
   last, 209–10, 224–25; lower-
   priced, 167, 168, 194–95; multiple lines confusion, 175–76,
   194–95; Portfolio (Vera), 52–53,
   54, 59, 65, 66, 68, 72, 81; silhouettes, 57, 59, 69, 72, 82, 92,
   97, 109, 123, 124, 130, 132,
   163, 179, 182, 197, 210; sportswear, 190–91, 197–99. *See also*
   Men's wear
Costello, Tom, 52
Coty (co.), 58
Coty Awards (American Critics
   Awards for Fashion), 58, 123,
   135, 147, 163, 186, 204; PE
   nominated, 65, 72, 83, 104, 180;
   PE won, 89–91, 104, 194
Coty Hall of Fame, 122
Council of Fashion Designers of
   America (CFDA), 122–23, 179,
   186, 203–4; awards, 123, 180,
   204, 208–9, 216–18
Couture, 53, 118, 165, 194
Coward, Noel, 181
Cox, Denton, 232
Crysler, Larry, 119–21
Cunningham, Bill, 55

Cutty Sark Men's Fashion Award, 180

Daily News Record (DNR), 56, 58, 61, 98, 110, 117, 169
Davis, Bette, 16
de la Renta, Oscar, 68–69, 203, 216–17
Delauney, Sonia, 190, 191, 192, 193, 194
Dell'Olio, Louis, 58
Diana, princess of Wales, xix
Donovan, Carrie, 137, 151, 225
Dreamgirls (show), 118
Drier, Melissa, 98, 102
Duka, John, 46, 61, 71, 79, 125, 131
Dunham, Bruce, 137
D'Urban (co.), 186

Elle, 61
Ellis, Edwin, 1, 2, 4, 7, 236; death of, 95, 111–12, 151–52
Ellis, Perry Edwin: burial, 238; character, 3, 141, 229; childhood, 1–5; death, 95–96, 108, 122, 225, 229–30, 231–32, 234, 237; as designer, xv, 38–39, 51–52, 53–54, 55, 70, 76–77, 83, 97–98, 109, 113–14, 122, 129–32, 146; design statement, 35, 129, 145–46; education, 5–12, 17–18, 20, 147–48; ego, 26, 68, 79–80, 104, 133–34; employment, 19–32, 33–47; fashion statement, 58, 81, 98, 104, 121, 124; fathering a child, 179, 190, 198, 199, 214; friends, 29, 42–43, 101, 108; generosity, 4–5, 6, 27–29, 101–2, 141–42, 156; homes, 43–44, 45, 153–54, 158, 178, 182, 183–85, 209, 213, 236, 237; homosexuality, 41–42, 79, 106–7, 158–59; illness, 122, 202, 203, 209, 210–11, 214–15, 217, 218–19, 221–23, 224, 229;

influence of, on fashion, xxii–xxiii, 115–16; "inner circle," 147, 151, 189; legacy, 189, 209; lovers, 42–43, 77–79, 95, 106–7, 108, 147–48, 149, 150, 151–52, 158–59, 201–2, 213, 219; manner of dressing, 3, 7–8, 20, 28, 36, 79, 84, 102–3, 120, 151; memorial service, xiii–xiv; military service, 12–17, 27; neglect of business, 202–3, 207; obsession with detail, 66, 126–27; perfectionism, 45, 65–66, 111, 127–28, 129, 155, 172, 184, 195; personal characteristics, xiv, 5, 6, 26–27, 43, 76–77, 91, 104, 106, 113, 141–42, 209; physical appearance, 4, 11, 41, 76, 78–79, 210, 217, 223; privacy, 26, 79–80, 111–12, 135–36, 229; pursuit of rich and famous, 77, 100–101, 135; relationships with women, 10–11, 77, 106; sense of humor, xiv, 5, 8–9, 45, 107–8, 113, 221, 229; shyness, insecurity, 3–4, 6, 11–12, 129, 152, 229; staff, 85, 88, 106, 127, 128, 129–30, 132, 156, 195–97, 233–34; star status, 91, 96, 100–101, 112, 118, 126, 127, 128, 134, 135–36, 144, 179; travel, 7, 49–50, 106–7, 195, 202, 214; uncontrolled spending, 66, 67, 75, 85, 114–15, 142–44, 160, 161, 172; wealth, 137, 146, 153–54, 237; will, 236–37; work with students, 103, 179, 186–87; as world-class designer, 112, 145–46, 147
Ellis, Tyler Alexandra Gallagher, 43, 199, 200, 209, 214, 215, 221, 233, 236, 237, 238
Ellis, Winifred Alene Roundtree, 1, 2, 3, 4, 5, 6, 7, 137, 208, 225, 236, 237, 238
Ellis family, 2, 4

Esquire, 61
Etro (designer), 131, 132

Fabric, 3, 85, 106, 121, 138, 142;
inspiration for PE clothes, 130–33
Fairchild, John, 56, 58, 63, 110,
111–12, 194
Fairchild Publications, 56, 61, 96
Fashion: business of, 138–39; evolution of, xvi–xxiii; high, 93, 146,
162; influence of PE on, xxii–
xxiii, 115–16; social change and,
33–34, 40
Fashion Calendar, The, 133
Fashion industry, xv–xvi, 59, 61,
204; and AIDS, 223; costs in,
65; and fashion press, 62–63;
gimmicks in, 99–100; as global
operation, 138–39; PE and,
112–13
Fashion Institute of Technology
(F.I.T.), 90, 103, 187
Fashion press, 54–55, 57–58, 81,
83, 99, 104, 118, 122, 180, 193,
194, 225; PE courted, 39, 60–61,
62–63, 137, 144; power of,
60–63
Finlay, Ruth, 133
Fire Island, 79, 158
Flannery, Catherine Burke, 237
Fortier, Karen, 196–97, 203–4, 223
Fragrance line, 171, 204–5, 213–14,
234
Frederick the Great, xx
Frost Bros., 71

Galcotti, Sergio, 113
Gallagher, Barbara, 189–90, 199,
233, 238
Gallo, Anita, 122
Garr, Terri, 182
Gempp, Kathy, 24–25, 26, 32
Genesco, Inc., 155
Gentlemen's Quarterly, 61
George, Phyllis, 117

Gernreich, Rudy, xxii, 218
Ghandi, Indira, xix
Glamour, 38, 55, 61
Goodman, Shirley, 90
Gottfried, Carolyn, 54, 55, 56, 66,
96, 100
Graves, Thomas A., Jr., 188–89
Grief Companies, 130, 155, 224
Greschner, Ron, 179
Guilder, Jean, 38, 39, 43–44, 50,
52, 55

Haas, Robert, 176–77, 220–22
Haight-Ashbury, xxi, 33
Hall, Jerry, 99
Halston, 34, 48, 49
Halston VI license, 71
Hambrecht Terrell International, 74,
125, 185
Harper's Bazaar, 61
Hashim, Koko, 60, 70
Hawks, Kitty, 217
Hemingway, Mariel, 179, 193
Henri Bendel, 109, 119
Hepburn Audrey, 16
Hepburn, Katharine, 16, 186,
208–9, 218
Hobson, Jade, 105
Home furnishings line, 155
Hong Kong, 138
Honsberger, Barbara, 60
Horvitz, Sandy, 55
Hudson, Rock, 214, 231
Hutton, Lauren, 117
Hyde, Nina, 90, 102

Interstoff fabric show, 85–86, 108,
131, 133, 152–53
Interviews with PE, 3, 12, 17,
21–22, 150, 178, 221–22
Irving, Amy, 181
Isman, Erwin, 72–73, 74, 75, 80,
85, 89, 113–14, 138, 142, 143;
on PE, 113, 115–16, 128–29,
135, 139–40; on PE as busi-

nessman, 165, 166, 169; president, Perry Ellis Sportswear, Inc., 118, 126, 161–62, 163

Jefferson, Thomas, 9
Jerry Magnin (boutique), 119, 120
Jockey International, 206
John Henry line, 71, 170
John Meyer of Norwich (co.), 22–23, 34, 35, 36–38, 39, 40–41, 46, 47, 49, 59, 73, 77
Jolly, Alison, xvii
Jones, Edward M., 118–19, 121, 154, 156, 157, 158, 194, 195, 213, 214, 217, 232; and death of Barker, 216; left PE business, 203, 235; on PE, 135; and PE illness, 219–20; president and CEO, PE business, 163–64, 165–66, 167, 168, 169, 172–75, 199; rejoined PE business, 206–7, 208
Jones, John, 120
Jordache Jeans, 99

Kahn, Madeline, 181
Kamali, Norma, 132
Kaplan, Mort, 149
Kaposi's sarcoma, 201, 202, 231
Karan, Donna, xiv, 58, 203
Karrakase family, 2
Kashimyama (co.), 185–86
Kennedy, Jackie, xv, 14, 34, 95
Kennedy, John Fitzgerald, 14
Kenzo, 50, 57, 59, 84, 105
Kieselstein-Cord, Barry, 82, 104–5, 122, 163, 211
Kieselstein-Cord, CeCe, 105
Kirkland, Sally, 47
Klein, Anne, xxii, 58
Klein, Calvin, xiv, xv, xxii, 48, 63, 84, 85, 89, 99, 101, 112, 113, 121, 123, 197, 203, 223; and CFDA awards, 209, 216–17, 218; men's wear company, 164; sig-

nature logo, 100; underwear line, 206
Kolhman, Lynn, 136, 151
Krascella, Jed, xiv, 54, 73, 80, 81, 85, 88, 105, 107, 127, 129, 130, 131, 139–40, 156, 168, 196, 207, 209, 224, 225; design work following PE death, 233, 235; resignation, 234
Krieger, Henry, 118
Krim, Mathilde, 211–12, 231

Lacoste, René, xxii
Lagerfeld, Karl, 50, 110, 111
LaMonica, Barbara, 83
Lauren, Ralph, xiv, xv, xxi, 63, 69, 85, 99, 101, 112, 121, 166, 182, 197, 216–17; home furnishings line, 155; signature logo, 100
Lawler, Carol, 130–31
Lee, Peggy, 142, 153, 169, 170, 237
Leeds, Dalia, 71
Leeds, Laurence C., Jr., 65, 66, 67, 70–71, 80, 99, 114, 156–57, 232–33, 235; and PE/Manhattan Industries conflict, 160, 167, 169–70, 171, 180–81
Lesser, Stanley, 66, 67
Levi Strauss and Company, 168, 171, 173, 174, 175, 176, 177, 185, 197, 204, 220
Liberace, 231
Licensing ventures, 67, 68, 71–72, 91–92, 95, 105, 124, 129, 154–55, 166, 185–86, 205, 206, 207, 213–14, 232, 234; failures, 172–73; Manhattan Industries and, 157, 160–61, 164, 168, 171; PE control over, 155–56; revenues, 137, 146, 154; with Vera Companies, 180–81
Liebeskind, Mimi, 83
Locke, Edith, 55
Los Angeles Times, 61–62, 230

Lubar, Rea, 52, 54–55, 56, 60, 77, 89–90, 91, 218; on PE, 101

"M" (magazine), 56, 123
McCardell, Claire, xxii, 34, 109
McDonald, Robert, 42–43, 46, 77, 108, 136, 151, 189, 190, 217, 218, 223; and death of Barker, 208; and PE illness, death, 225; PE trustee, 236–37; president, Perry Ellis International, 177, 219, 221, 232, 233, 234–35
McFadden, Mary, 83, 203
Machado, China, 54
Macy's California, 204
Mademoiselle, 55, 61
Mallonee, Gordon, 21, 22–23, 31
Manhattan Industries, 47, 52, 54, 65, 66, 124, 125, 154, 181, 234; costs to, of PE extravagance, 114–15; and death of PE, 232–33; financial troubles, 235–36; losses on PE lines, 112; M.I. Group, 72; Pelican division, 172; PE conflict with, 75, 85, 142–44, 160–77, 178, 183, 207; PE contractual arrangements with, 66–68, 98–99, 136, 146, 155, 156–57, 164; Perry Ellis division, 66, 70–71; and PE men's collections, 119; profits, PE collections, 118
Manogue, Amanda, 126–27, 224
Marcos, Imelda, xix
Marcus, Richard, 134
Markham, Beryl, 221
Marshall Field and Co., 204–5
Martex (co.), 155
Martin, Mavis, xiv
Medici, Lorenzo de, xviii
Meliora Quartet, xiv
Men's wear, xxi–xxii, 83, 95, 146, 164–65, 174–75; collections, 68, 69, 98–99, 103–4, 110, 118–21, 157, 181–82; tailored line, 155

Menswear (magazine), 58, 123
Meo, Eddie, 179
Merrill, Dina, 90
Meyer, Arlene, 223
Meyer, John 22–23, 24, 31–32, 34–35, 36–37, 38, 39, 46, 55
Metropolitan Museum of Art, Costume Institute, 215
Miller, Phillip, 102, 134, 204–5, 235
Miller & Rhoads (department store), 19–32, 80
Minskoff organization, 74
Models, 58, 59–60, 107, 118, 134, 136, 140
Mondale, Joan, 95, 100
Monroe, James, 9
Moore, Nonnie, 55
Mori, Hanae, 110
Morris, Bernadine, 50, 55, 90, 122, 215
Morrisroe, Patricia, 126–27, 190, 224
Motomora, Horoshi, 107

Nakash brothers, 99
Neiman Marcus, 70, 83–84, 102, 134–35
Neimark, Ira, 235
Neumann, Vera, 47, 49
Neuville, Charlotte, 52
Newman, Claire, 53
New York magazine, 126–27
New York Times, 55, 61–62, 71, 74, 79, 103, 105, 122, 125, 157, 176, 230
New York Times Magazine, 46, 66–67, 84, 131
New York University, 17, 18, 20, 148
Norell, Norman, xxii
Norfolk Academy, 5
Norkland, Matt, 140
Norstan Industries, 124
North American Flying Service, 137

O'Hara, Frank 45
Old Dominion University (Norfolk, Va.), 7–8, 9, 17
Oliver, Barbara, 6
O'Neal, Tatum, 163
Ozer, Bernie, 70

Parsons School of Design, 53, 103, 186–87
Pasteur Institute (Paris), 214, 231
Pastor, Patricia, 53–54, 73, 81, 105, 107, 126, 127, 129, 130, 131, 136, 139–40, 147, 156, 168, 187, 196, 207, 209, 224, 225; collection design following PE death, 233, 235
Patterson, Belknap, Webb and Tyler (law firm), 148–49, 237
Pelican Industries, 124
Percheck, Frank, 15
Peron, Eva Duarte, xix
Perry Ellis clothes, 50, 54; designs, 37; details, 38, 59, 82, 100, 197; problems with fit, 140–41; witty, irreverent, xiv, 50, 57, 72, 81–82, 93, 98, 118, 180, 198
Perry Ellis International, 41, 43, 67, 68, 99, 107, 124–25, 129, 137, 146, 148–49, 154, 156, 157, 164, 177, 181, 203, 219, 232, 233, 234, 237; Barker president of, 149–50, 166–67, 171, 176; expansion, 206; profits, 236
"Perry Ellis look," 106, 126
Perry Ellis Men, Ltd., 164, 172
Perry Ellis showroom, 40, 45, 74–75, 80–81, 117–18, 125–26, 142–43, 167, 197
Perry Ellis Sportswear, Inc., 66, 68, 70–71, 72–73, 76, 113–15, 118, 124–25, 126, 128, 139, 143, 163–64, 168, 172; financial troubles, 144, 156–57, 162
Perry Ellis Sportswear, Ltd., 98–99, 119, 124–25

"Perry Ellis style," 44
Perry Ellis Trust, 149, 236–37
Perry family, 2
Perse, Tommy, 120
Personal appearances, 99–100, 101, 134–35, 157, 169, 205
Peters, Bernadette, 163
Poiret, Paul, xx
Poisson, Jeanne Antoinette (Madame de Pompadour), xix
Price, Sarah, 20–21, 24, 25–26, 27, 29, 41
Purri, Michael, 223–24

Radd, Norman, 22
Raleigh, Sir Walter, xxi
Raymond, Robert, 203, 208, 209, 216, 217, 223
Reagan, Doria, 95
Reagan, Nancy, xv, xix, 95
Reagan, Ron, Jr., 95, 182
Reagan, Ronald, 94
Renown (co.), 91, 92, 107, 185–86
Retailers, 61, 70, 71, 81, 83, 84, 96, 109, 118, 122, 162, 183, 193, 199; and PE death, 231, 235; and PE men's collections, 118, 119, 121
Rhodes, Zandra, 110
Rivers, Larry, 45
Rizzo, Frank, 187, 188
Robbins, Stephanie, 140
Robertson, Cliff, 90
Rockman, Frank, 49, 51, 52, 53, 60
Roosevelt, Eleanor, xix
Rosenberg, Jean, 120–21
Rosensweig, David, 135
Rosenthal, Mitch, 217
Ross, Robert, 94
Rossellini, Isabella, 179
Roundtree family, 2
Rudolph, Paul, 42
Ruttenstein, Kalman, 55, 70, 83, 84, 101, 124

Ryall, Lise, 140
Rykiel, Sonia, 117

Saint Laurent, Yves, 57, 63, 65, 97,
  113, 155, 171, 192
Saks Fifth Avenue, 181–82, 205
Saltzman, Ellin, 235
Santa Fe Festival Theatre, 181
Sarandon, Susan, 179, 181
Sawyer, Dorothy, 21
Schiaperelli, Elsa, 50
Schiro, Anne Marie, 55
Schoen, Julia, 50
Schumaker, Avis, 6
Schwartz, Barry, 113
Seventh Avenue ("Fashion Avenue")
  (New York City), 64–65, 203
Shaw, Matt, 46, 47
Shea, John, 183
Shoe, line, 155
Sicart, Regine, 54
Signature style(s) (PE), 57, 59, 69,
  81, 82, 93, 98, 100, 109, 120,
  133, 198, 205
Simon, Neil, 181
Sinatra, Frank, 10
Smith, Willie, 8–9
Social change, 22, 33–34, 146
Society for Ethical Culture, xiii–xiv
Solomon, Zachary, 232–33
Sportswear, xxi–xxii, 54, 68–69, 93,
  198, 204; collections, 190–91,
  197–99; moderate-priced,
  166–67, 168, 174
Steinberg, Ed, 30–31
Stern, Milton, 171
Stern's (store), 18
Streep, Meryl, 135
Stutz, Geraldine, 109, 119, 223,
  235
Sunny Day, A (store), 30–31, 32
Suppon, Charles, 54, 58
Sweaters (PE), 82, 92–93, 97,
  123–24, 154, 179–80, 191, 198;
  signature, 205

Swindell, Troy, 7–8, 9–10, 13–18,
  25, 27, 44, 213

Tailoring, (PE), 82–83, 97, 179
Taylor, Elizabeth, 181, 223
Terrell, James, 29, 40, 42, 44, 45,
  48, 74–75, 77, 117, 125, 135,
  136, 153–54, 170, 183–84, 185,
  189, 212, 225, 237; on PE,
  49–50, 151, 190; PE loan to,
  101–2
Thalhimer's (department store), 19
Thatcher, Margaret, xix
Thayer, Jim, 170–71
Theater costume design, 181
Tiegs, Cheryl, 117
Trigere, Pauline, xxii
Tropper, Robert (Beau), 77–79,
  106–7, 108, 119, 136, 151, 189
Traub, Marvin, 169, 235
Traub and Lesser (law firm), 66
Tyler, John, 9
Tyler, Suzanne, 10–12

Underwood, Patricia, 104, 127
Ungaro, Emmanuel, 97

Valentino, 97, 171
Vanderbilt, Gloria, 100
Vangelis, 123, 190
Vera Companies, The, 32, 46–47,
  49, 52, 71, 73, 77, 124; PE li-
  censing arrangements with,
  180–81
Vera Sportswear, 46, 51, 52, 54, 68
Versace, Gianni, xxiii
Villager (co.), 22, 34
Vionnet, Mademoiselle, xx
Visions Stern (co.), 171, 213–14
Vogue, 3, 12, 17, 21–22, 55, 61
Vreeland, Diana, 204

"W" (magazine), 56, 58, 95
W. R. Grace & Company, 46
Waldbauer, Mr., 238

Ward, Rachel, 183
Warhol, Andy, 90, 117
Washington, Harold, 205
Washington Post, 61–62, 102, 230
Water Island, 79, 105, 136, 138, 147, 148, 153, 158, 178, 182, 195–97, 202, 236, 237
Weaver, Sigourney, 135, 179
Webber, Bruce, 197, 204
Weekes, Miss, 4
Weir, June, 54, 55
Weiser, Jon, 120
Weitz, John, xxii, 34
West, Bonnie, 90
William and Mary (college), 7, 9–10, 12, 20, 103, 148; *Alumni Gazette*, 11, 12; PE gifts to, 188
Williams, Cathy, 56, 60
Wilson, Jimmy, 155
Women's Wear Daily (*WWD*), 50, 54, 56, 58, 60, 61, 68, 70, 72, 76, 83, 92, 96, 107, 109, 121–22, 143, 150, 156, 163, 164, 179, 182, 232–33; attacks on PE, 110–12, 180, 191–94, 198, 199; interview with PE, 221–22
Woodrow Wilson High School, 5–7
Woolrich, Jane, 102–3
World Health Organization, 230
Worth, Charles Frederick, xx
Wren, Sir Christopher, 9

Yagi Tsusho Kaisha, Ltd., 91–92, 185
Yospin, Jerry, 22, 23, 25, 26, 27–28, 29, 30, 31–32, 40, 41, 43, 47

Zelnick, Michael, 167

TT
505
E55
M66
1988

Moor, Jonathan.

Perry Ellis

$17.95

DATE			

E55 M66 1988